X-MEN

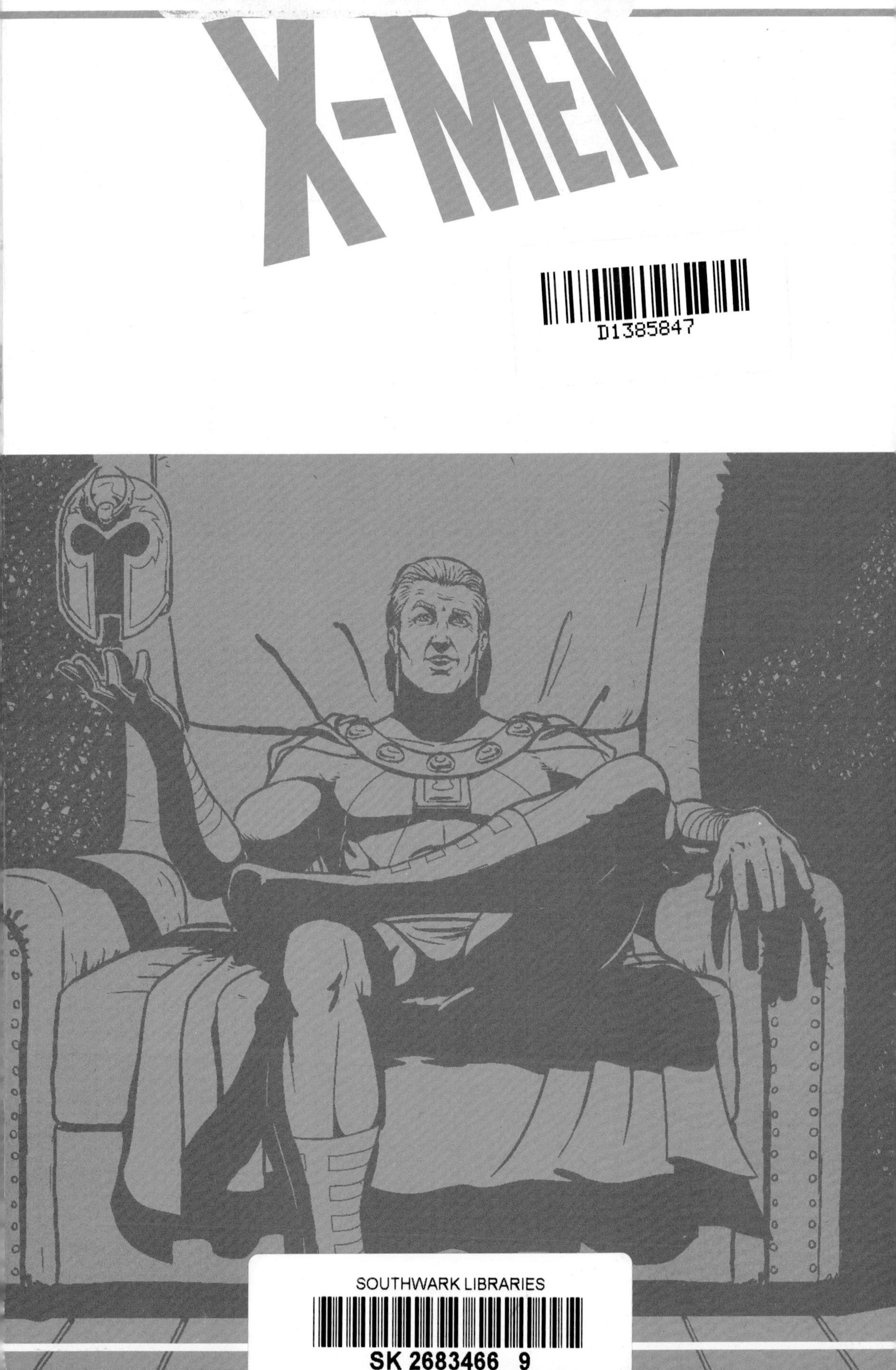

COLLECTION EDITOR: **JENNIFER GRÜNWALD**
ASSISTANT EDITOR: **CAITLIN O'CONNELL**
ASSOCIATE MANAGING EDITOR: **KATERI WOODY**
EDITOR, SPECIAL PROJECTS: **MARK D. BEAZLEY**
VP PRODUCTION & SPECIAL PROJECTS: **JEFF YOUNGQUIST**
SVP PRINT, SALES & MARKETING: **DAVID GABRIEL**
BOOK DESIGN: **JEFF POWELL**

EDITOR IN CHIEF: **C.B. CEBULSKI**
CHIEF CREATIVE OFFICER: **JOE QUESADA**
PRESIDENT: **DAN BUCKLEY**
EXECUTIVE PRODUCER: **ALAN FINE**

X-MEN: UNCANNY ORIGINS. Contains material originally published in magazine form as X-MEN: SEASON ONE and UNCANNY X-MEN #1. First printing 2018. ISBN 978-0-7851-5646-8. Published by MARVEL WORLDWIDE, INC., a subsidiary of MARVEL ENTERTAINMENT, LLC. OFFICE OF PUBLICATION: 135 West 50th Street, New York, NY 10020. Copyright © 2018 MARVEL No similarity between any of the names, characters, persons, and/or institutions in this magazine with those of any living or dead person or institution is intended, and any such similarity which may exist is purely coincidental. **Printed in Canada.** DAN BUCKLEY, President, Marvel Entertainment; JOHN NEE, Publisher; JOE QUESADA, Chief Creative Officer; TOM BREVOORT, SVP of Publishing; DAVID BOGART, SVP of Business Affairs & Operations, Publishing & Partnership; DAVID GABRIEL, SVP of Sales & Marketing, Publishing; JEFF YOUNGQUIST, VP of Production & Special Projects; DAN CARR, Executive Director of Publishing Technology; ALEX MORALES, Director of Publishing Operations; DAN EDINGTON, Managing Editor; SUSAN CRESPI, Production Manager; STAN LEE, Chairman Emeritus. For information regarding advertising in Marvel Comics or on Marvel.com, please contact Vit DeBellis, Custom Solutions & Integrated Advertising Manager, at vdebellis@marvel.com. For Marvel subscription inquiries, please call 888-511-5480. **Manufactured between 8/17/2018 and 9/18/2018 by SOLISCO PRINTERS, SCOTT, QC, CANADA.**

10 9 8 7 6 5 4 3 2 1

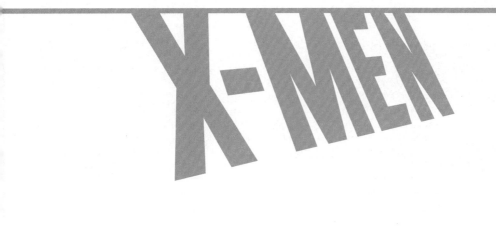

X-MEN

WRITER
DENNIS HOPELESS
ARTIST
JAMIE McKELVIE
WITH
MIKE NORTON
COLORIST
MATTHEW WILSON
LETTERER
VC'S CLAYTON COWLES
COVER ARTIST
JULIAN TOTINO TEDESCO

EDITORS
ALEJANDRO ARBONA
AND
JORDAN D. WHITE

X-MEN CREATED BY STAN LEE & JACK KIRBY

UNCANNY ORIGINS

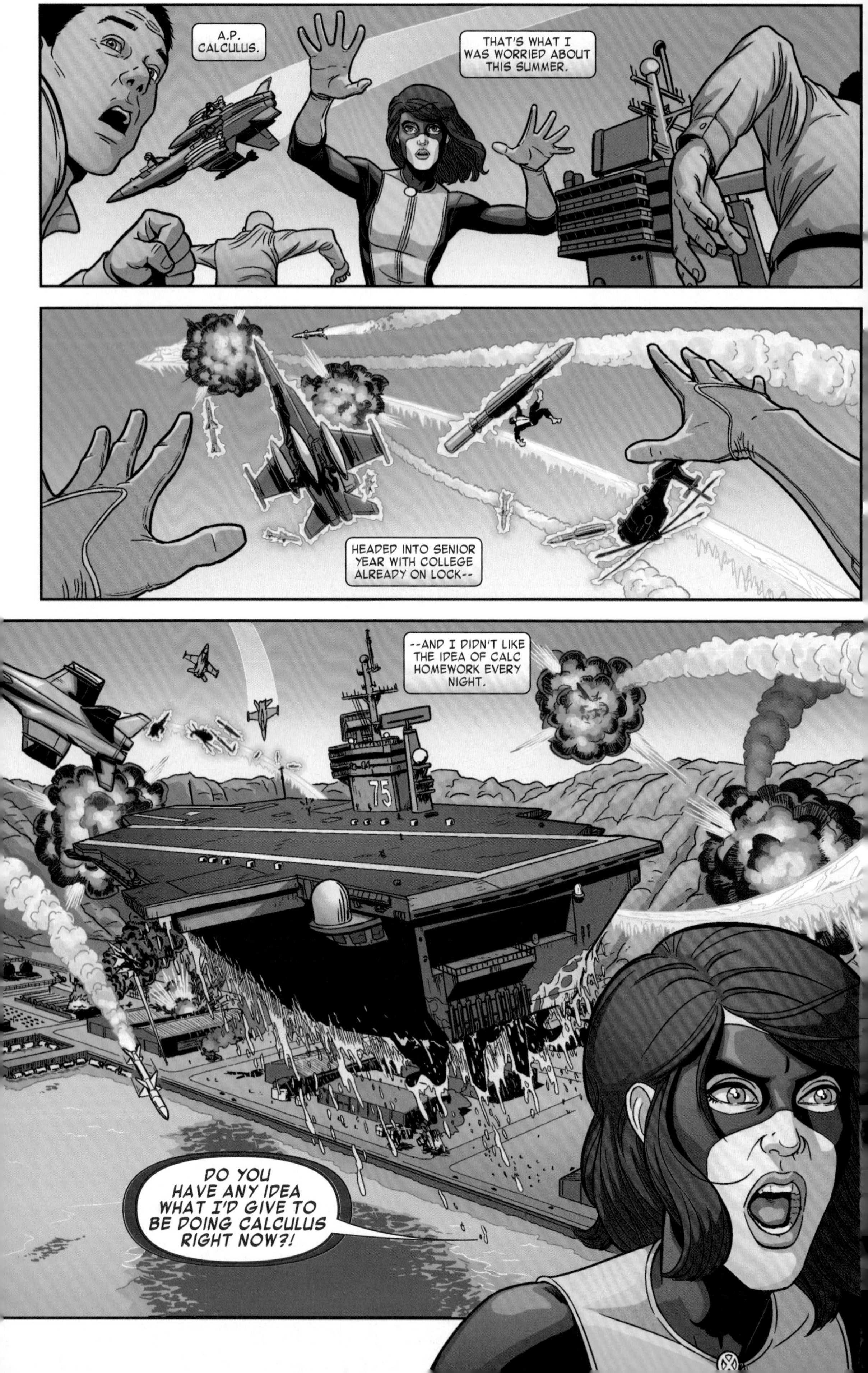
A.P. CALCULUS.
THAT'S WHAT I WAS WORRIED ABOUT THIS SUMMER.
HEADED INTO SENIOR YEAR WITH COLLEGE ALREADY ON LOCK--
--AND I DIDN'T LIKE THE IDEA OF CALC HOMEWORK EVERY NIGHT.
75
DO YOU HAVE ANY IDEA WHAT I'D GIVE TO BE DOING CALCULUS RIGHT NOW?!

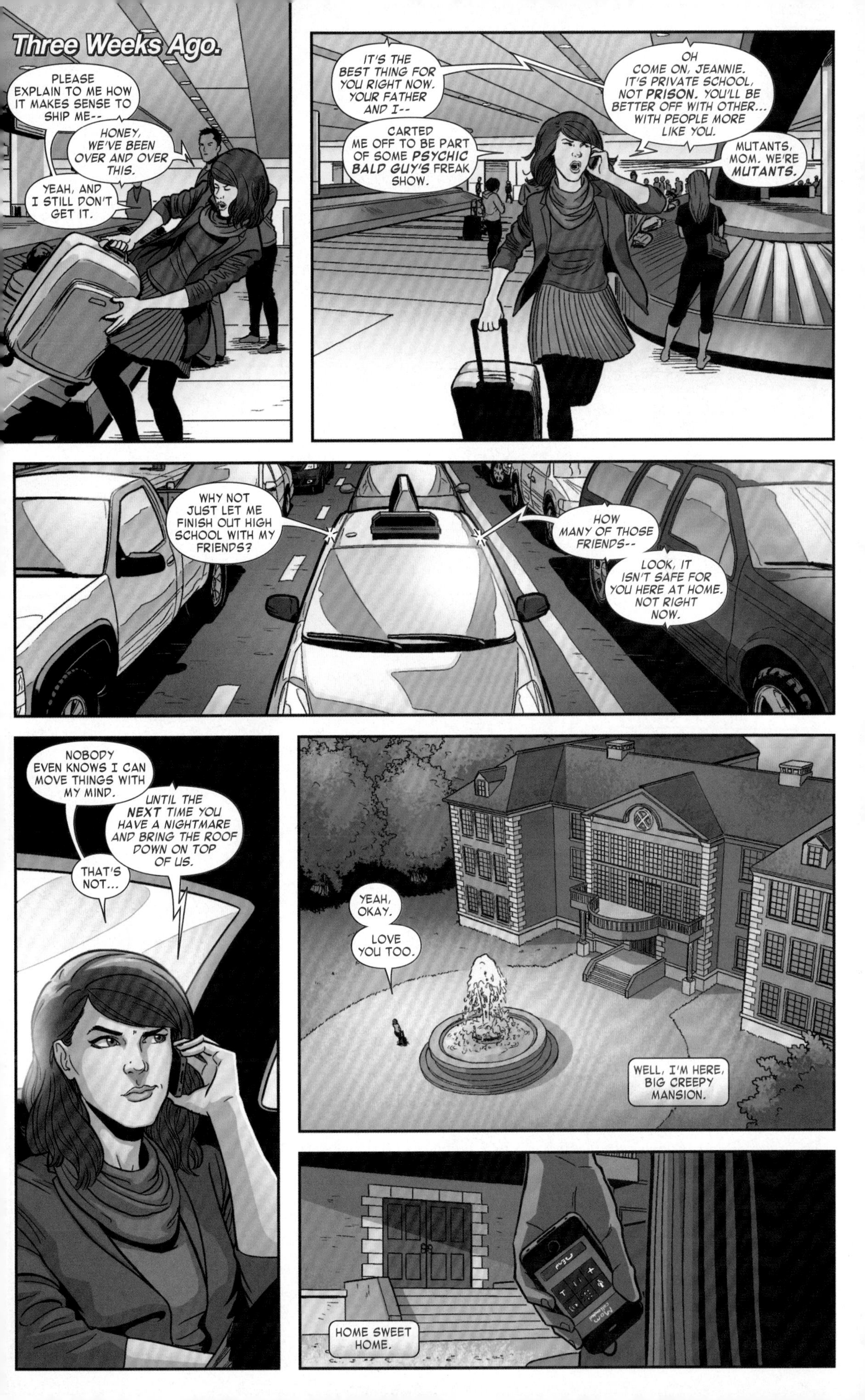
Three Weeks Ago.
PLEASE EXPLAIN TO ME HOW IT MAKES SENSE TO SHIP ME--
HONEY, WE'VE BEEN OVER AND OVER THIS.
YEAH, AND I STILL DON'T GET IT.
IT'S THE BEST THING FOR YOU RIGHT NOW. YOUR FATHER AND I--
CARTED ME OFF TO BE PART OF SOME PSYCHIC BALD GUY'S FREAK SHOW.
OH COME ON, JEANNIE. IT'S PRIVATE SCHOOL, NOT PRISON. YOU'LL BE BETTER OFF WITH OTHER... WITH PEOPLE MORE LIKE YOU.
MUTANTS, MOM. WE'RE MUTANTS.
WHY NOT JUST LET ME FINISH OUT HIGH SCHOOL WITH MY FRIENDS?
HOW MANY OF THOSE FRIENDS--
LOOK, IT ISN'T SAFE FOR YOU HERE AT HOME. NOT RIGHT NOW.
NOBODY EVEN KNOWS I CAN MOVE THINGS WITH MY MIND.
UNTIL THE NEXT TIME YOU HAVE A NIGHTMARE AND BRING THE ROOF DOWN ON TOP OF US.
THAT'S NOT...
YEAH, OKAY.
LOVE YOU TOO.
WELL, I'M HERE, BIG CREEPY MANSION.
HOME SWEET HOME.

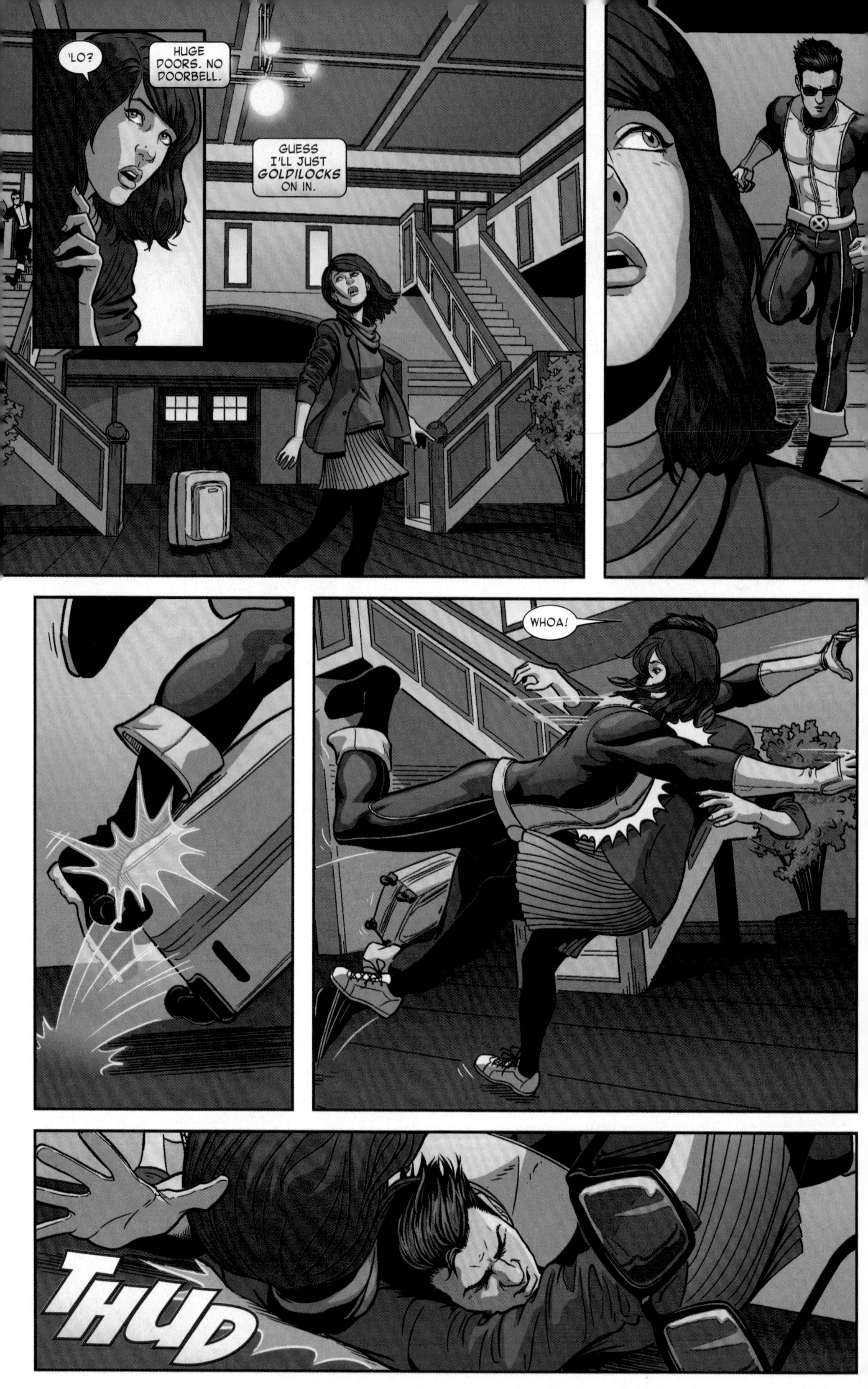
'LO?
HUGE DOORS. NO DOORBELL.
GUESS I'LL JUST GOLDILOCKS ON IN.
WHOA!
THUD

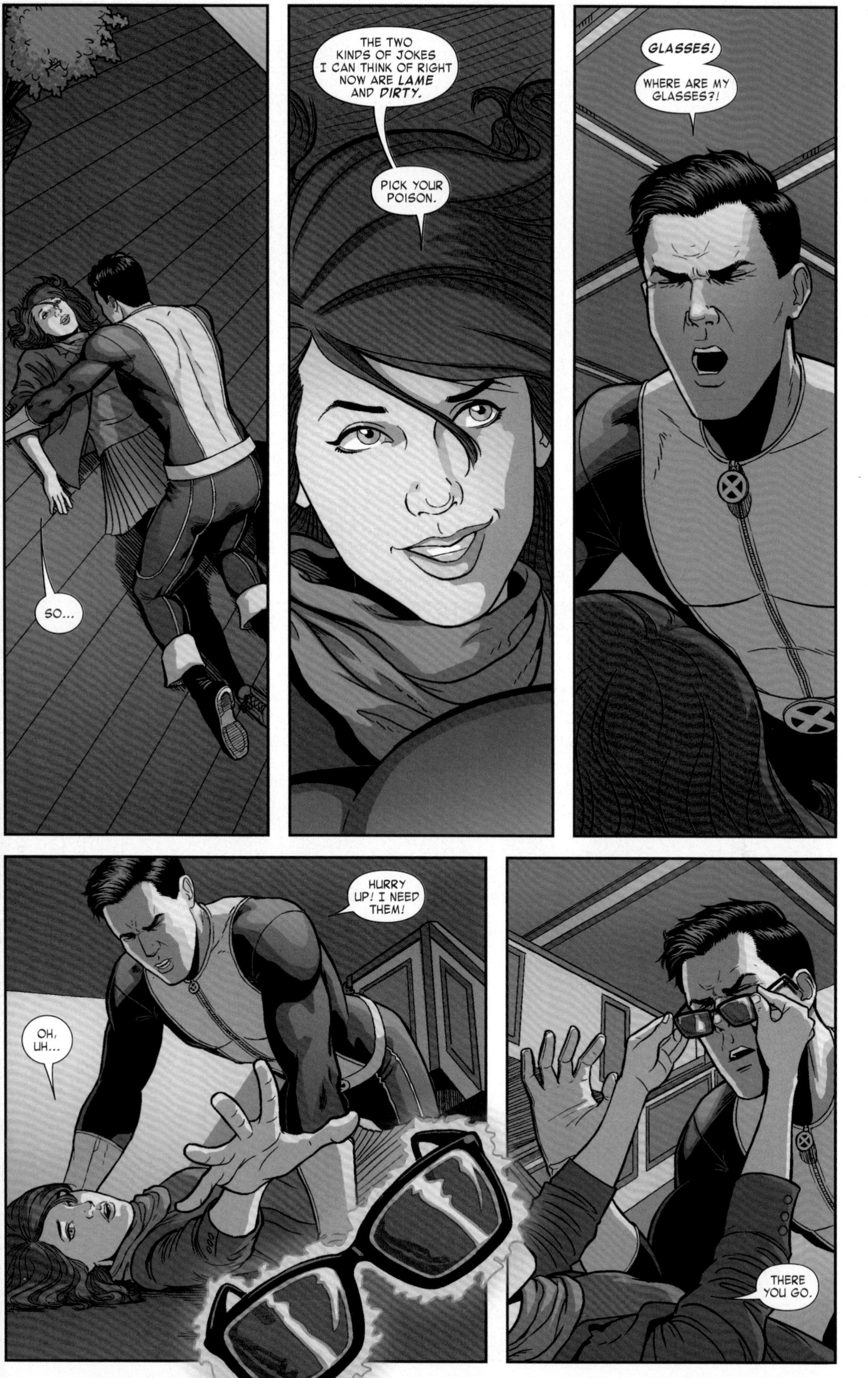

SO...
THE TWO KINDS OF JOKES I CAN THINK OF RIGHT NOW ARE LAME AND DIRTY.
PICK YOUR POISON.
GLASSES!
WHERE ARE MY GLASSES?!
OH, UH...
HURRY UP! I NEED THEM!
THERE YOU GO.

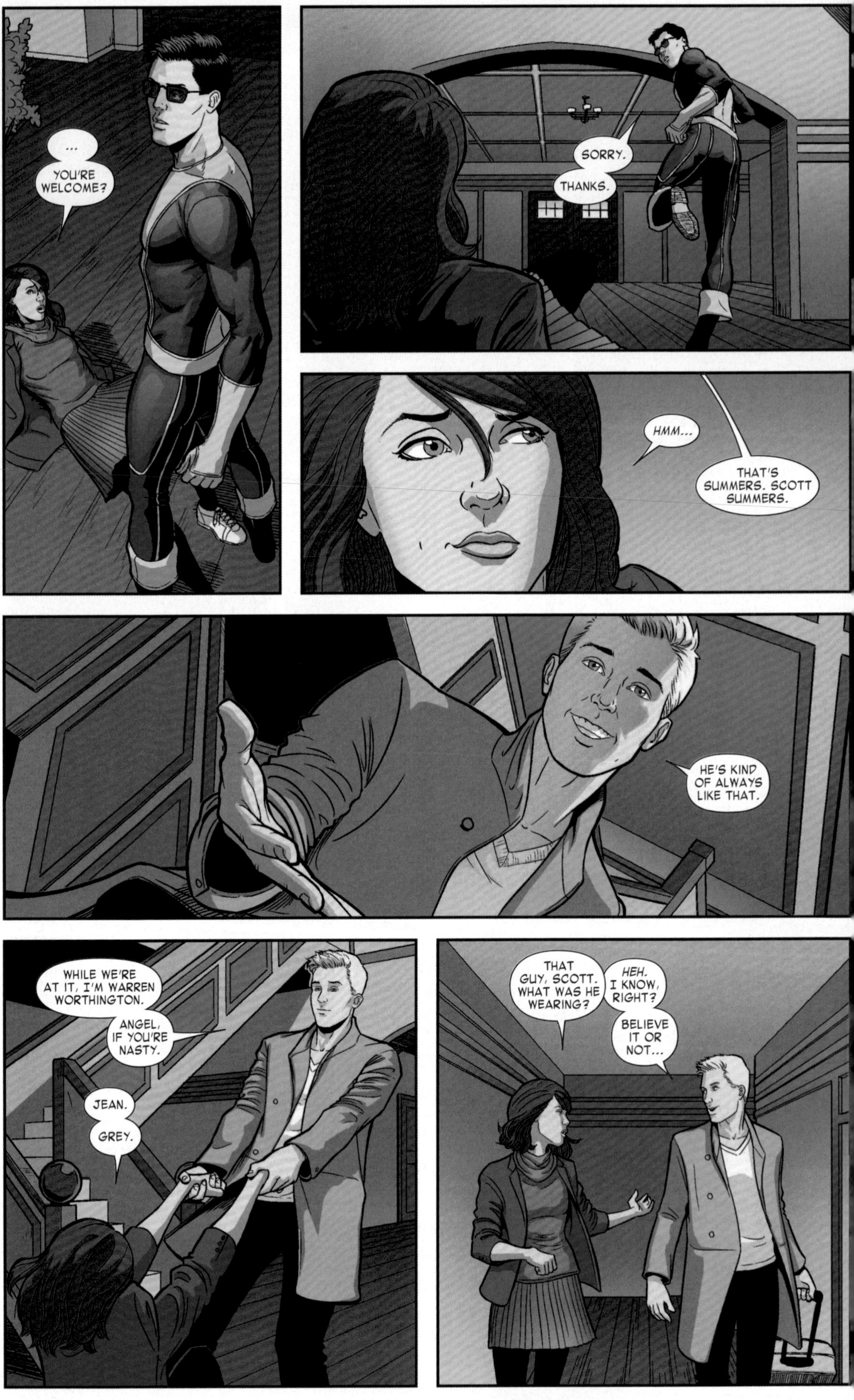
...
YOU'RE WELCOME?
SORRY.
THANKS.
HMM...
THAT'S SUMMERS. SCOTT SUMMERS.
HE'S KIND OF ALWAYS LIKE THAT.
WHILE WE'RE AT IT, I'M WARREN WORTHINGTON.
ANGEL, IF YOU'RE NASTY.
JEAN.
GREY.
THAT GUY, SCOTT. WHAT WAS HE WEARING?
HEH. I KNOW, RIGHT?
BELIEVE IT OR NOT...

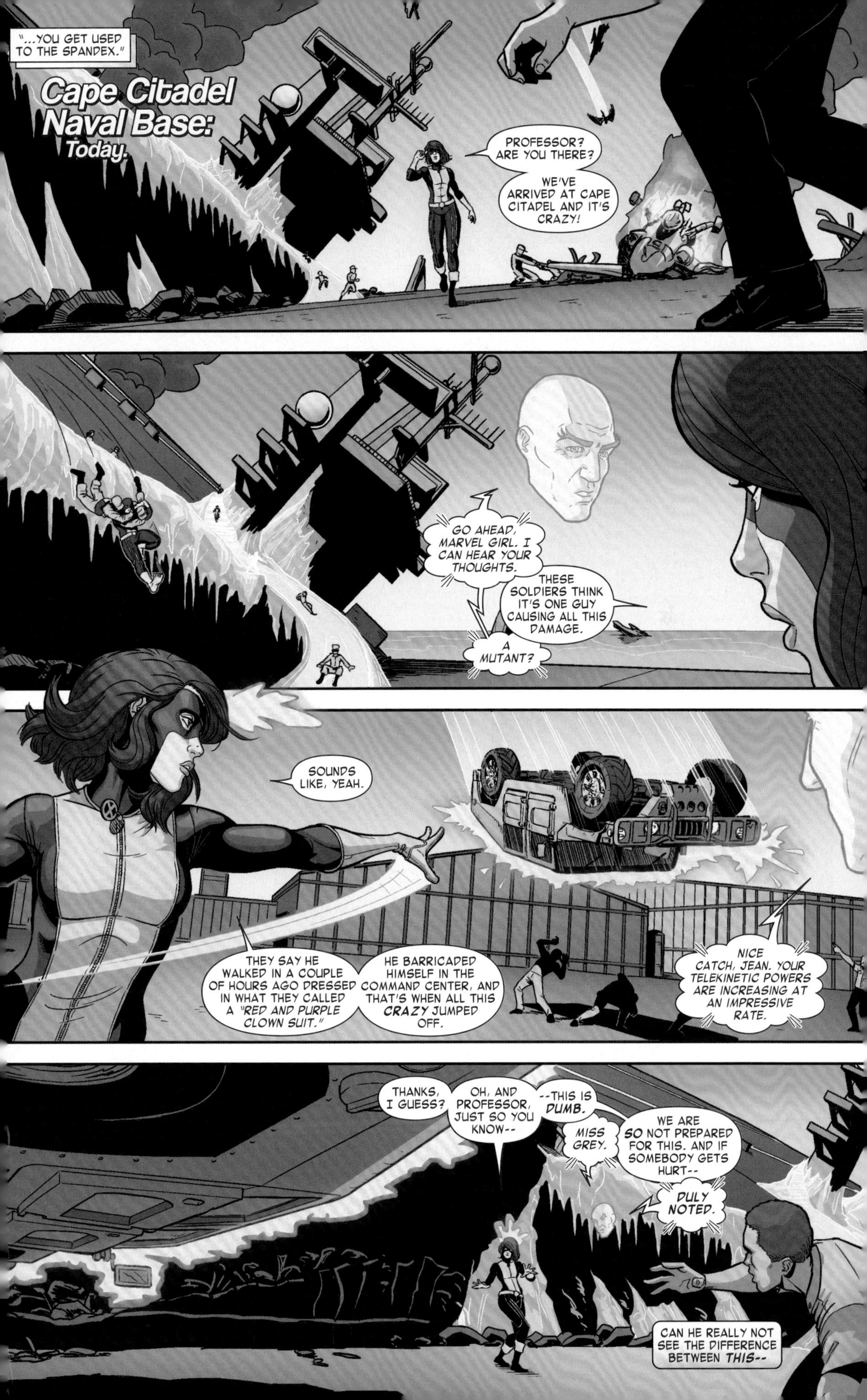

"...YOU GET USED TO THE SPANDEX."
Cape Citadel Naval Base: Today.
PROFESSOR? ARE YOU THERE?
WE'VE ARRIVED AT CAPE CITADEL AND IT'S CRAZY!
GO AHEAD, MARVEL GIRL. I CAN HEAR YOUR THOUGHTS.
THESE SOLDIERS THINK IT'S ONE GUY CAUSING ALL THIS DAMAGE.
A MUTANT?
SOUNDS LIKE, YEAH.
THEY SAY HE WALKED IN A COUPLE OF HOURS AGO DRESSED IN WHAT THEY CALLED A "RED AND PURPLE CLOWN SUIT."
HE BARRICADED HIMSELF IN THE COMMAND CENTER, AND THAT'S WHEN ALL THIS CRAZY JUMPED OFF.
NICE CATCH, JEAN. YOUR TELEKINETIC POWERS ARE INCREASING AT AN IMPRESSIVE RATE.
THANKS, I GUESS?
OH, AND PROFESSOR, JUST SO YOU KNOW--
--THIS IS DUMB.
MISS GREY.
WE ARE SO NOT PREPARED FOR THIS. AND IF SOMEBODY GETS HURT--
DULY NOTED.
CAN HE REALLY NOT SEE THE DIFFERENCE BETWEEN THIS--

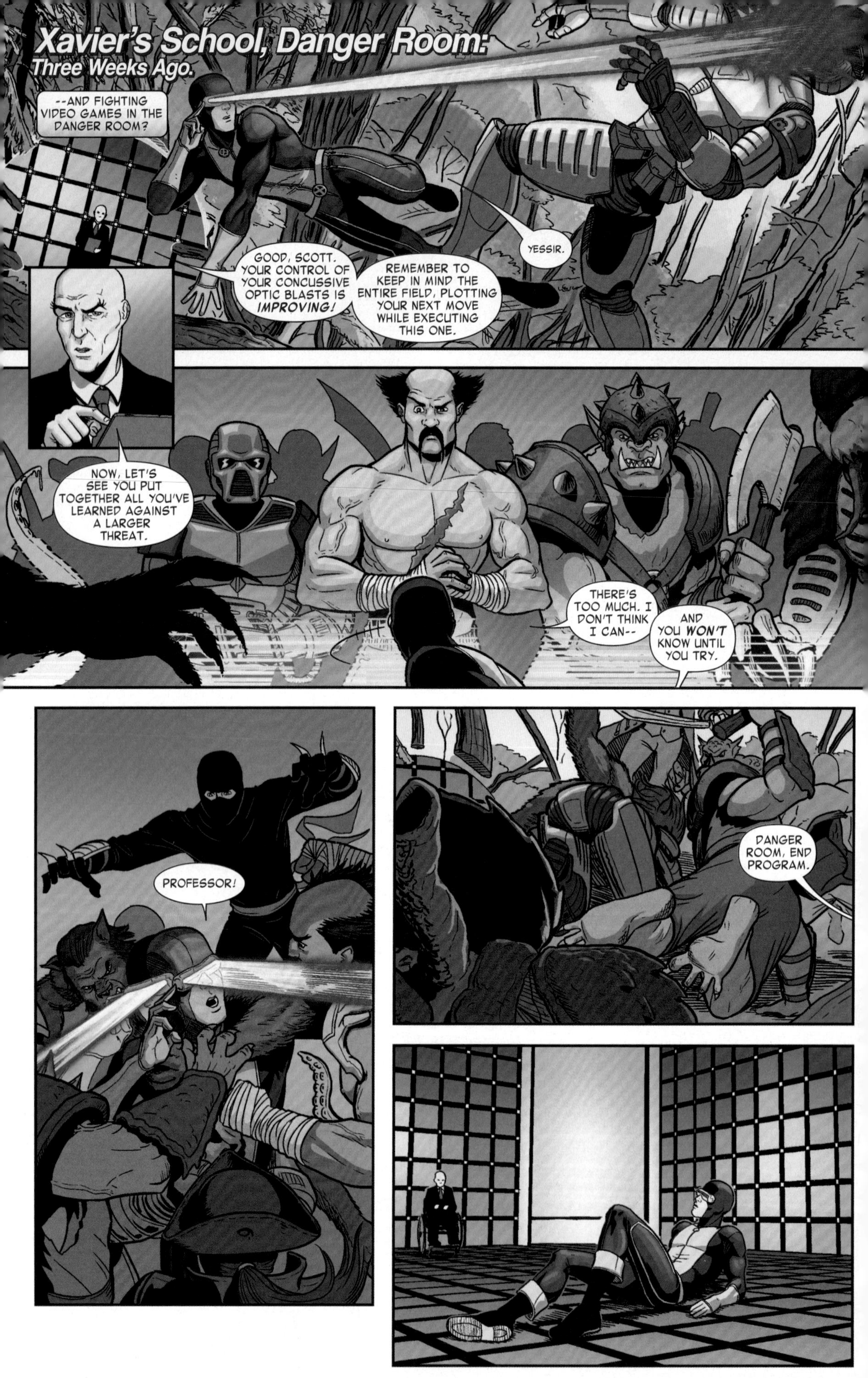
Xavier's School, Danger Room:
Three Weeks Ago.
--AND FIGHTING VIDEO GAMES IN THE DANGER ROOM?
GOOD, SCOTT. YOUR CONTROL OF YOUR CONCUSSIVE OPTIC BLASTS IS IMPROVING!
REMEMBER TO KEEP IN MIND THE ENTIRE FIELD, PLOTTING YOUR NEXT MOVE WHILE EXECUTING THIS ONE.
YESSIR.
NOW, LET'S SEE YOU PUT TOGETHER ALL YOU'VE LEARNED AGAINST A LARGER THREAT.
THERE'S TOO MUCH. I DON'T THINK I CAN--
AND YOU WON'T KNOW UNTIL YOU TRY.
PROFESSOR!
DANGER ROOM, END PROGRAM.

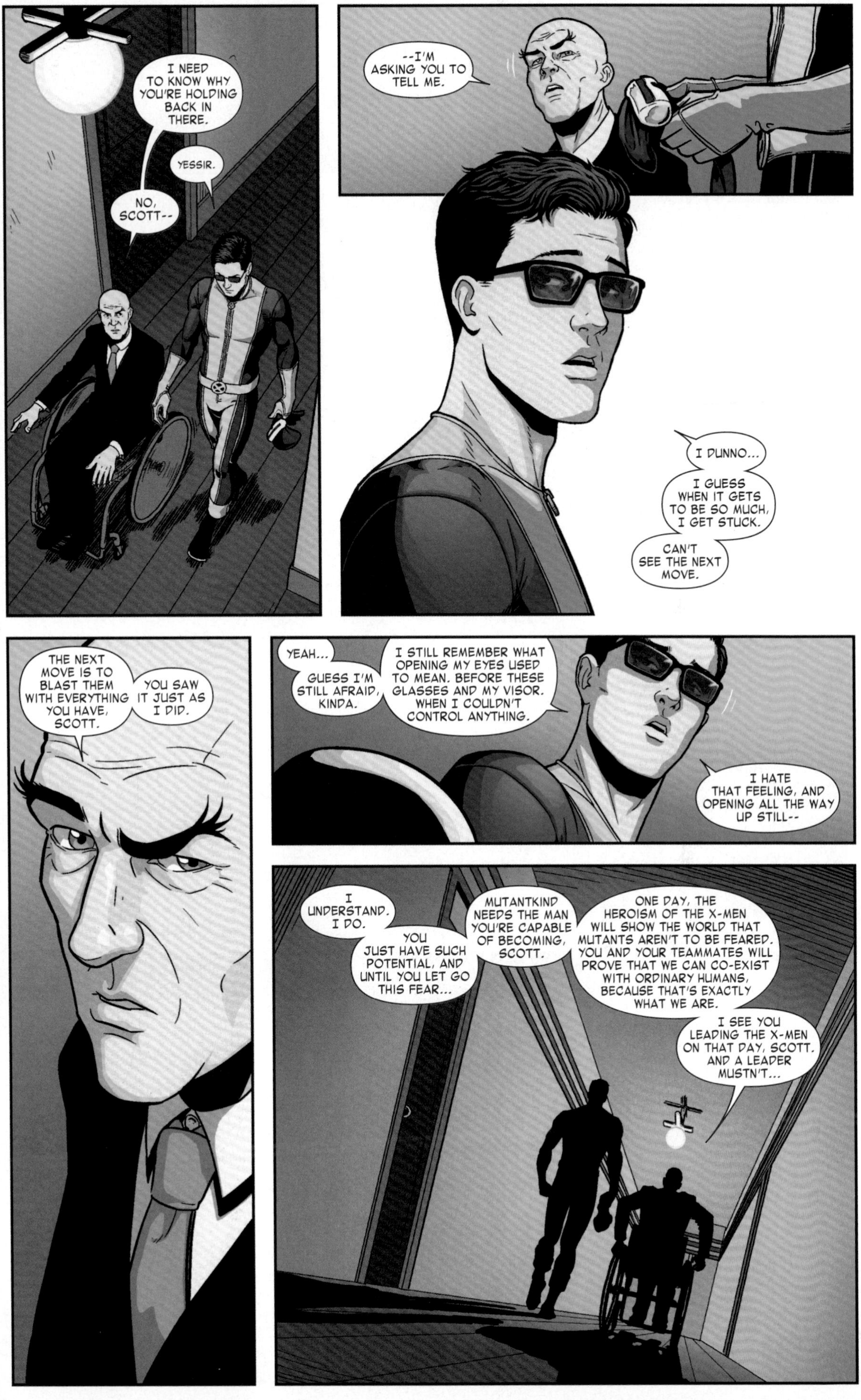
I NEED TO KNOW WHY YOU'RE HOLDING BACK IN THERE.
YESSIR.
NO, SCOTT--
--I'M ASKING YOU TO TELL ME.
I DUNNO...
I GUESS WHEN IT GETS TO BE SO MUCH, I GET STUCK.
CAN'T SEE THE NEXT MOVE.
THE NEXT MOVE IS TO BLAST THEM WITH EVERYTHING YOU HAVE, SCOTT.
YOU SAW IT JUST AS I DID.
YEAH...
GUESS I'M STILL AFRAID, KINDA.
I STILL REMEMBER WHAT OPENING MY EYES USED TO MEAN. BEFORE THESE GLASSES AND MY VISOR. WHEN I COULDN'T CONTROL ANYTHING.
I HATE THAT FEELING, AND OPENING ALL THE WAY UP STILL--
I UNDERSTAND. I DO.
YOU JUST HAVE SUCH POTENTIAL, AND UNTIL YOU LET GO THIS FEAR...
MUTANTKIND NEEDS THE MAN YOU'RE CAPABLE OF BECOMING, SCOTT.
ONE DAY, THE HEROISM OF THE X-MEN WILL SHOW THE WORLD THAT MUTANTS AREN'T TO BE FEARED. YOU AND YOUR TEAMMATES WILL PROVE THAT WE CAN CO-EXIST WITH ORDINARY HUMANS, BECAUSE THAT'S EXACTLY WHAT WE ARE.
I SEE YOU LEADING THE X-MEN ON THAT DAY, SCOTT. AND A LEADER MUSTN'T...

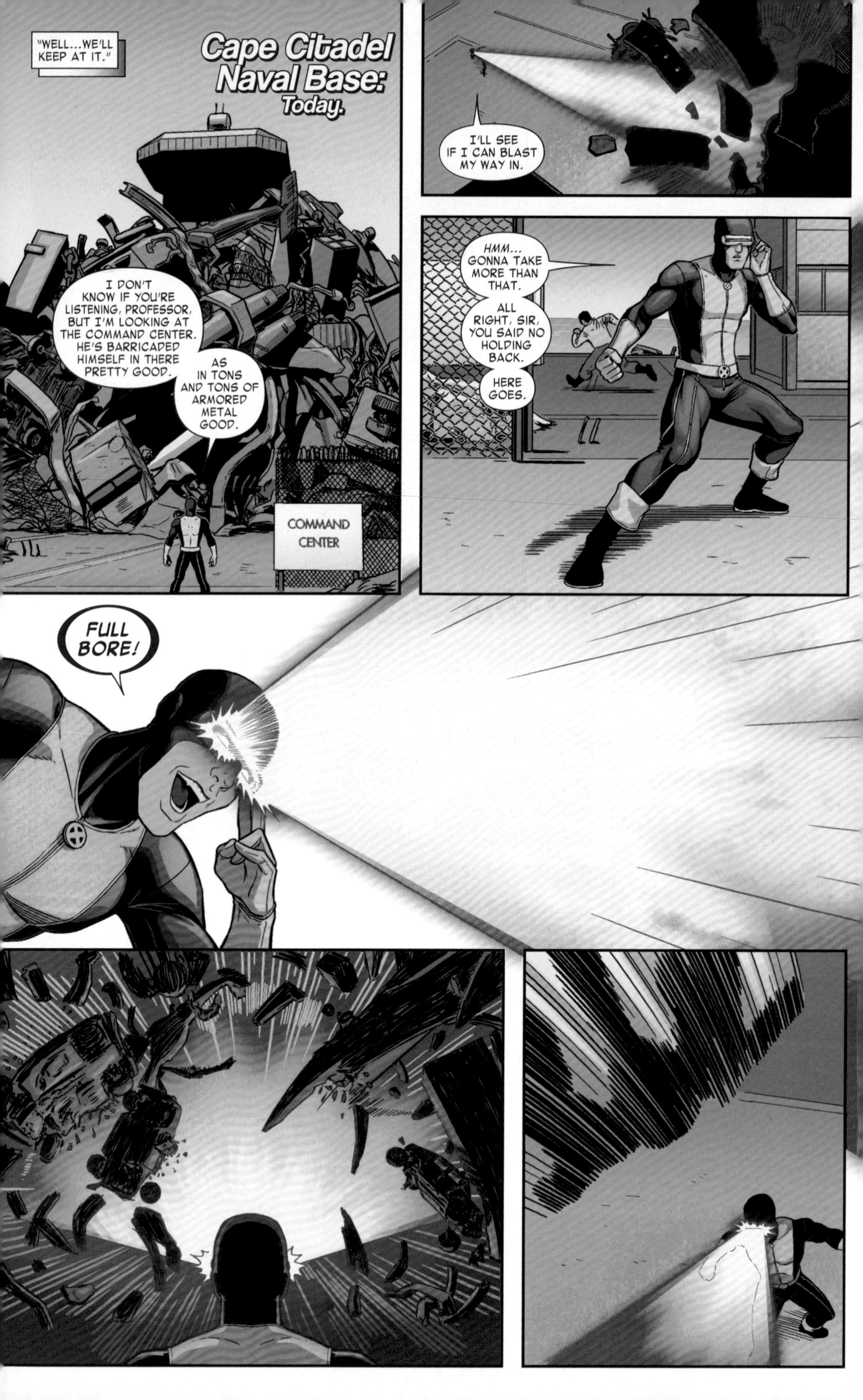
"WELL...WE'LL KEEP AT IT."
Cape Citadel Naval Base: Today.
I DON'T KNOW IF YOU'RE LISTENING, PROFESSOR, BUT I'M LOOKING AT THE COMMAND CENTER. HE'S BARRICADED HIMSELF IN THERE PRETTY GOOD.
AS IN TONS AND TONS OF ARMORED METAL GOOD.
COMMAND CENTER
I'LL SEE IF I CAN BLAST MY WAY IN.
HMM... GONNA TAKE MORE THAN THAT.
ALL RIGHT, SIR, YOU SAID NO HOLDING BACK.
HERE GOES.
FULL BORE!

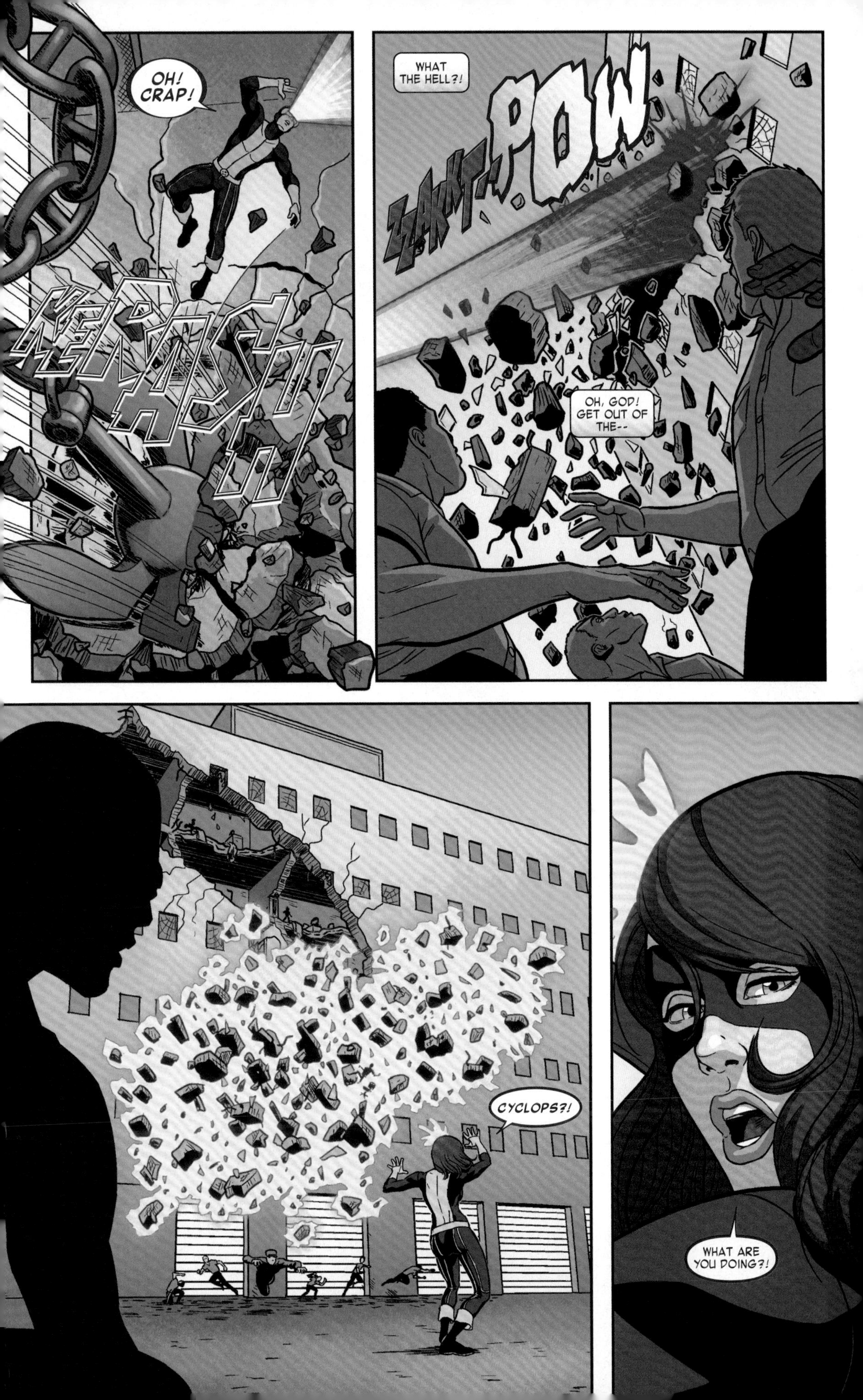
OH! CRAP!
WHAT THE HELL?!
POW
OH, GOD! GET OUT OF THE--
CYCLOPS?!
WHAT ARE YOU DOING?!

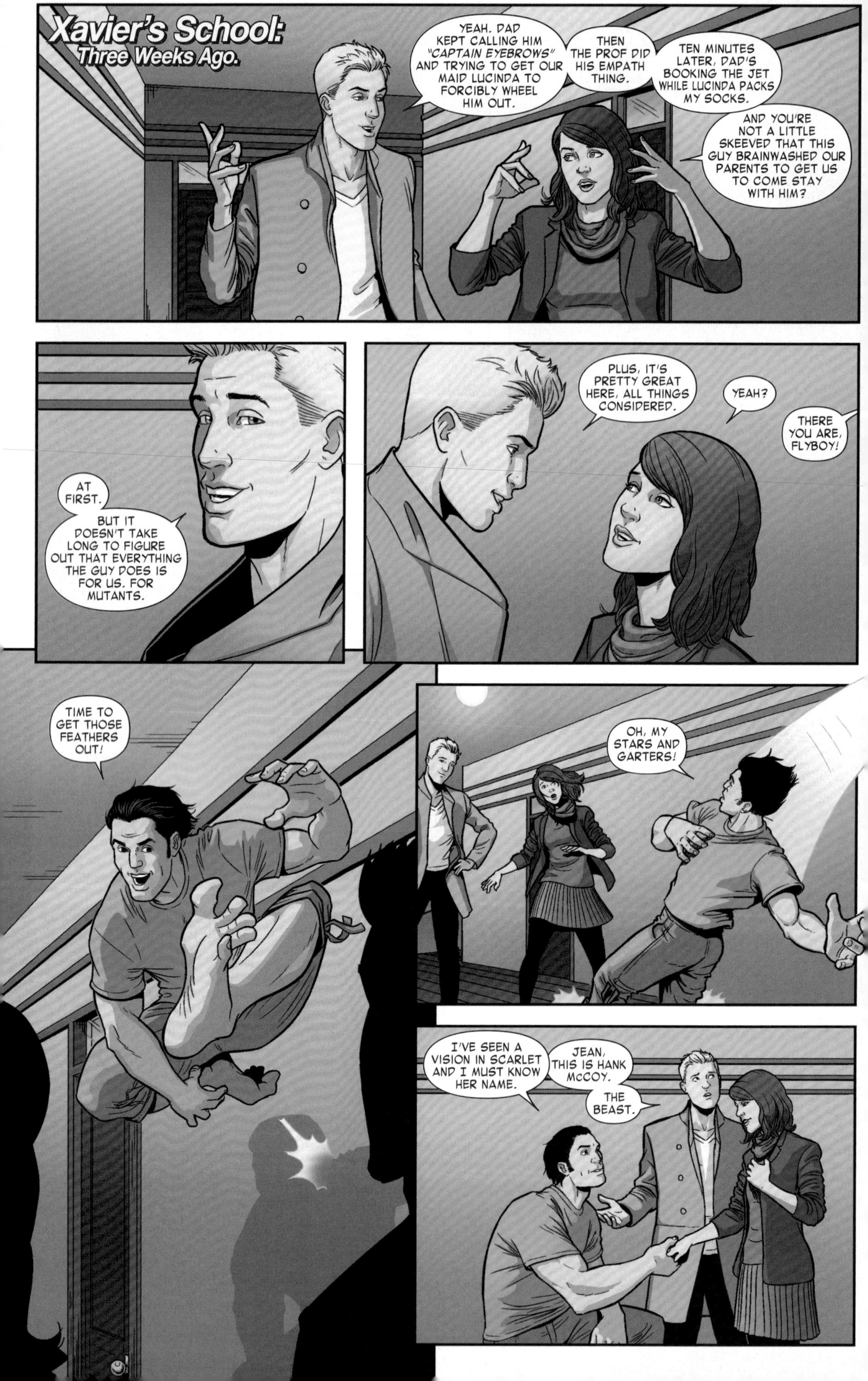
Xavier's School: Three Weeks Ago.
YEAH. DAD KEPT CALLING HIM "CAPTAIN EYEBROWS" AND TRYING TO GET OUR MAID LUCINDA TO FORCIBLY WHEEL HIM OUT.
THEN THE PROF DID HIS EMPATH THING.
TEN MINUTES LATER, DAD'S BOOKING THE JET WHILE LUCINDA PACKS MY SOCKS.
AND YOU'RE NOT A LITTLE SKEEVED THAT THIS GUY BRAINWASHED OUR PARENTS TO GET US TO COME STAY WITH HIM?
AT FIRST.
BUT IT DOESN'T TAKE LONG TO FIGURE OUT THAT EVERYTHING THE GUY DOES IS FOR US. FOR MUTANTS.
PLUS, IT'S PRETTY GREAT HERE, ALL THINGS CONSIDERED.
YEAH?
THERE YOU ARE, FLYBOY!
TIME TO GET THOSE FEATHERS OUT!
OH, MY STARS AND GARTERS!
I'VE SEEN A VISION IN SCARLET AND I MUST KNOW HER NAME.
JEAN, THIS IS HANK McCOY.
THE BEAST.

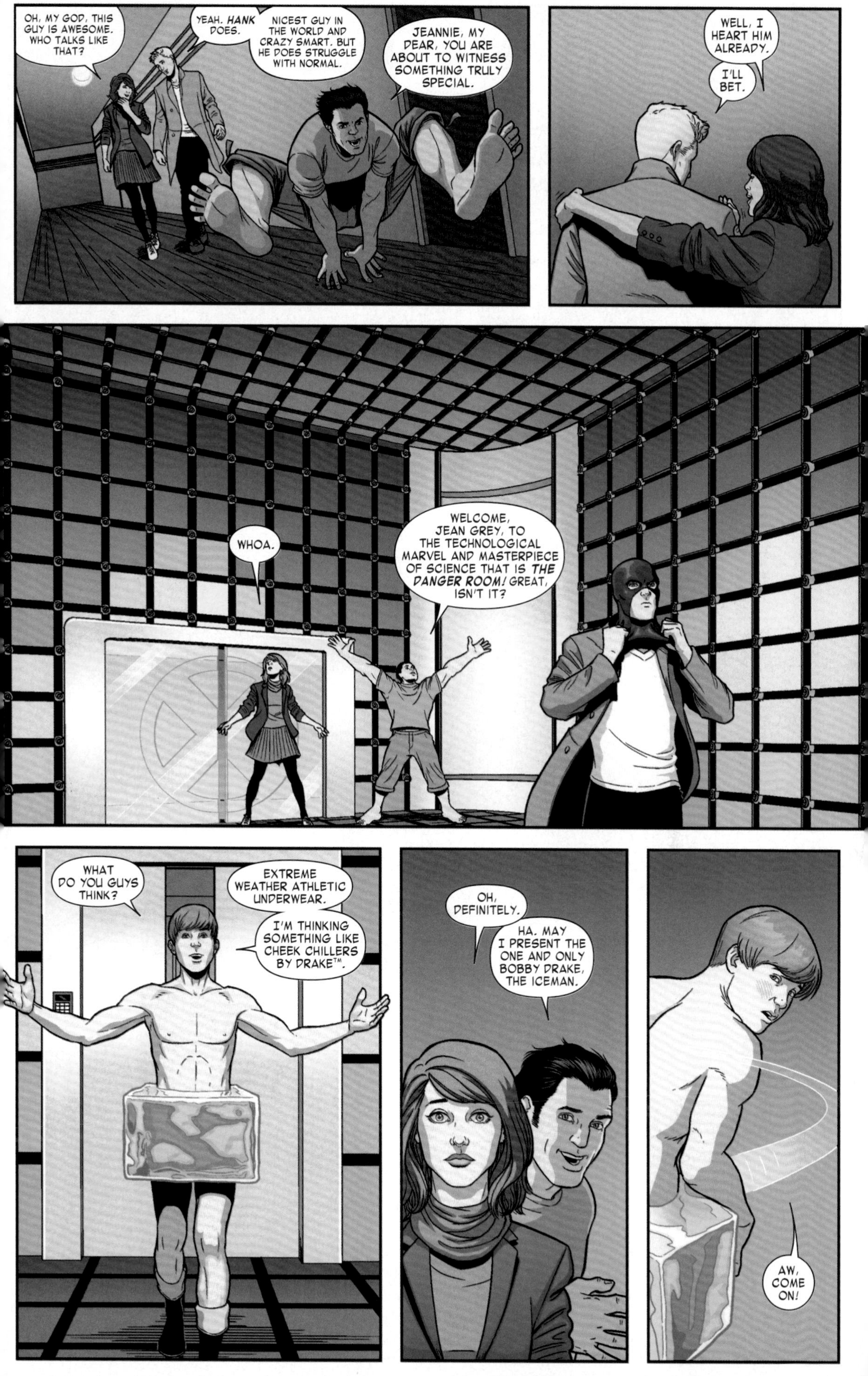
OH, MY GOD, THIS GUY IS AWESOME. WHO TALKS LIKE THAT?
YEAH. HANK DOES.
NICEST GUY IN THE WORLD AND CRAZY SMART. BUT HE DOES STRUGGLE WITH NORMAL.
JEANNIE, MY DEAR, YOU ARE ABOUT TO WITNESS SOMETHING TRULY SPECIAL.
WELL, I HEART HIM ALREADY.
I'LL BET.
WHOA.
WELCOME, JEAN GREY, TO THE TECHNOLOGICAL MARVEL AND MASTERPIECE OF SCIENCE THAT IS THE DANGER ROOM! GREAT, ISN'T IT?
WHAT DO YOU GUYS THINK?
EXTREME WEATHER ATHLETIC UNDERWEAR.
I'M THINKING SOMETHING LIKE CHEEK CHILLERS BY DRAKE™.
OH, DEFINITELY.
HA. MAY I PRESENT THE ONE AND ONLY BOBBY DRAKE, THE ICEMAN.
AW, COME ON!

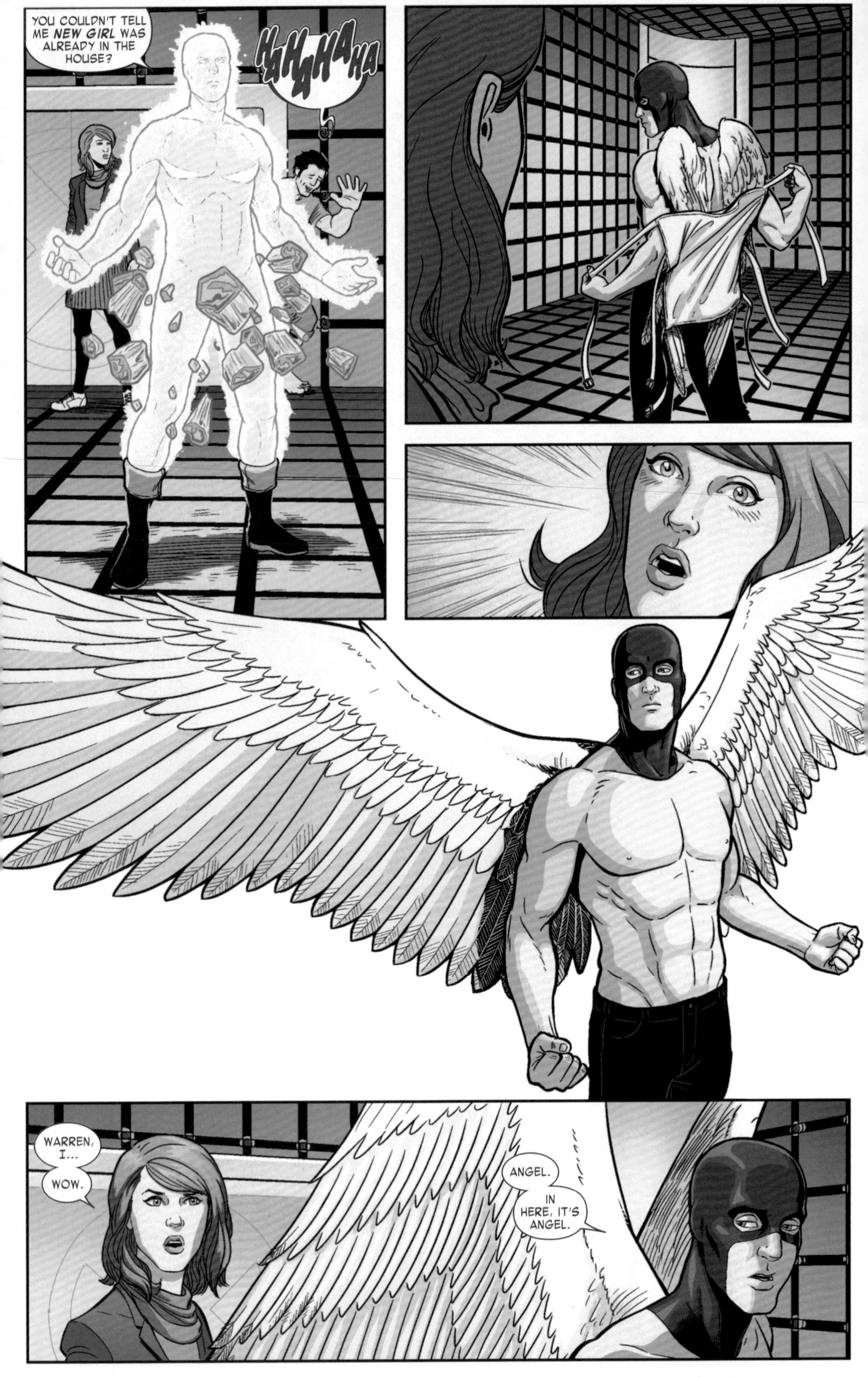
YOU COULDN'T TELL ME NEW GIRL WAS ALREADY IN THE HOUSE?
HAHAHAHAHA
WARREN, I...
WOW.
ANGEL.
IN HERE, IT'S ANGEL.

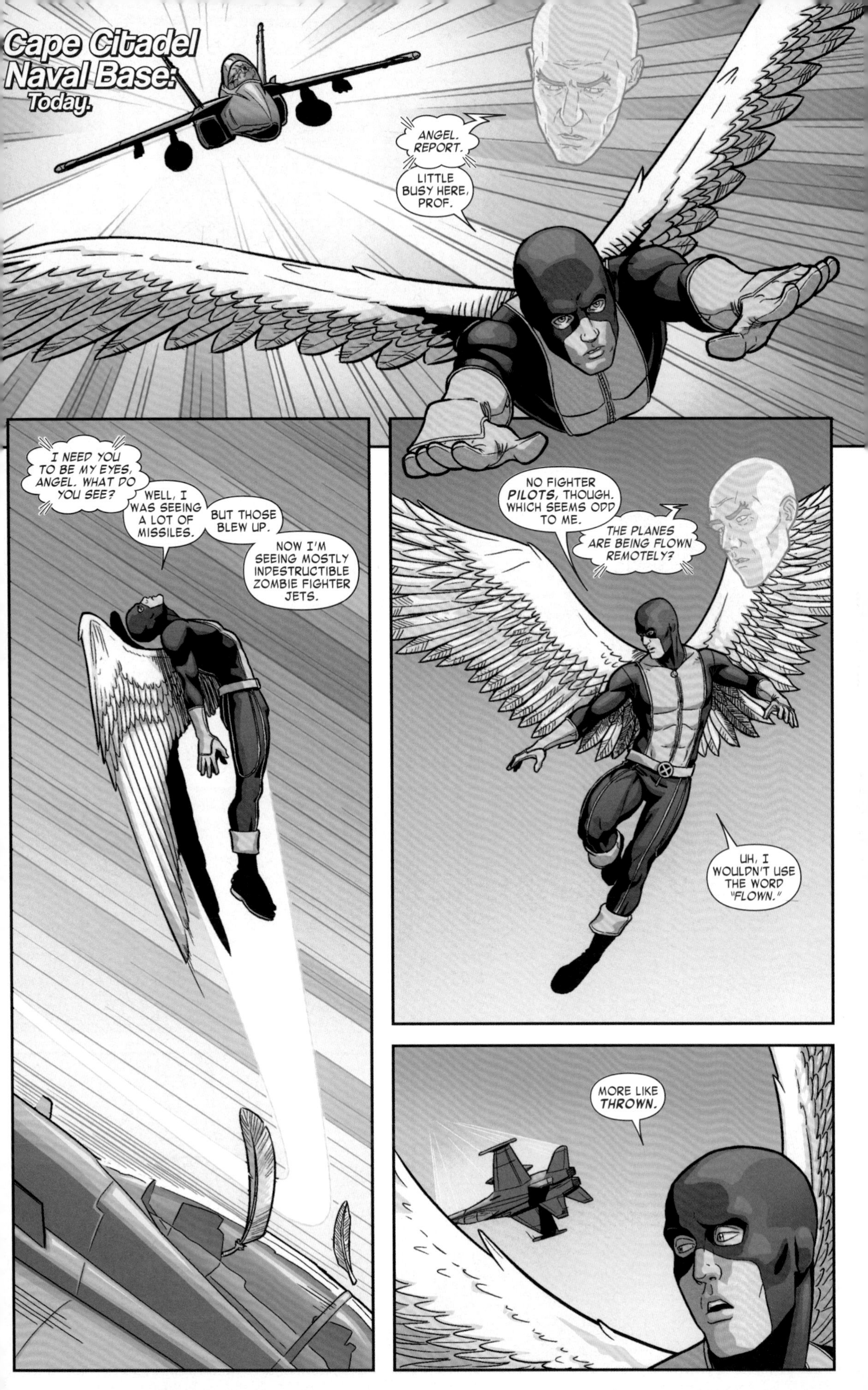
Cape Citadel Naval Base: Today.
ANGEL. REPORT.
LITTLE BUSY HERE, PROF.
I NEED YOU TO BE MY EYES, ANGEL. WHAT DO YOU SEE?
WELL, I WAS SEEING A LOT OF MISSILES.
BUT THOSE BLEW UP.
NOW I'M SEEING MOSTLY INDESTRUCTIBLE ZOMBIE FIGHTER JETS.
NO FIGHTER PILOTS, THOUGH. WHICH SEEMS ODD TO ME.
THE PLANES ARE BEING FLOWN REMOTELY?
UH, I WOULDN'T USE THE WORD "FLOWN."
MORE LIKE THROWN.

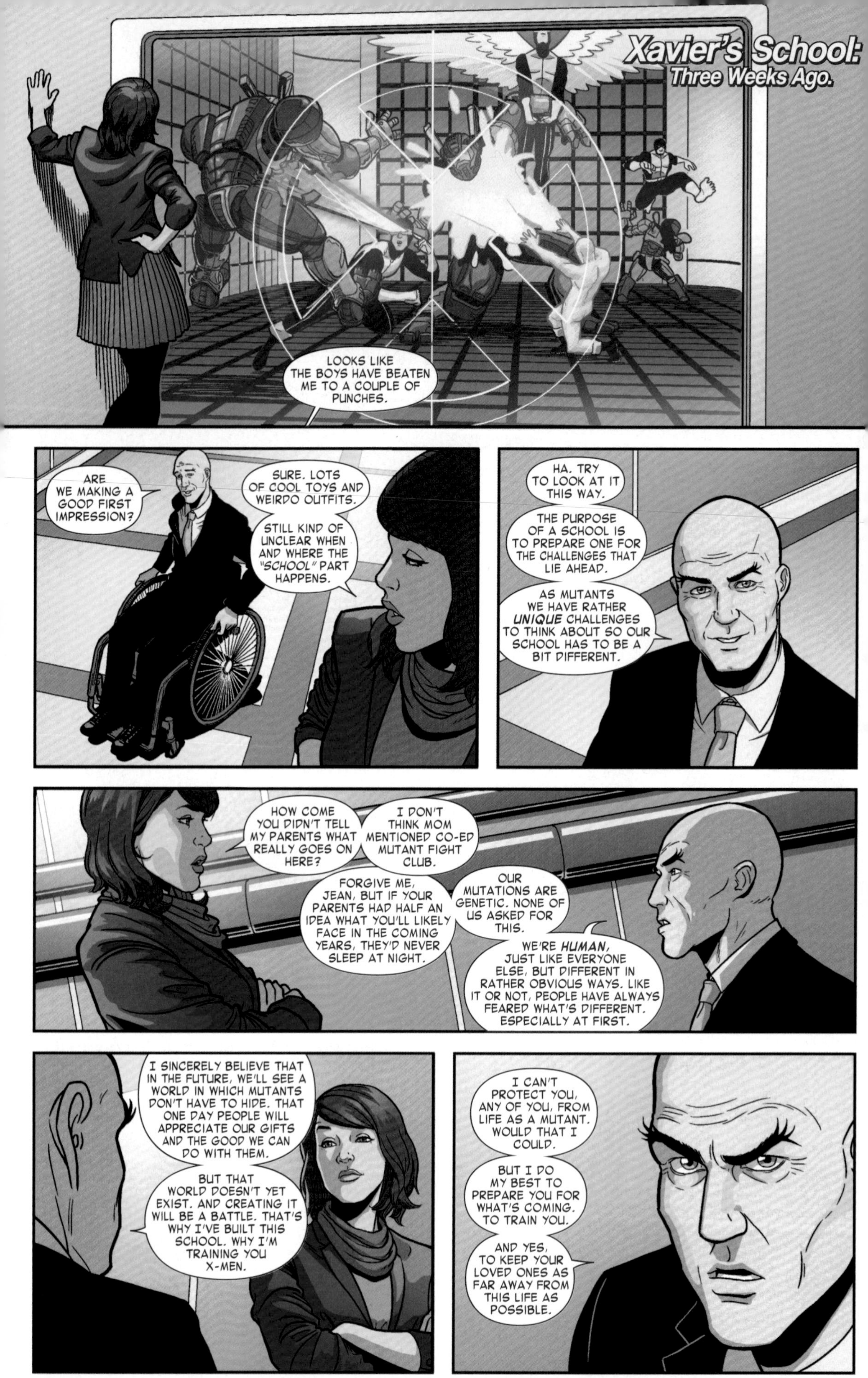
Xavier's School: Three Weeks Ago.
LOOKS LIKE THE BOYS HAVE BEATEN ME TO A COUPLE OF PUNCHES.
ARE WE MAKING A GOOD FIRST IMPRESSION?
SURE. LOTS OF COOL TOYS AND WEIRDO OUTFITS.
STILL KIND OF UNCLEAR WHEN AND WHERE THE "SCHOOL" PART HAPPENS.
HA. TRY TO LOOK AT IT THIS WAY.
THE PURPOSE OF A SCHOOL IS TO PREPARE ONE FOR THE CHALLENGES THAT LIE AHEAD.
AS MUTANTS WE HAVE RATHER UNIQUE CHALLENGES TO THINK ABOUT SO OUR SCHOOL HAS TO BE A BIT DIFFERENT.
HOW COME YOU DIDN'T TELL MY PARENTS WHAT REALLY GOES ON HERE?
I DON'T THINK MOM MENTIONED CO-ED MUTANT FIGHT CLUB.
FORGIVE ME, JEAN, BUT IF YOUR PARENTS HAD HALF AN IDEA WHAT YOU'LL LIKELY FACE IN THE COMING YEARS, THEY'D NEVER SLEEP AT NIGHT.
OUR MUTATIONS ARE GENETIC. NONE OF US ASKED FOR THIS.
WE'RE HUMAN, JUST LIKE EVERYONE ELSE, BUT DIFFERENT IN RATHER OBVIOUS WAYS. LIKE IT OR NOT, PEOPLE HAVE ALWAYS FEARED WHAT'S DIFFERENT. ESPECIALLY AT FIRST.
I SINCERELY BELIEVE THAT IN THE FUTURE, WE'LL SEE A WORLD IN WHICH MUTANTS DON'T HAVE TO HIDE. THAT ONE DAY PEOPLE WILL APPRECIATE OUR GIFTS AND THE GOOD WE CAN DO WITH THEM.
BUT THAT WORLD DOESN'T YET EXIST. AND CREATING IT WILL BE A BATTLE. THAT'S WHY I'VE BUILT THIS SCHOOL. WHY I'M TRAINING YOU X-MEN.
I CAN'T PROTECT YOU, ANY OF YOU, FROM LIFE AS A MUTANT. WOULD THAT I COULD.
BUT I DO MY BEST TO PREPARE YOU FOR WHAT'S COMING. TO TRAIN YOU.
AND YES, TO KEEP YOUR LOVED ONES AS FAR AWAY FROM THIS LIFE AS POSSIBLE.

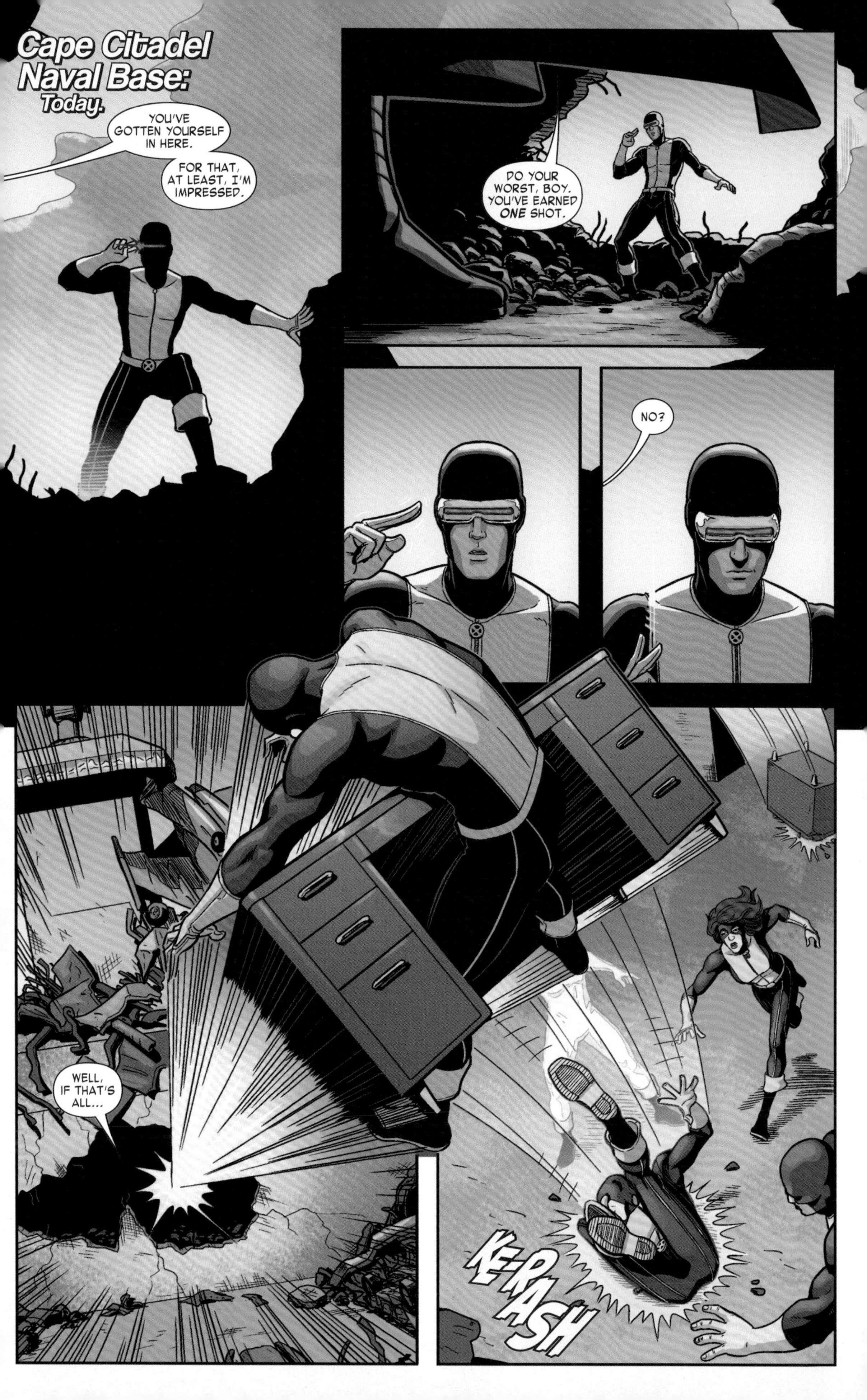
Cape Citadel Naval Base: Today.
YOU'VE GOTTEN YOURSELF IN HERE.
FOR THAT, AT LEAST, I'M IMPRESSED.
DO YOUR WORST, BOY. YOU'VE EARNED ONE SHOT.
NO?
WELL, IF THAT'S ALL...
KE-RASH

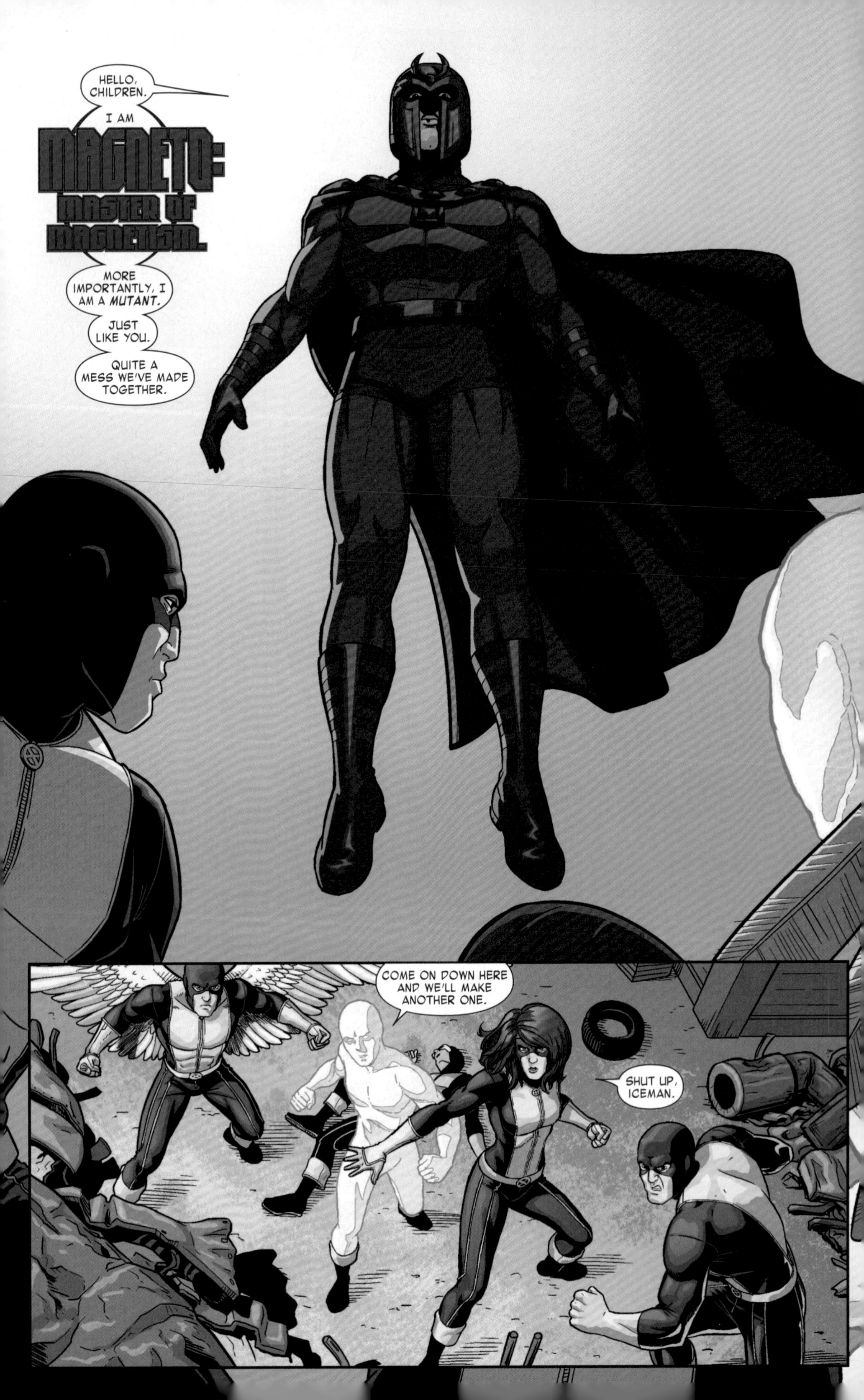
HELLO, CHILDREN.
I AM
MAGNETO: MASTER OF MAGNETISM.
MORE IMPORTANTLY, I AM A *MUTANT.*
JUST LIKE YOU.
QUITE A MESS WE'VE MADE TOGETHER.
COME ON DOWN HERE AND WE'LL MAKE ANOTHER ONE.
SHUT UP, ICEMAN.

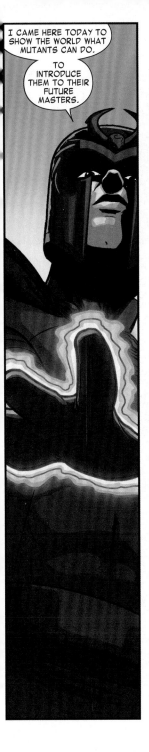

I CAME HERE TODAY TO SHOW THE WORLD WHAT MUTANTS CAN DO.

TO INTRODUCE THEM TO THEIR FUTURE MASTERS.

THANK YOU FOR THE *HELP.*

WHERE'S HE GOING?

JUST THE ONE WAY TO FIND OUT.

GUYS! DON'T BE STUPID.

HE LEFT. IT'S OVER.

IT IS *SO* NOT OVER.

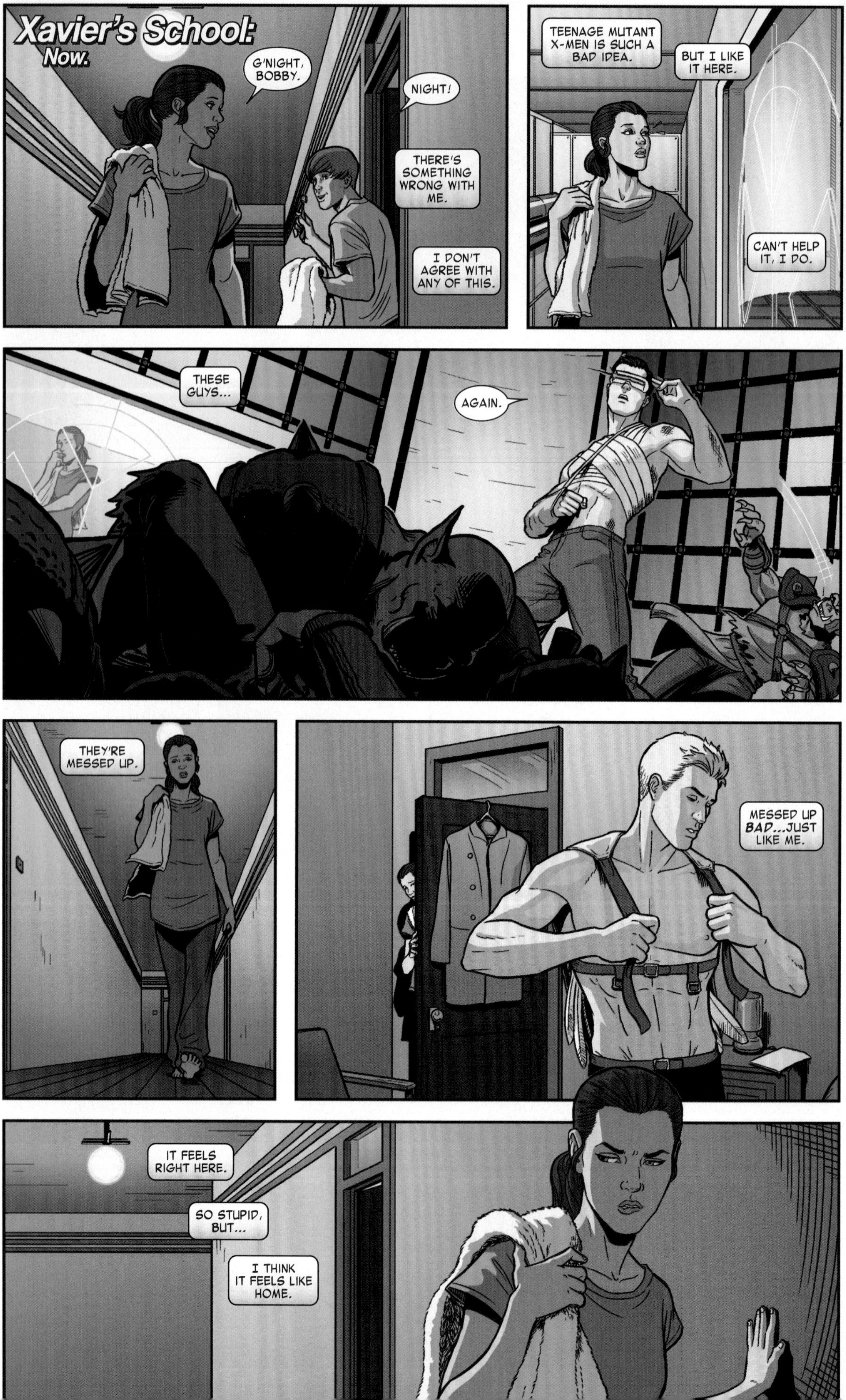

Xavier's School: Now.
G'NIGHT, BOBBY.
NIGHT!
THERE'S SOMETHING WRONG WITH ME.
I DON'T AGREE WITH ANY OF THIS.
TEENAGE MUTANT X-MEN IS SUCH A BAD IDEA.
BUT I LIKE IT HERE.
CAN'T HELP IT, I DO.
THESE GUYS...
AGAIN.
THEY'RE MESSED UP.
MESSED UP BAD...JUST LIKE ME.
IT FEELS RIGHT HERE.
SO STUPID, BUT...
I THINK IT FEELS LIKE HOME.

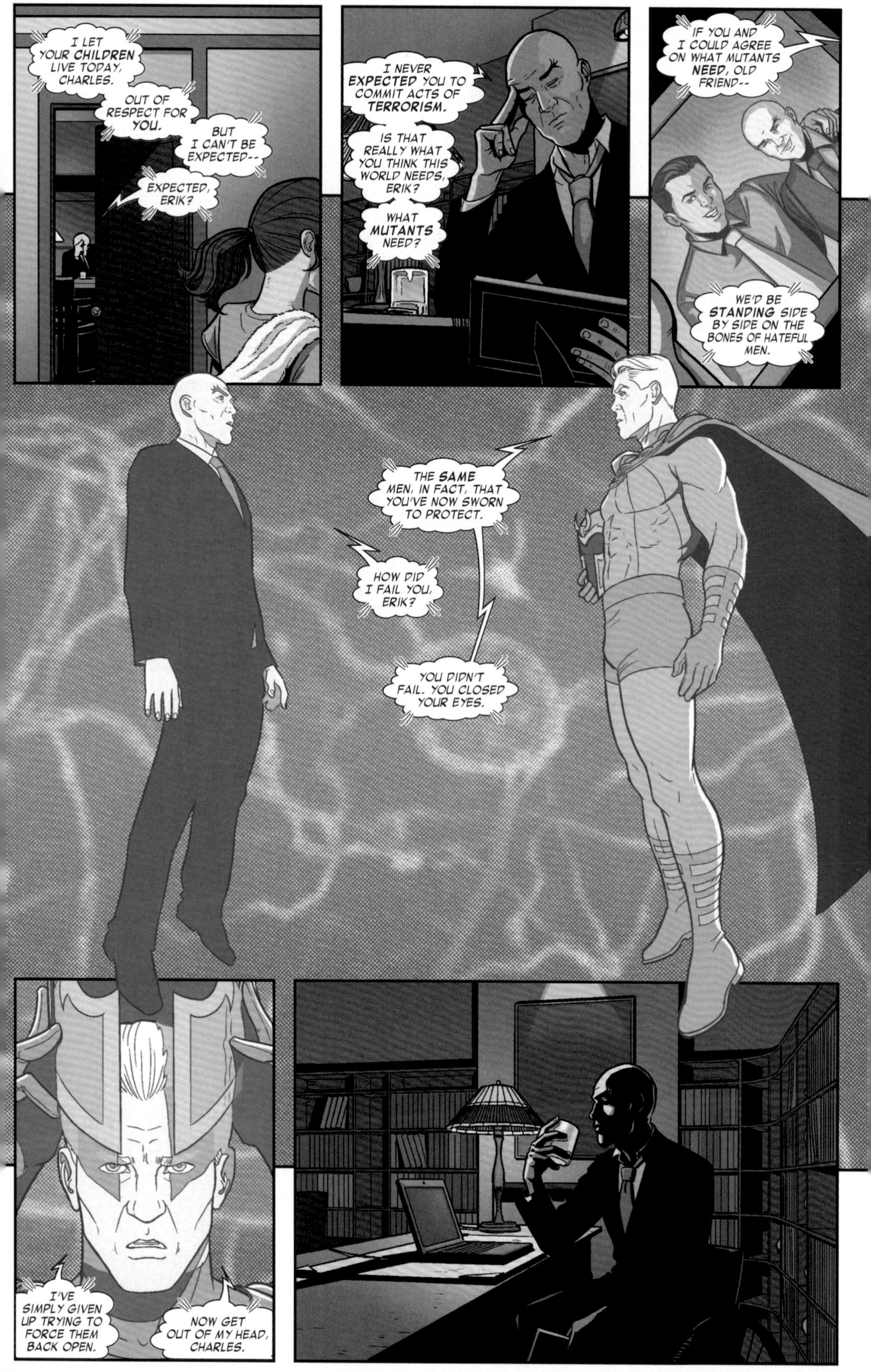
I LET YOUR CHILDREN LIVE TODAY, CHARLES.
OUT OF RESPECT FOR YOU.
BUT I CAN'T BE EXPECTED--
EXPECTED, ERIK?
I NEVER EXPECTED YOU TO COMMIT ACTS OF TERRORISM.
IS THAT REALLY WHAT YOU THINK THIS WORLD NEEDS, ERIK?
WHAT MUTANTS NEED?
IF YOU AND I COULD AGREE ON WHAT MUTANTS NEED, OLD FRIEND--
WE'D BE STANDING SIDE BY SIDE ON THE BONES OF HATEFUL MEN.
THE SAME MEN, IN FACT, THAT YOU'VE NOW SWORN TO PROTECT.
HOW DID I FAIL YOU, ERIK?
YOU DIDN'T FAIL. YOU CLOSED YOUR EYES.
I'VE SIMPLY GIVEN UP TRYING TO FORCE THEM BACK OPEN.
NOW GET OUT OF MY HEAD, CHARLES.

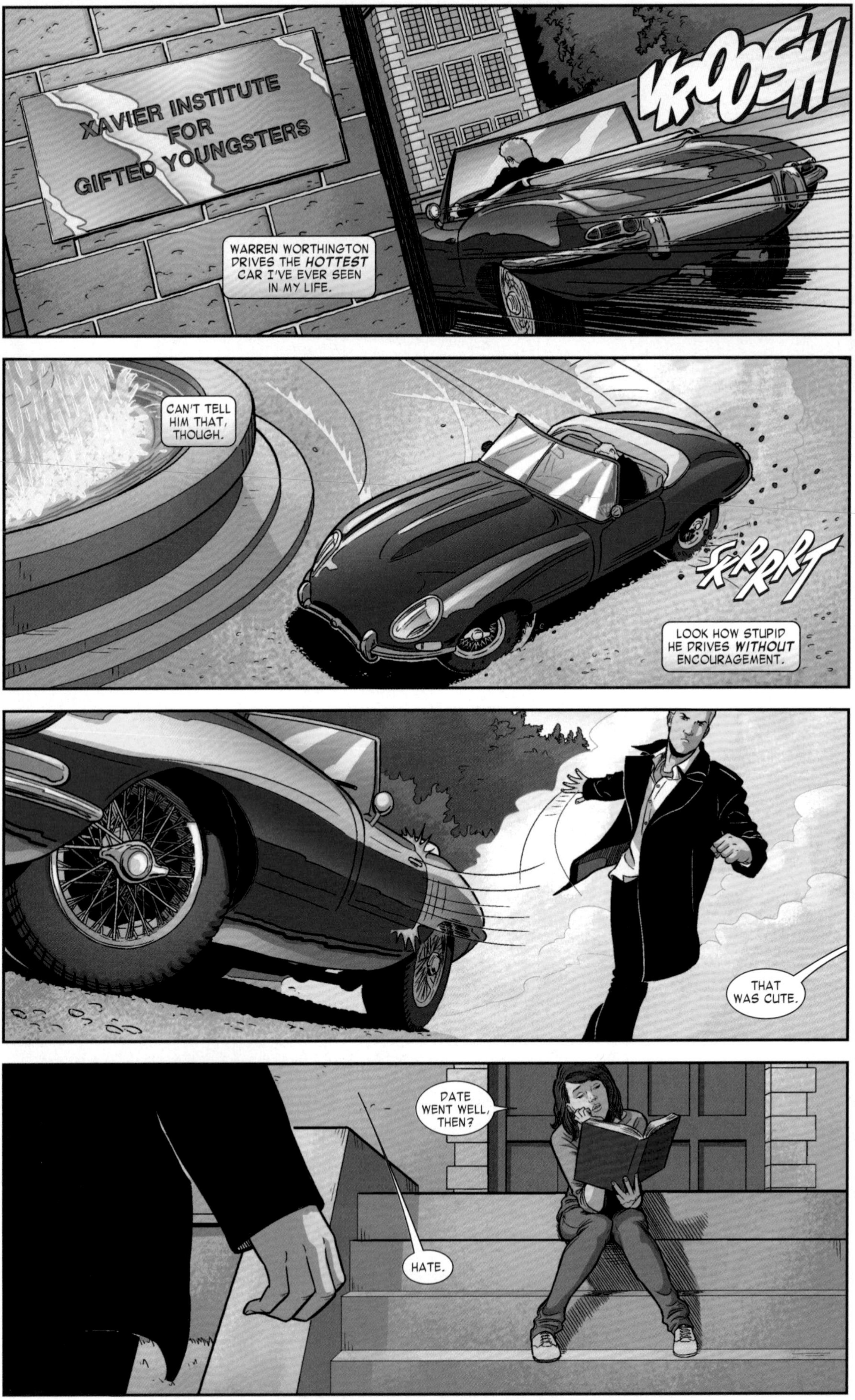
XAVIER INSTITUTE FOR GIFTED YOUNGSTERS
VROOSH
WARREN WORTHINGTON DRIVES THE HOTTEST CAR I'VE EVER SEEN IN MY LIFE.
CAN'T TELL HIM THAT, THOUGH.
SKRRRT
LOOK HOW STUPID HE DRIVES WITHOUT ENCOURAGEMENT.
THAT WAS CUTE.
DATE WENT WELL, THEN?
HATE.

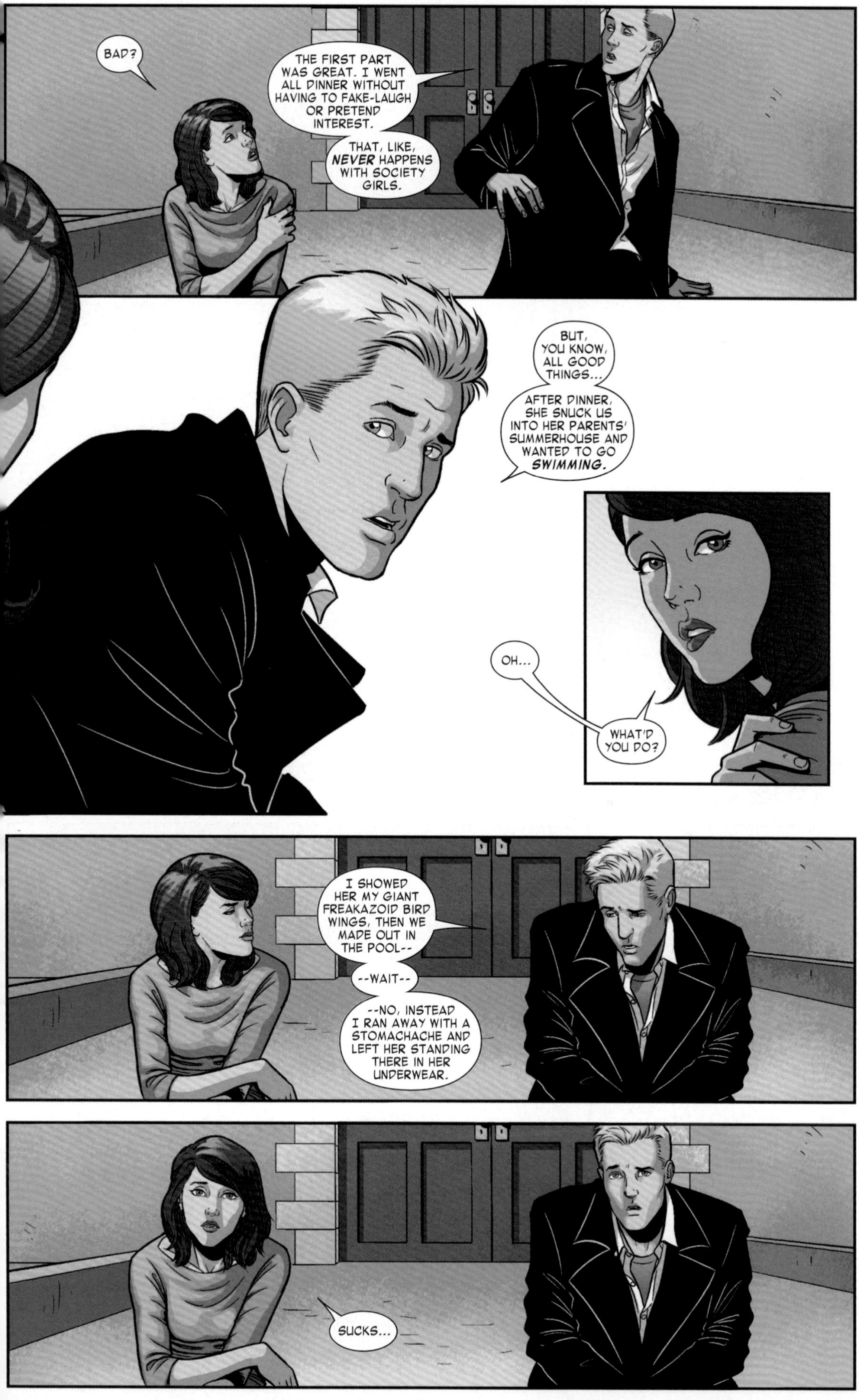
BAD?
THE FIRST PART WAS GREAT. I WENT ALL DINNER WITHOUT HAVING TO FAKE-LAUGH OR PRETEND INTEREST.
THAT, LIKE, NEVER HAPPENS WITH SOCIETY GIRLS.
BUT, YOU KNOW, ALL GOOD THINGS...
AFTER DINNER, SHE SNUCK US INTO HER PARENTS' SUMMERHOUSE AND WANTED TO GO SWIMMING.
OH...
WHAT'D YOU DO?
I SHOWED HER MY GIANT FREAKAZOID BIRD WINGS, THEN WE MADE OUT IN THE POOL--
--WAIT--
--NO, INSTEAD I RAN AWAY WITH A STOMACHACHE AND LEFT HER STANDING THERE IN HER UNDERWEAR.
SUCKS...

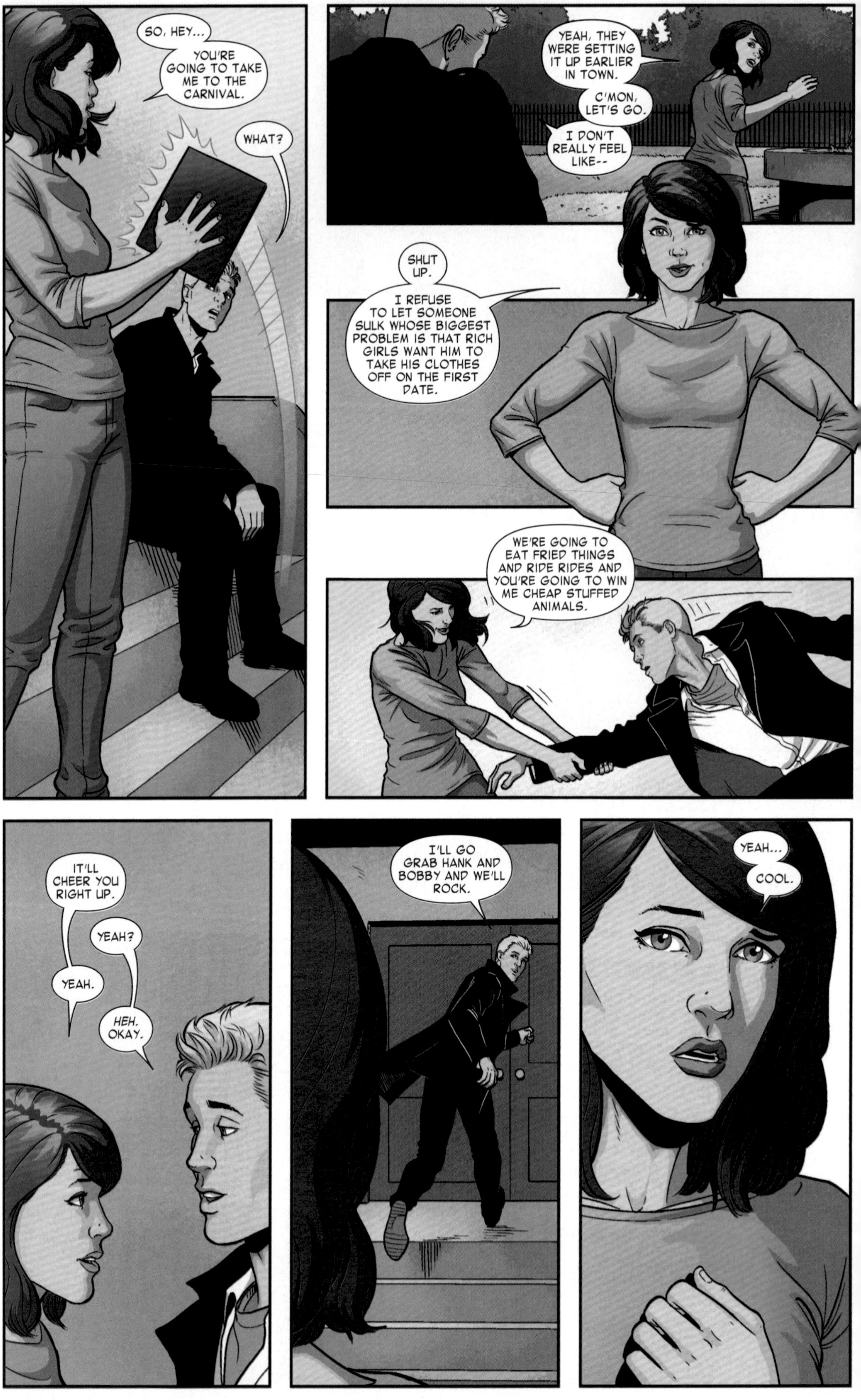
SO, HEY...
YOU'RE GOING TO TAKE ME TO THE CARNIVAL.
WHAT?
YEAH, THEY WERE SETTING IT UP EARLIER IN TOWN.
C'MON, LET'S GO.
I DON'T REALLY FEEL LIKE--
SHUT UP.
I REFUSE TO LET SOMEONE SULK WHOSE BIGGEST PROBLEM IS THAT RICH GIRLS WANT HIM TO TAKE HIS CLOTHES OFF ON THE FIRST DATE.
WE'RE GOING TO EAT FRIED THINGS AND RIDE RIDES AND YOU'RE GOING TO WIN ME CHEAP STUFFED ANIMALS.
IT'LL CHEER YOU RIGHT UP.
YEAH?
YEAH.
HEH. OKAY.
I'LL GO GRAB HANK AND BOBBY AND WE'LL ROCK.
YEAH...
COOL.

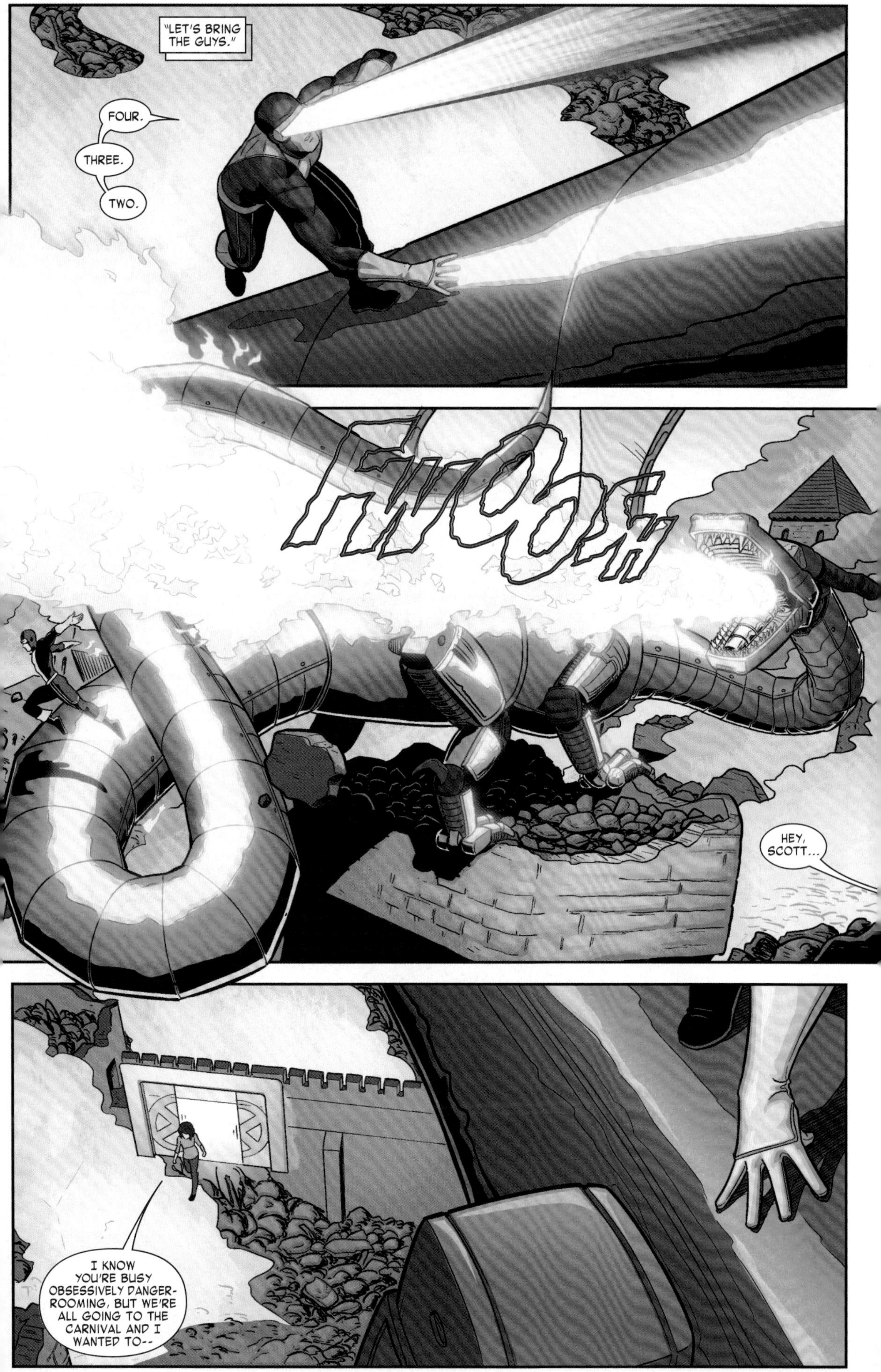
"LET'S BRING THE GUYS."
FOUR.
THREE.
TWO.
FWOOSH
HEY, SCOTT...
I KNOW YOU'RE BUSY OBSESSIVELY DANGER-ROOMING, BUT WE'RE ALL GOING TO THE CARNIVAL AND I WANTED TO--

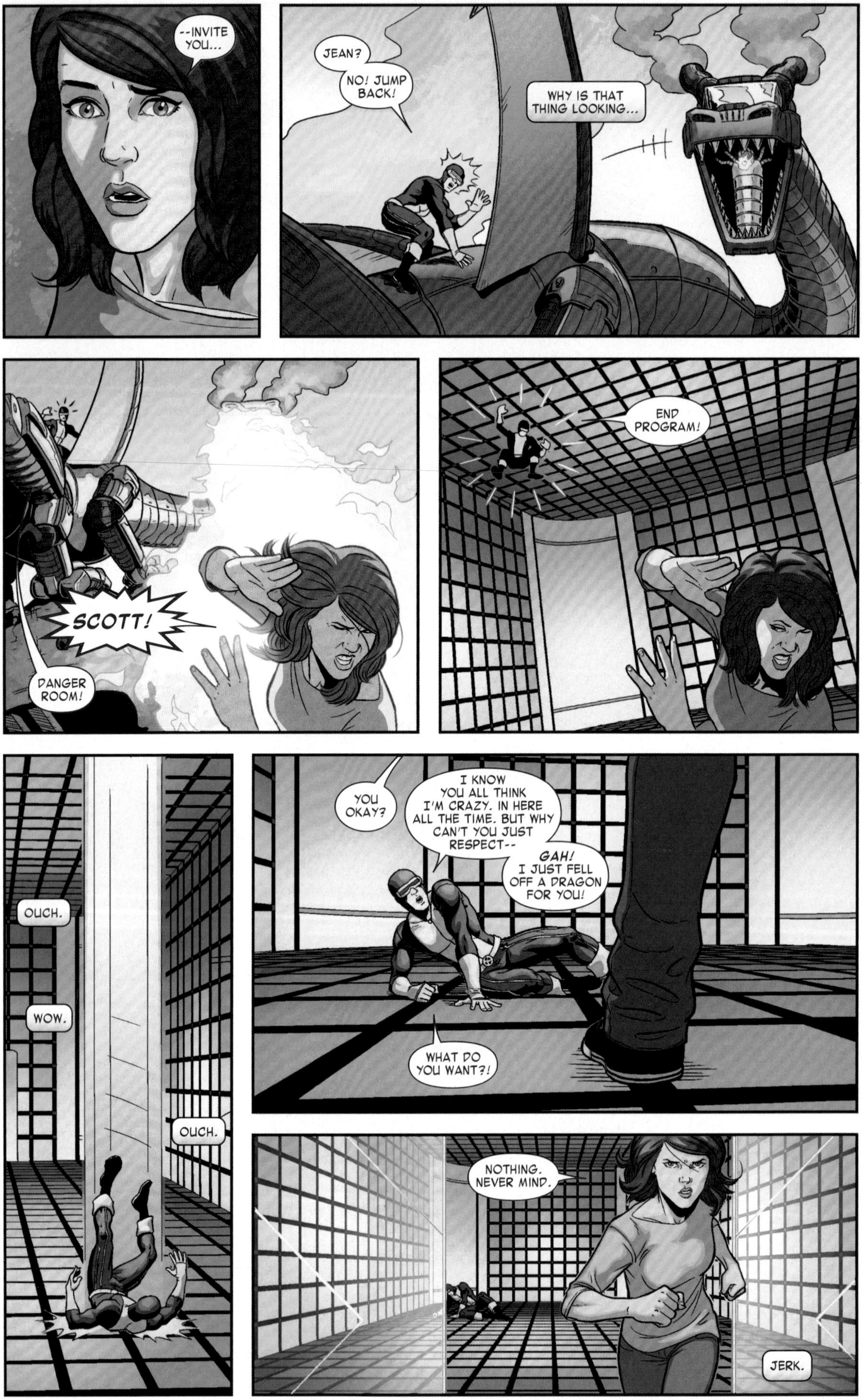
--INVITE YOU...
JEAN?
NO! JUMP BACK!
WHY IS THAT THING LOOKING...
SCOTT!
DANGER ROOM!
END PROGRAM!
OUCH.
WOW.
OUCH.
YOU OKAY?
I KNOW YOU ALL THINK I'M CRAZY. IN HERE ALL THE TIME. BUT WHY CAN'T YOU JUST RESPECT--
GAH! I JUST FELL OFF A DRAGON FOR YOU!
WHAT DO YOU WANT?!
NOTHING. NEVER MIND.
JERK.

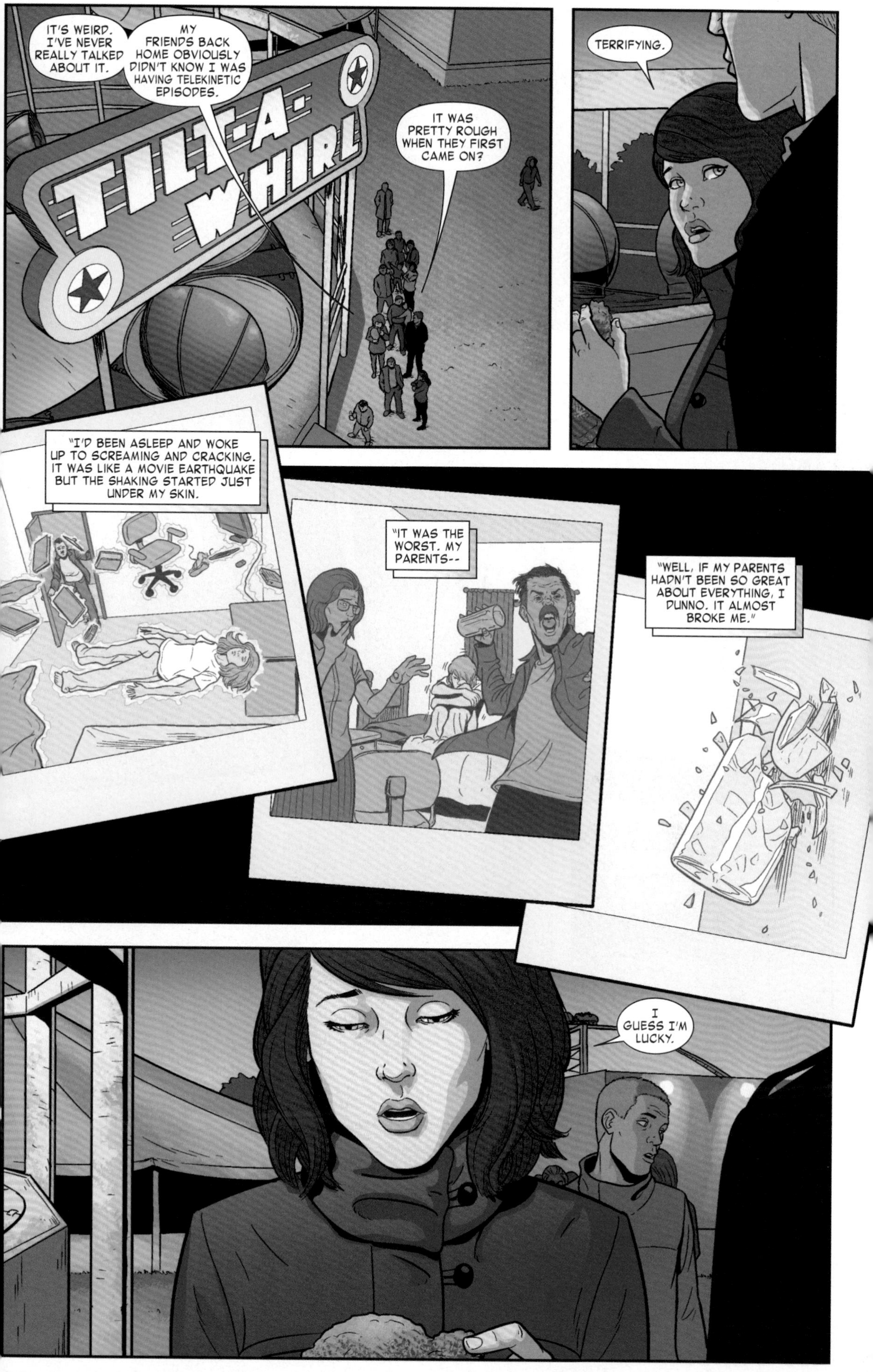
TILT-A-WHIRL
IT'S WEIRD. I'VE NEVER REALLY TALKED ABOUT IT.
MY FRIENDS BACK HOME OBVIOUSLY DIDN'T KNOW I WAS HAVING TELEKINETIC EPISODES.
IT WAS PRETTY ROUGH WHEN THEY FIRST CAME ON?
TERRIFYING.
"I'D BEEN ASLEEP AND WOKE UP TO SCREAMING AND CRACKING. IT WAS LIKE A MOVIE EARTHQUAKE BUT THE SHAKING STARTED JUST UNDER MY SKIN.
"IT WAS THE WORST. MY PARENTS--
"WELL, IF MY PARENTS HADN'T BEEN SO GREAT ABOUT EVERYTHING, I DUNNO. IT ALMOST BROKE ME."
I GUESS I'M LUCKY.

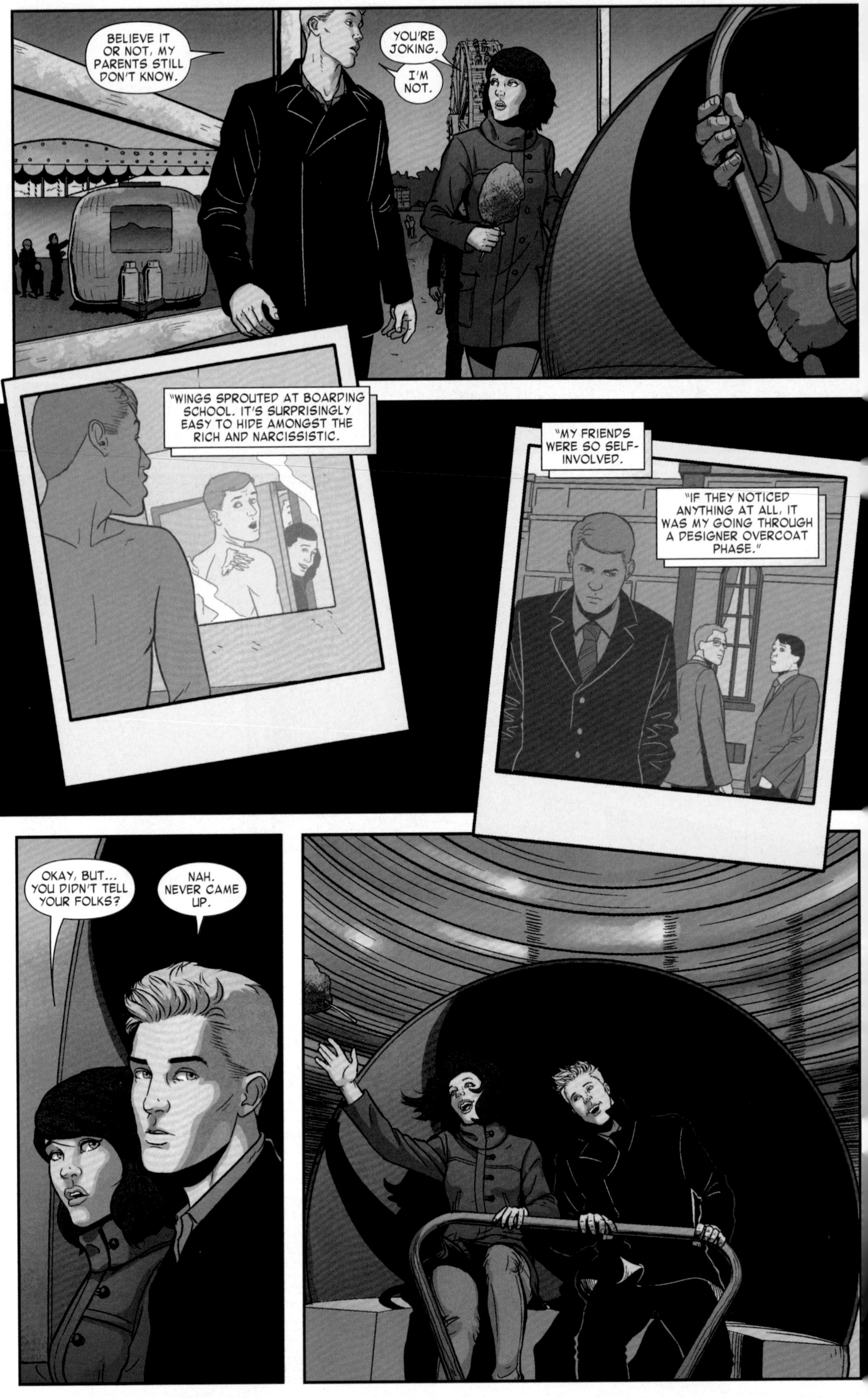
BELIEVE IT OR NOT, MY PARENTS STILL DON'T KNOW.
YOU'RE JOKING.
I'M NOT.
"WINGS SPROUTED AT BOARDING SCHOOL. IT'S SURPRISINGLY EASY TO HIDE AMONGST THE RICH AND NARCISSISTIC.
"MY FRIENDS WERE SO SELF-INVOLVED.
"IF THEY NOTICED ANYTHING AT ALL, IT WAS MY GOING THROUGH A DESIGNER OVERCOAT PHASE."
OKAY, BUT... YOU DIDN'T TELL YOUR FOLKS?
NAH. NEVER CAME UP.

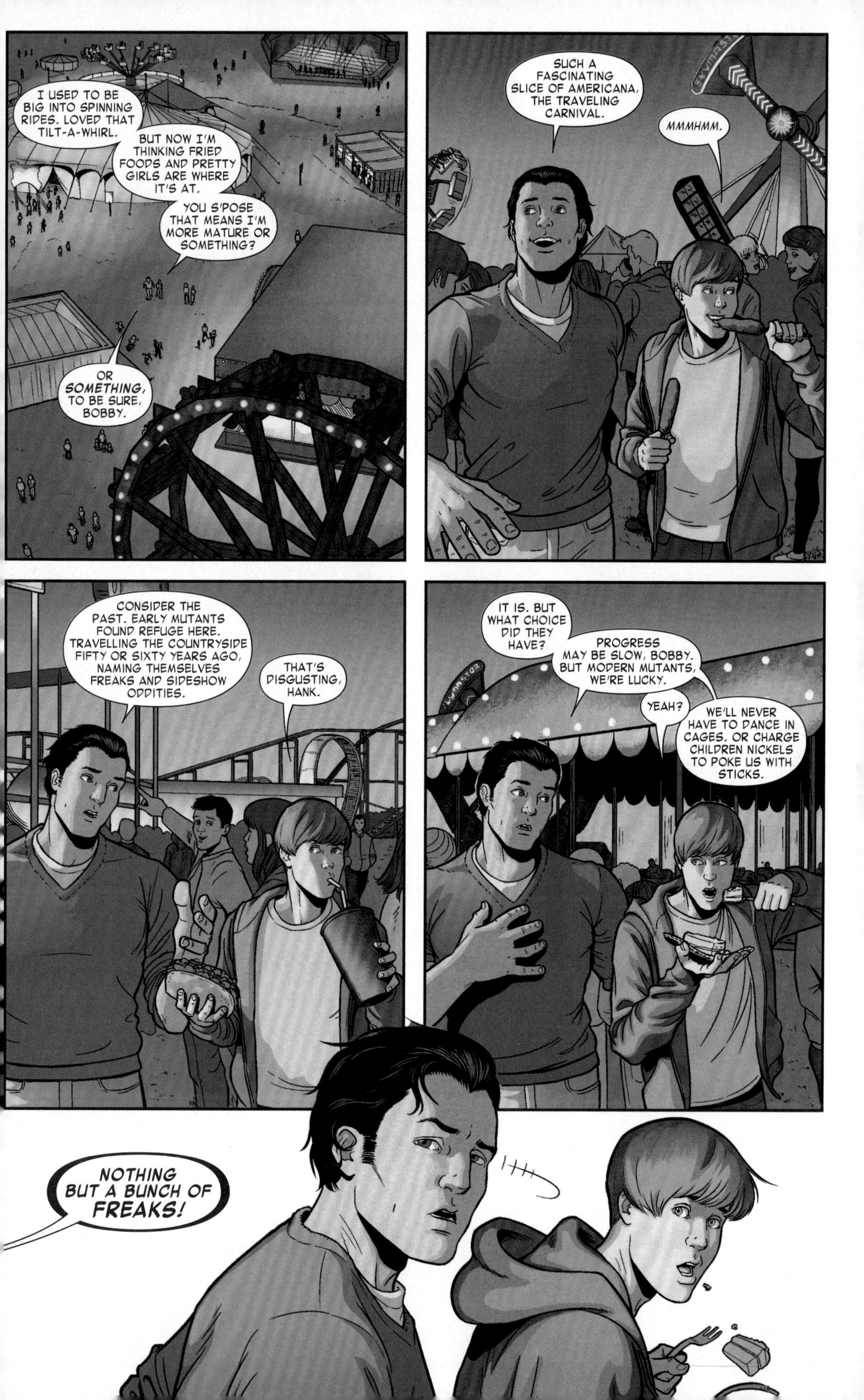
I USED TO BE BIG INTO SPINNING RIDES. LOVED THAT TILT-A-WHIRL.
BUT NOW I'M THINKING FRIED FOODS AND PRETTY GIRLS ARE WHERE IT'S AT.
YOU S'POSE THAT MEANS I'M MORE MATURE OR SOMETHING?
OR *SOMETHING*, TO BE SURE, BOBBY.
SUCH A FASCINATING SLICE OF AMERICANA, THE TRAVELING CARNIVAL.
MMMHMM.
CONSIDER THE PAST. EARLY MUTANTS FOUND REFUGE HERE. TRAVELLING THE COUNTRYSIDE FIFTY OR SIXTY YEARS AGO, NAMING THEMSELVES FREAKS AND SIDESHOW ODDITIES.
THAT'S DISGUSTING, HANK.
IT IS. BUT WHAT CHOICE DID THEY HAVE?
PROGRESS MAY BE SLOW, BOBBY. BUT MODERN MUTANTS, WE'RE LUCKY.
YEAH?
WE'LL NEVER HAVE TO DANCE IN CAGES. OR CHARGE CHILDREN NICKELS TO POKE US WITH STICKS.
NOTHING BUT A BUNCH OF **FREAKS!**

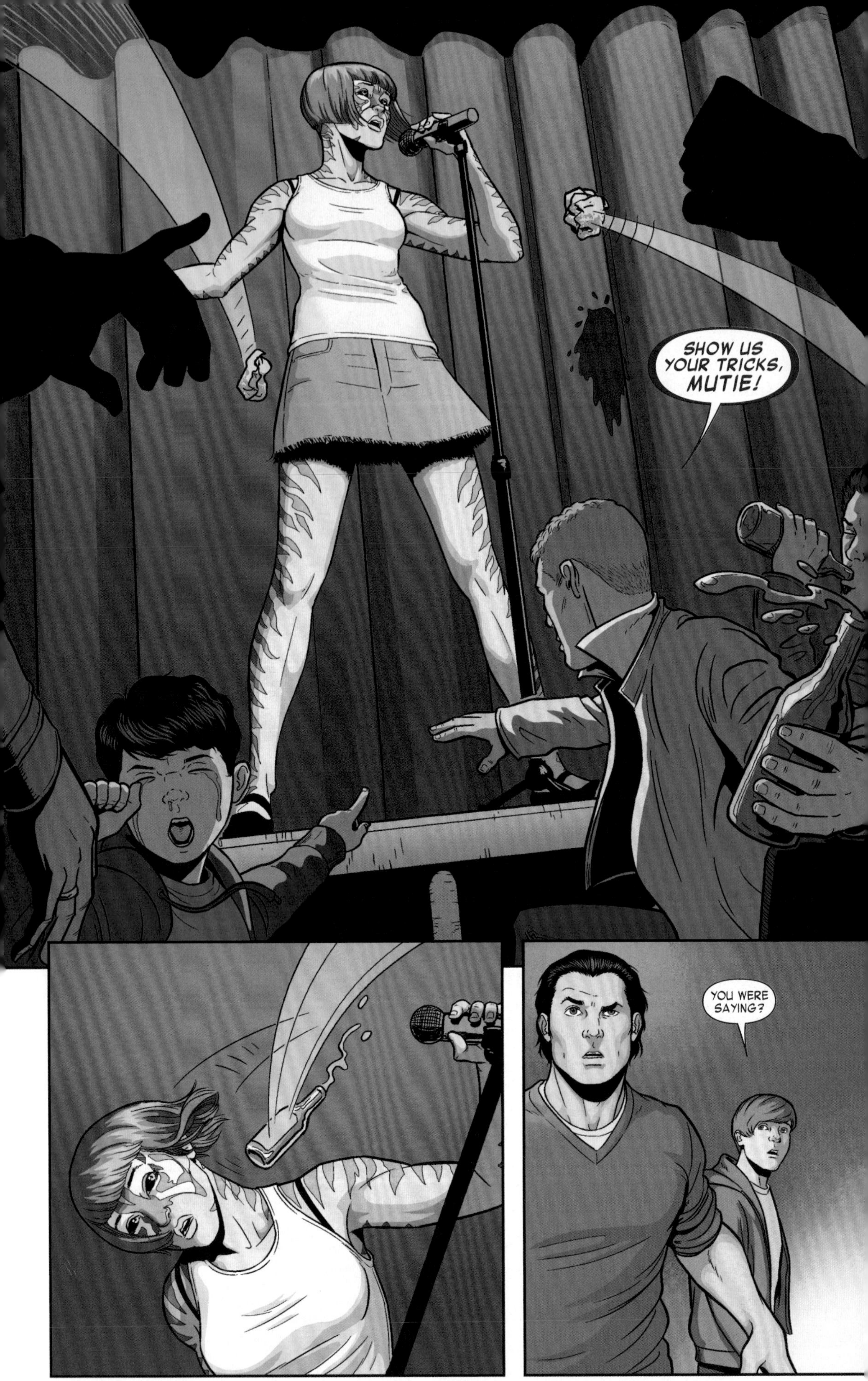
SHOW US
YOUR TRICKS,
MUTIE!
YOU WERE
SAYING?

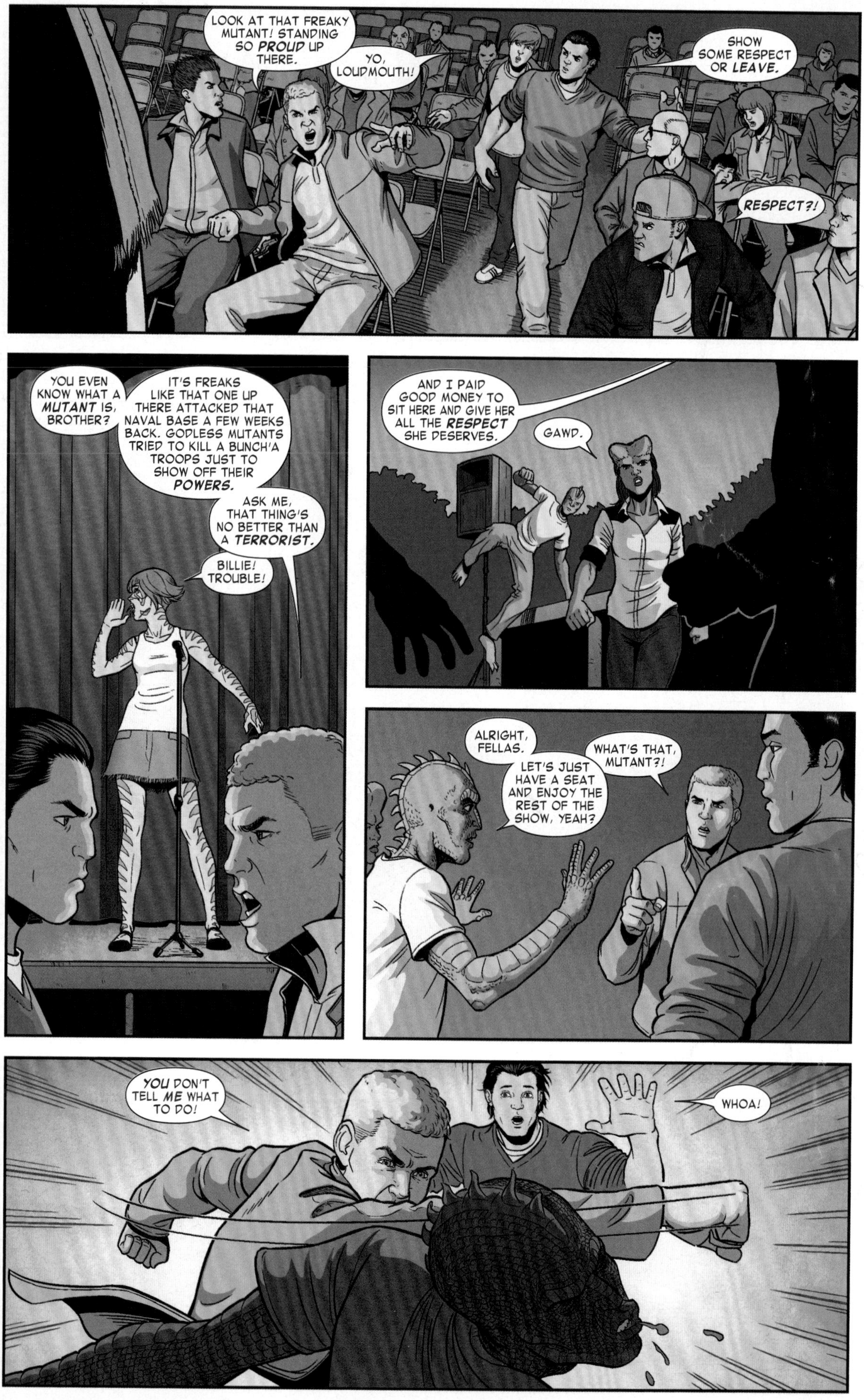

LOOK AT THAT FREAKY MUTANT! STANDING SO PROUD UP THERE.
YO, LOUDMOUTH!
SHOW SOME RESPECT OR LEAVE.
RESPECT?!
YOU EVEN KNOW WHAT A MUTANT IS, BROTHER?
IT'S FREAKS LIKE THAT ONE UP THERE ATTACKED THAT NAVAL BASE A FEW WEEKS BACK. GODLESS MUTANTS TRIED TO KILL A BUNCH'A TROOPS JUST TO SHOW OFF THEIR POWERS.
ASK ME, THAT THING'S NO BETTER THAN A TERRORIST.
BILLIE! TROUBLE!
AND I PAID GOOD MONEY TO SIT HERE AND GIVE HER ALL THE RESPECT SHE DESERVES.
GAWD.
ALRIGHT, FELLAS.
LET'S JUST HAVE A SEAT AND ENJOY THE REST OF THE SHOW, YEAH?
WHAT'S THAT, MUTANT?!
YOU DON'T TELL ME WHAT TO DO!
WHOA!

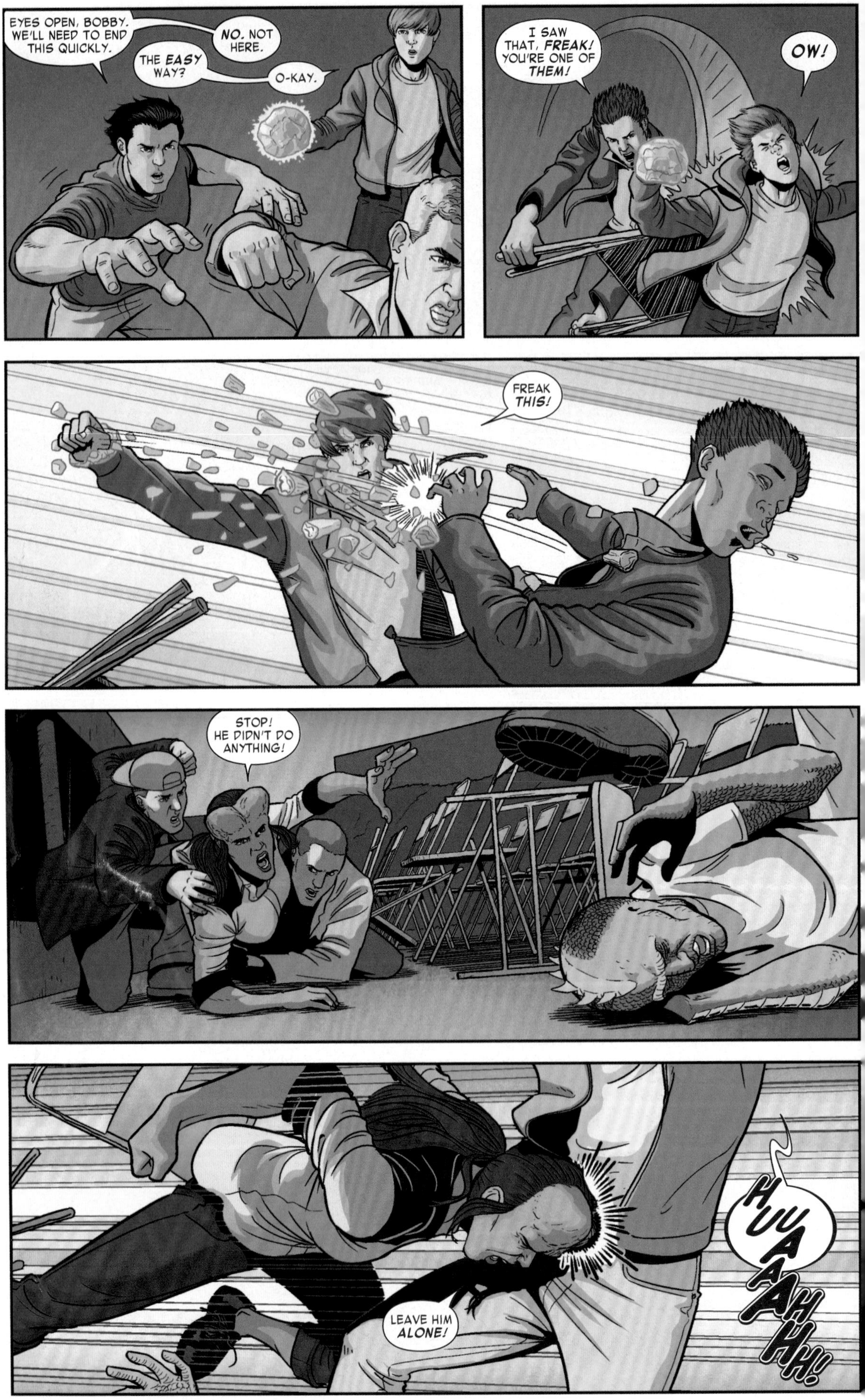
EYES OPEN, BOBBY. WE'LL NEED TO END THIS QUICKLY.
NO. NOT HERE.
THE EASY WAY?
O-KAY.
I SAW THAT, FREAK! YOU'RE ONE OF THEM!
OW!
FREAK THIS!
STOP! HE DIDN'T DO ANYTHING!
HUUAAAHHH!
LEAVE HIM ALONE!

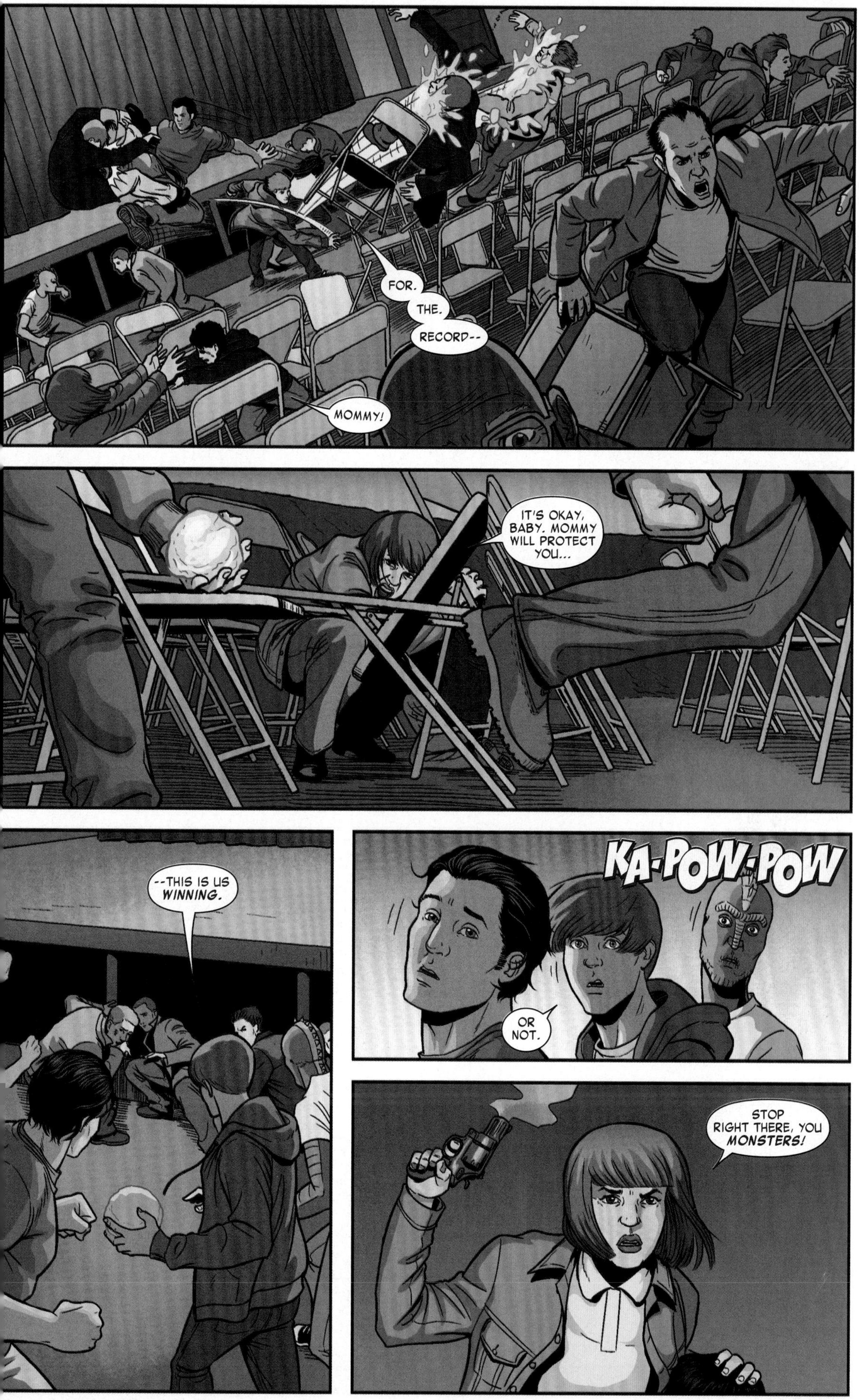
FOR.
THE.
RECORD--
MOMMY!
IT'S OKAY, BABY. MOMMY WILL PROTECT YOU...
--THIS IS US WINNING.
KA-POW-POW
OR NOT.
STOP RIGHT THERE, YOU MONSTERS!

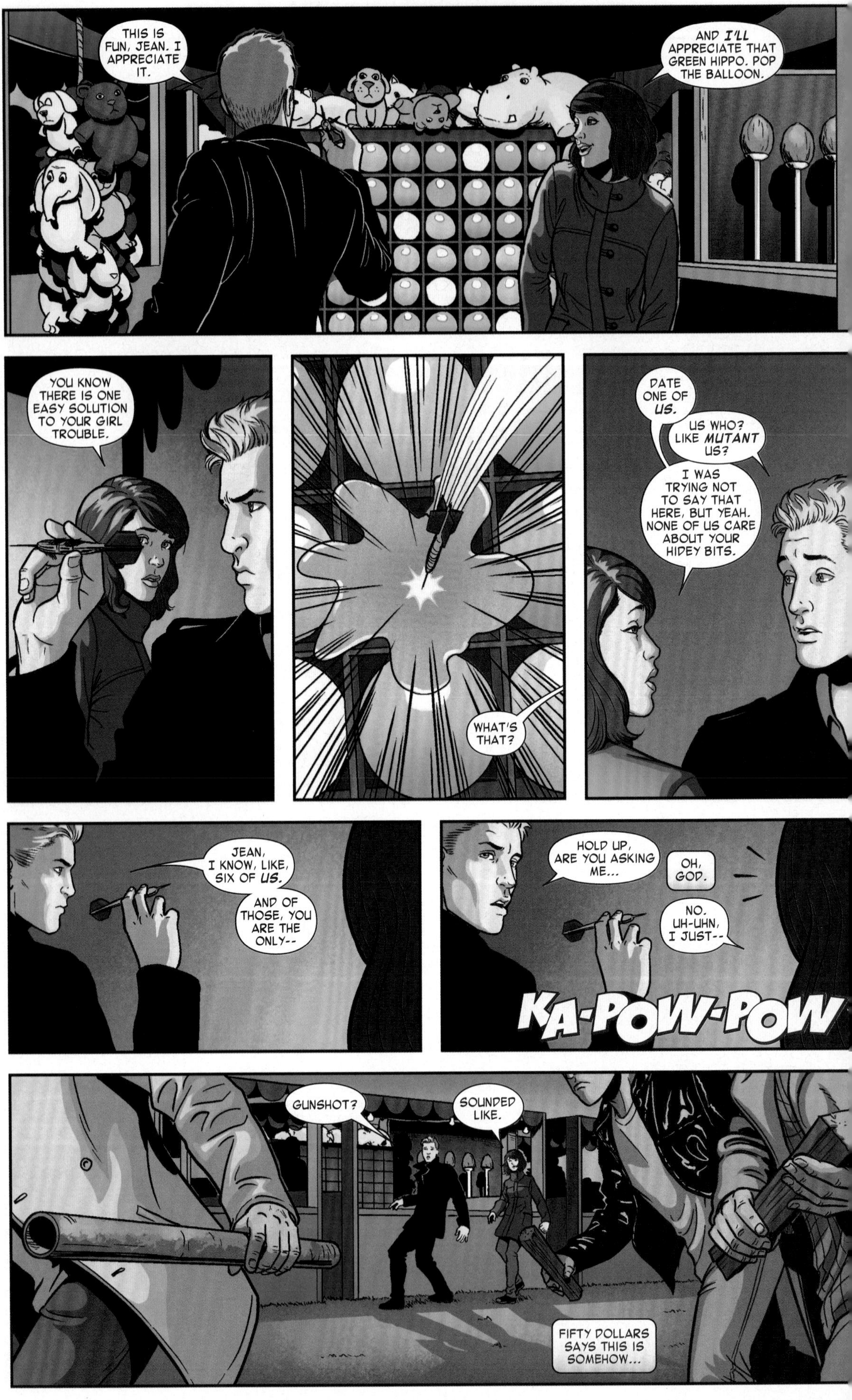
THIS IS FUN, JEAN. I APPRECIATE IT.
AND I'LL APPRECIATE THAT GREEN HIPPO. POP THE BALLOON.
YOU KNOW THERE IS ONE EASY SOLUTION TO YOUR GIRL TROUBLE.
WHAT'S THAT?
DATE ONE OF US.
US WHO? LIKE MUTANT US?
I WAS TRYING NOT TO SAY THAT HERE, BUT YEAH. NONE OF US CARE ABOUT YOUR HIDEY BITS.
JEAN, I KNOW, LIKE, SIX OF US.
AND OF THOSE, YOU ARE THE ONLY--
HOLD UP, ARE YOU ASKING ME...
OH, GOD.
NO. UH-UHN, I JUST--
KA-POW-POW
GUNSHOT?
SOUNDED LIKE.
FIFTY DOLLARS SAYS THIS IS SOMEHOW...

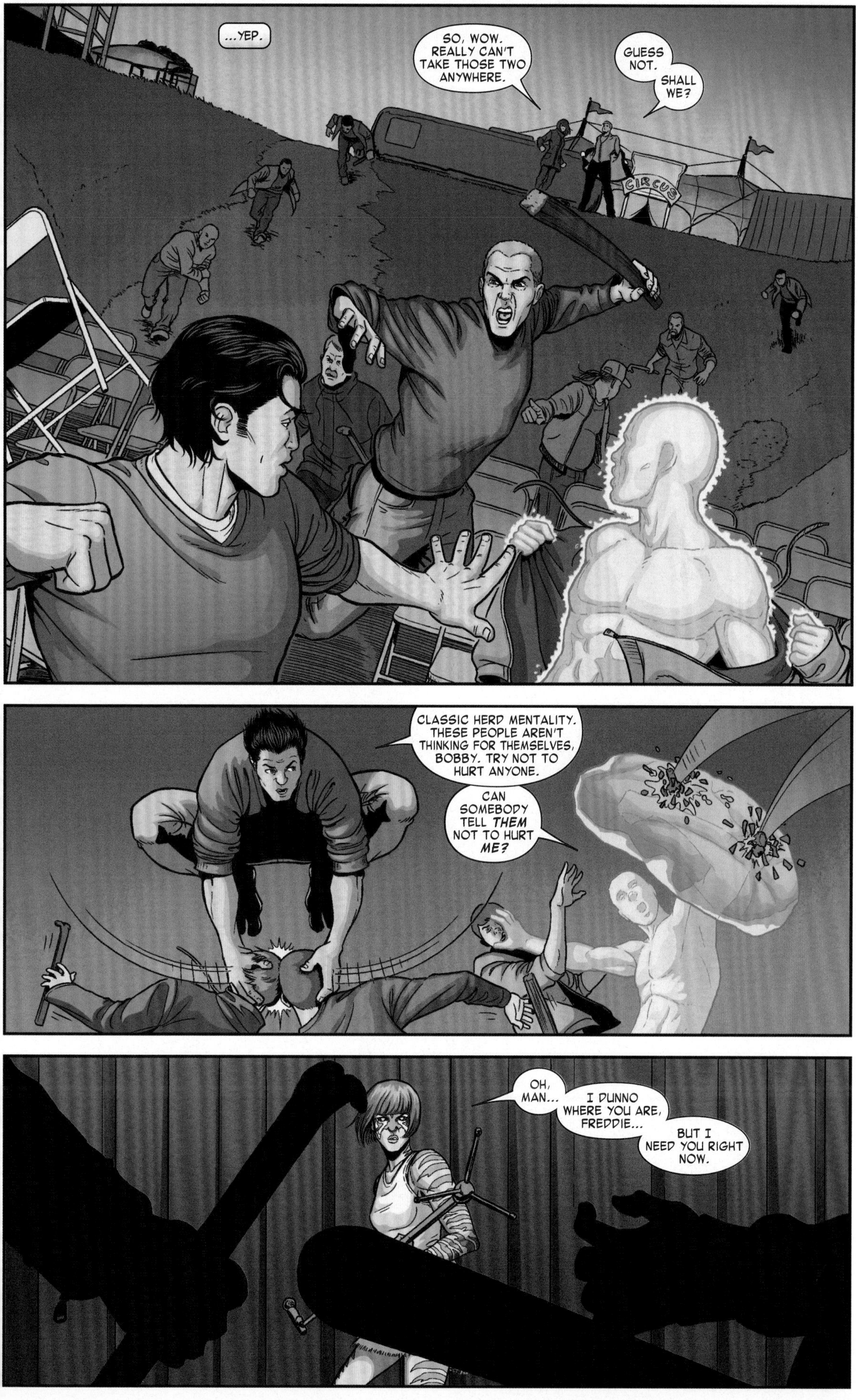
...YEP.
SO, WOW. REALLY CAN'T TAKE THOSE TWO ANYWHERE.
GUESS NOT.
SHALL WE?
CIRCUS
CLASSIC HERD MENTALITY. THESE PEOPLE AREN'T THINKING FOR THEMSELVES, BOBBY. TRY NOT TO HURT ANYONE.
CAN SOMEBODY TELL *THEM* NOT TO HURT *ME?*
OH, MAN...
I DUNNO WHERE YOU ARE, FREDDIE...
BUT I NEED YOU RIGHT NOW.

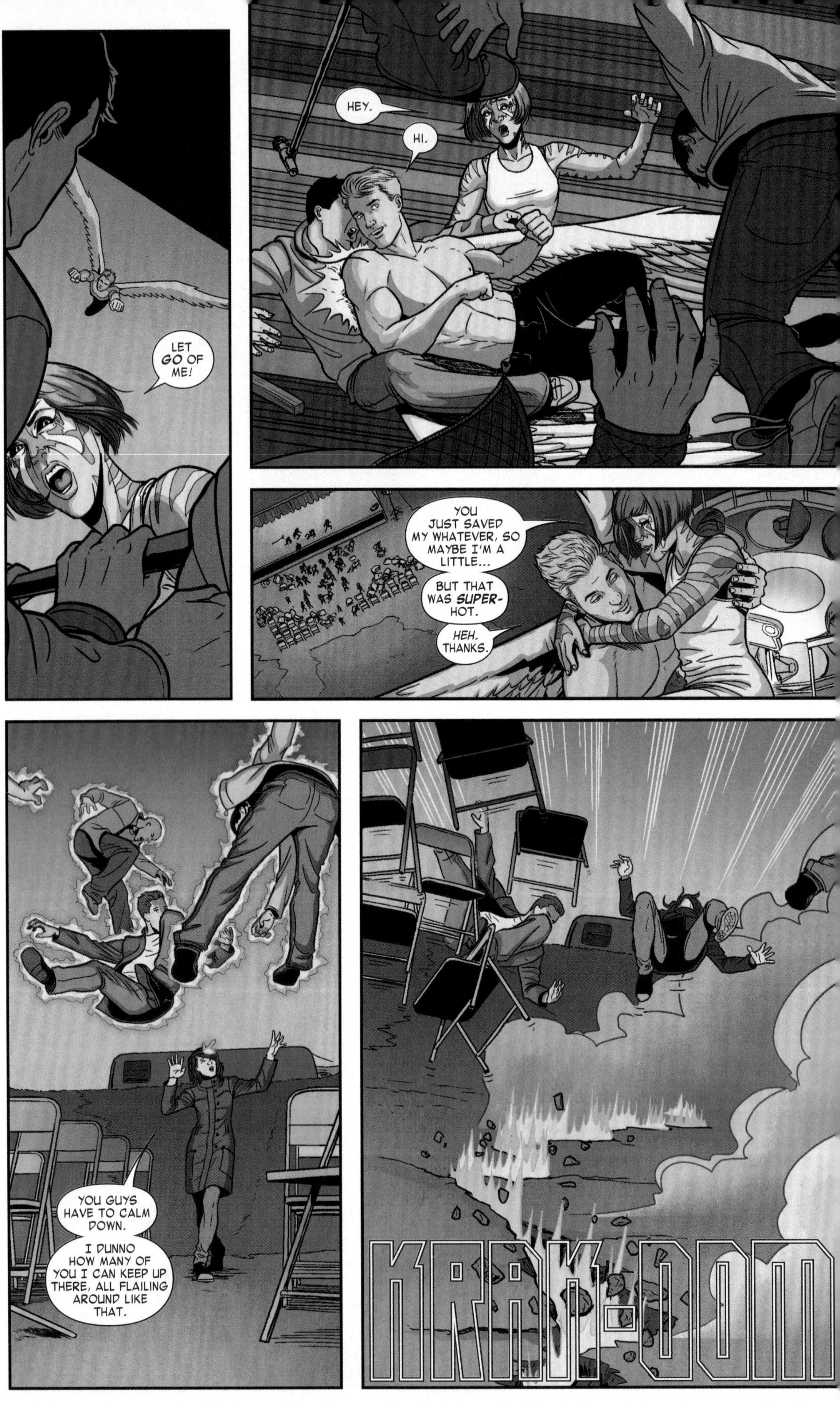
LET GO OF ME!
HEY.
HI.
YOU JUST SAVED MY WHATEVER, SO MAYBE I'M A LITTLE...
BUT THAT WAS SUPER-HOT.
HEH. THANKS.
YOU GUYS HAVE TO CALM DOWN.
I DUNNO HOW MANY OF YOU I CAN KEEP UP THERE, ALL FLAILING AROUND LIKE THAT.
KRAK-OOM

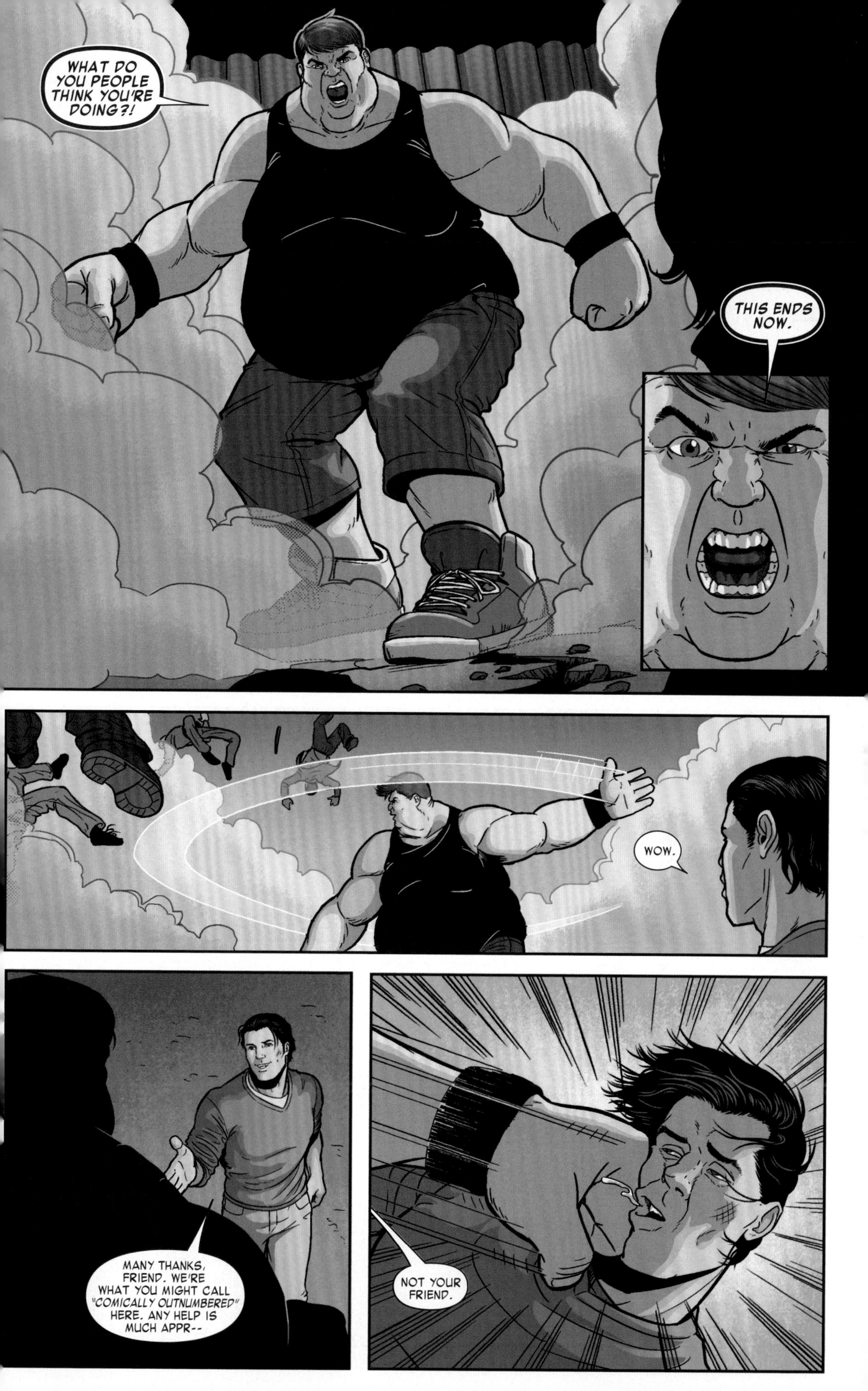
WHAT DO YOU PEOPLE THINK YOU'RE DOING?!
THIS ENDS NOW.
WOW.
MANY THANKS, FRIEND. WE'RE WHAT YOU MIGHT CALL "COMICALLY OUTNUMBERED" HERE. ANY HELP IS MUCH APPR--
NOT YOUR FRIEND.

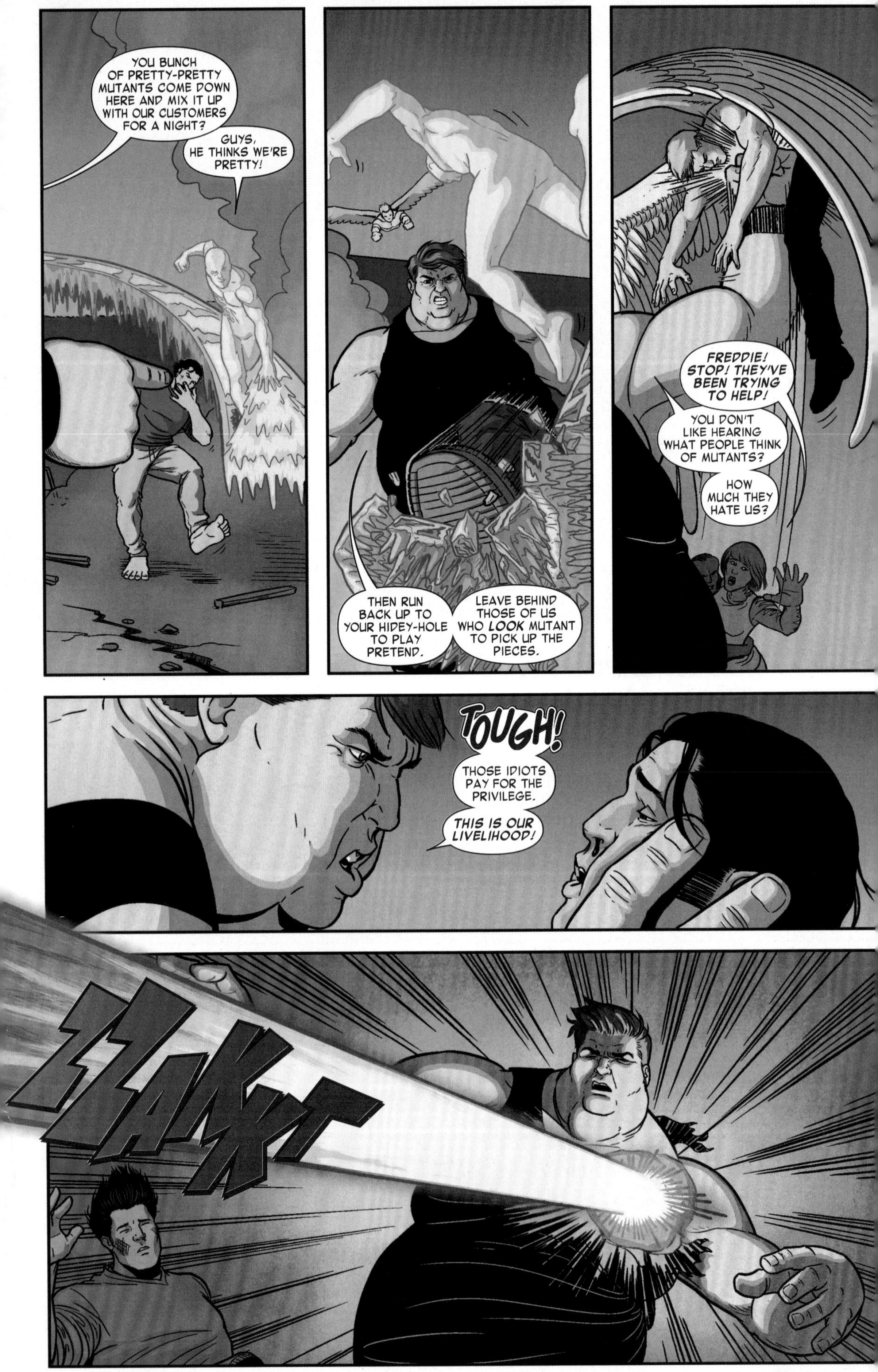
YOU BUNCH OF PRETTY-PRETTY MUTANTS COME DOWN HERE AND MIX IT UP WITH OUR CUSTOMERS FOR A NIGHT?
GUYS, HE THINKS WE'RE PRETTY!
THEN RUN BACK UP TO YOUR HIDEY-HOLE TO PLAY PRETEND.
LEAVE BEHIND THOSE OF US WHO LOOK MUTANT TO PICK UP THE PIECES.
FREDDIE! STOP! THEY'VE BEEN TRYING TO HELP!
YOU DON'T LIKE HEARING WHAT PEOPLE THINK OF MUTANTS?
HOW MUCH THEY HATE US?
TOUGH!
THOSE IDIOTS PAY FOR THE PRIVILEGE.
THIS IS OUR LIVELIHOOD!
ZZAKT

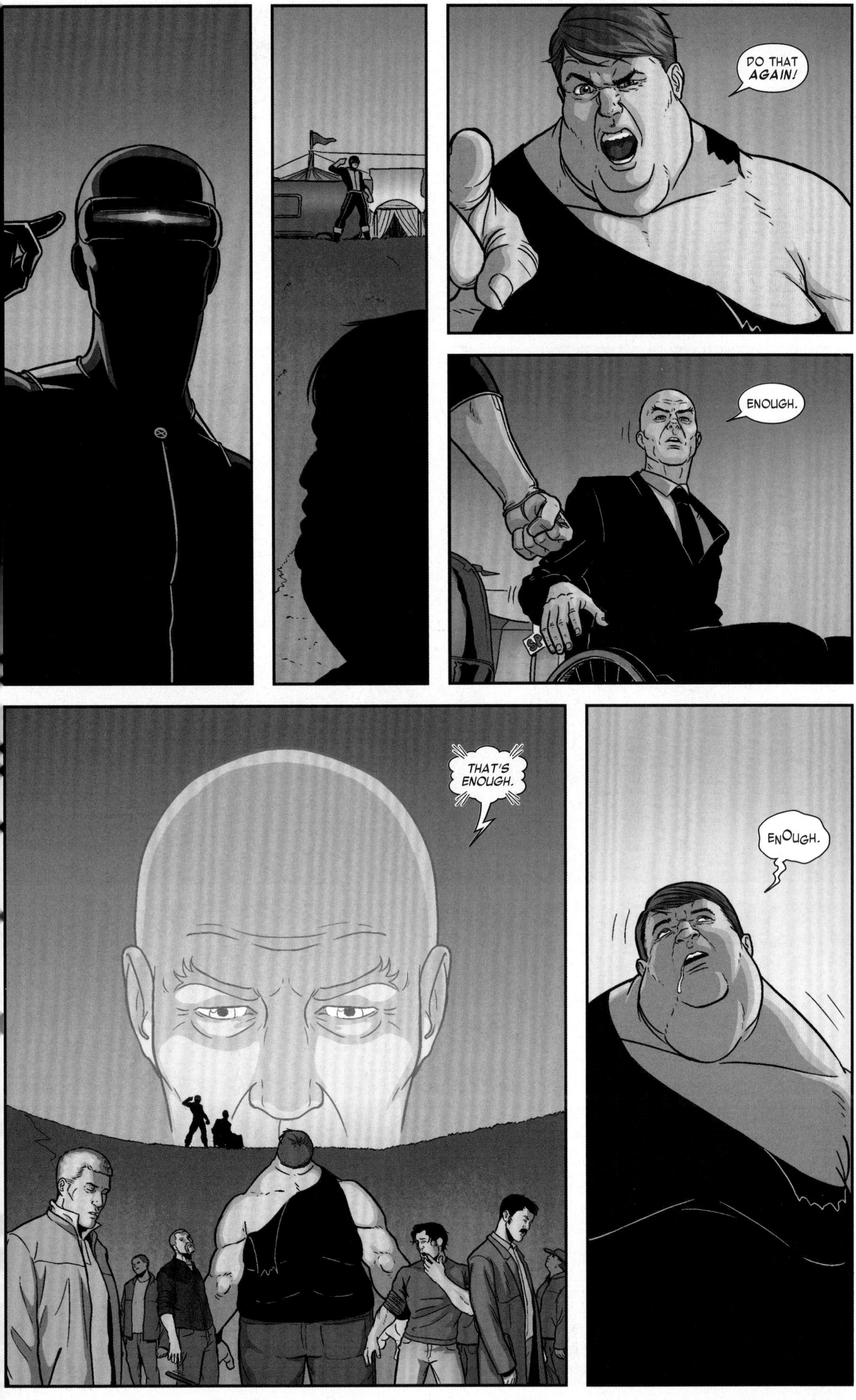
DO THAT AGAIN!
ENOUGH.
THAT'S ENOUGH.
ENOUGH.

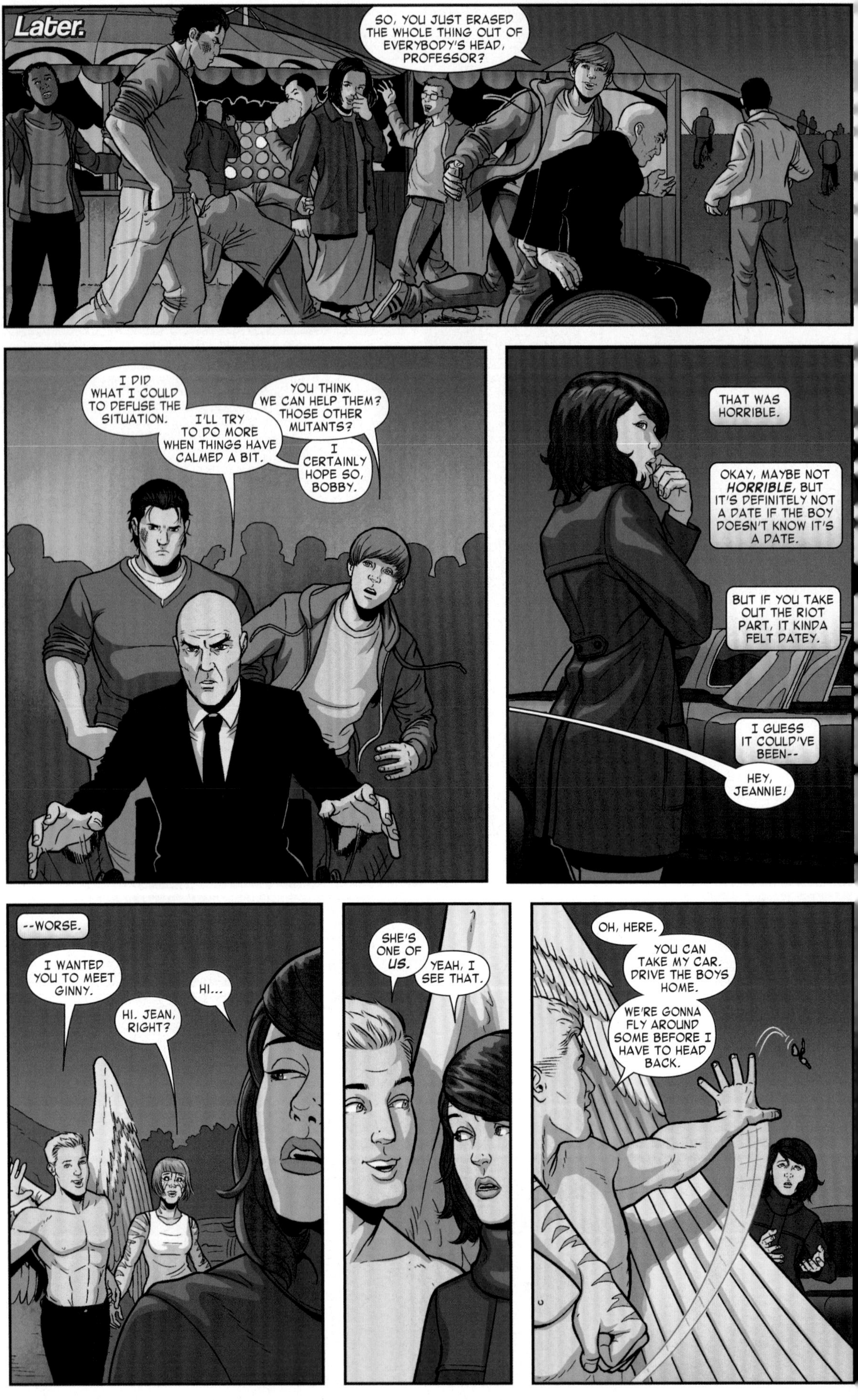
Later.
SO, YOU JUST ERASED THE WHOLE THING OUT OF EVERYBODY'S HEAD, PROFESSOR?
I DID WHAT I COULD TO DEFUSE THE SITUATION.
I'LL TRY TO DO MORE WHEN THINGS HAVE CALMED A BIT.
YOU THINK WE CAN HELP THEM? THOSE OTHER MUTANTS?
I CERTAINLY HOPE SO, BOBBY.
THAT WAS HORRIBLE.
OKAY, MAYBE NOT HORRIBLE, BUT IT'S DEFINITELY NOT A DATE IF THE BOY DOESN'T KNOW IT'S A DATE.
BUT IF YOU TAKE OUT THE RIOT PART, IT KINDA FELT DATEY.
I GUESS IT COULD'VE BEEN--
HEY, JEANNIE!
--WORSE.
I WANTED YOU TO MEET GINNY.
HI. JEAN, RIGHT?
HI...
SHE'S ONE OF US.
YEAH, I SEE THAT.
OH, HERE.
YOU CAN TAKE MY CAR. DRIVE THE BOYS HOME.
WE'RE GONNA FLY AROUND SOME BEFORE I HAVE TO HEAD BACK.

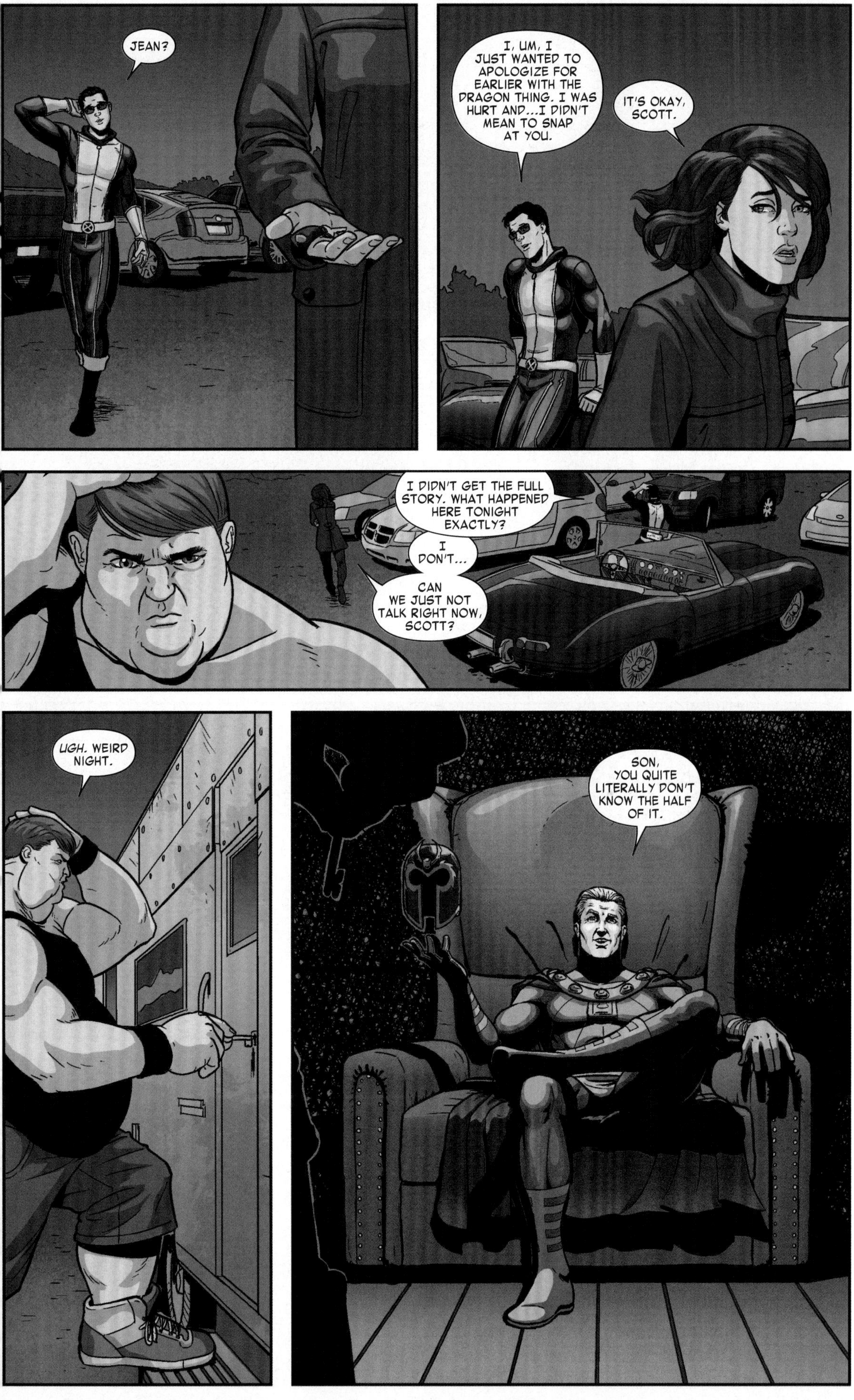
JEAN?
I, UM, I JUST WANTED TO APOLOGIZE FOR EARLIER WITH THE DRAGON THING. I WAS HURT AND...I DIDN'T MEAN TO SNAP AT YOU.
IT'S OKAY, SCOTT.
I DIDN'T GET THE FULL STORY. WHAT HAPPENED HERE TONIGHT EXACTLY?
I DON'T...
CAN WE JUST NOT TALK RIGHT NOW, SCOTT?
UGH. WEIRD NIGHT.
SON, YOU QUITE LITERALLY DON'T KNOW THE HALF OF IT.

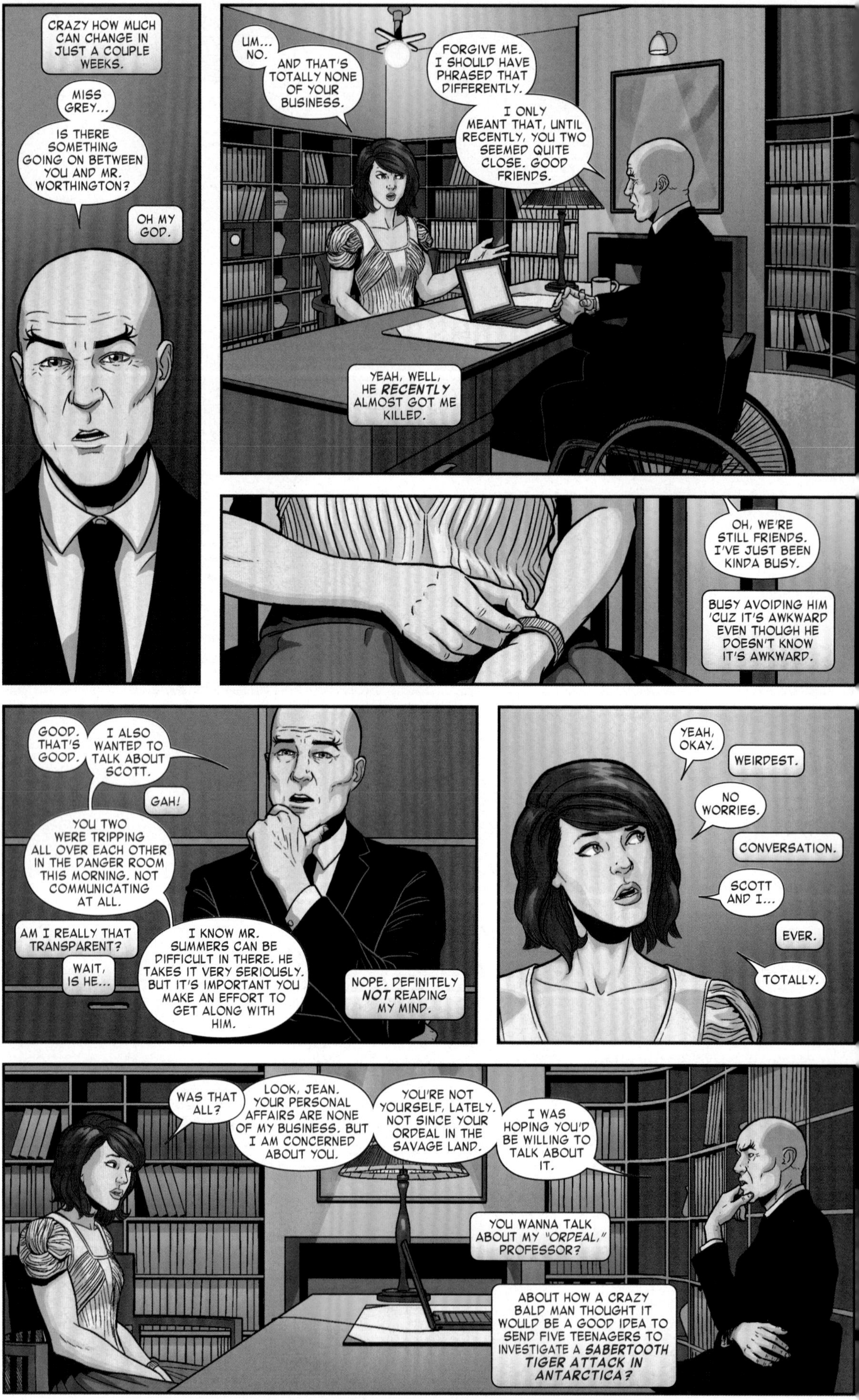

CRAZY HOW MUCH CAN CHANGE IN JUST A COUPLE WEEKS.
MISS GREY...
IS THERE SOMETHING GOING ON BETWEEN YOU AND MR. WORTHINGTON?
OH MY GOD.
UM... NO.
AND THAT'S TOTALLY NONE OF YOUR BUSINESS.
FORGIVE ME. I SHOULD HAVE PHRASED THAT DIFFERENTLY.
I ONLY MEANT THAT, UNTIL RECENTLY, YOU TWO SEEMED QUITE CLOSE. GOOD FRIENDS.
YEAH, WELL, HE *RECENTLY* ALMOST GOT ME KILLED.
OH, WE'RE STILL FRIENDS. I'VE JUST BEEN KINDA BUSY.
BUSY AVOIDING HIM 'CUZ IT'S AWKWARD EVEN THOUGH HE DOESN'T KNOW IT'S AWKWARD.
GOOD. THAT'S GOOD.
I ALSO WANTED TO TALK ABOUT SCOTT.
GAH!
YOU TWO WERE TRIPPING ALL OVER EACH OTHER IN THE DANGER ROOM THIS MORNING. NOT COMMUNICATING AT ALL.
AM I REALLY THAT TRANSPARENT?
WAIT, IS HE...
I KNOW MR. SUMMERS CAN BE DIFFICULT IN THERE. HE TAKES IT VERY SERIOUSLY. BUT IT'S IMPORTANT YOU MAKE AN EFFORT TO GET ALONG WITH HIM.
NOPE. DEFINITELY *NOT* READING MY MIND.
YEAH, OKAY.
WEIRDEST.
NO WORRIES.
CONVERSATION.
SCOTT AND I...
EVER.
TOTALLY.
WAS THAT ALL?
LOOK, JEAN. YOUR PERSONAL AFFAIRS ARE NONE OF MY BUSINESS. BUT I AM CONCERNED ABOUT YOU.
YOU'RE NOT YOURSELF, LATELY. NOT SINCE YOUR ORDEAL IN THE SAVAGE LAND.
I WAS HOPING YOU'D BE WILLING TO TALK ABOUT IT.
YOU WANNA TALK ABOUT MY "ORDEAL," PROFESSOR?
ABOUT HOW A CRAZY BALD MAN THOUGHT IT WOULD BE A GOOD IDEA TO SEND FIVE TEENAGERS TO INVESTIGATE A *SABERTOOTH TIGER ATTACK IN ANTARCTICA?*

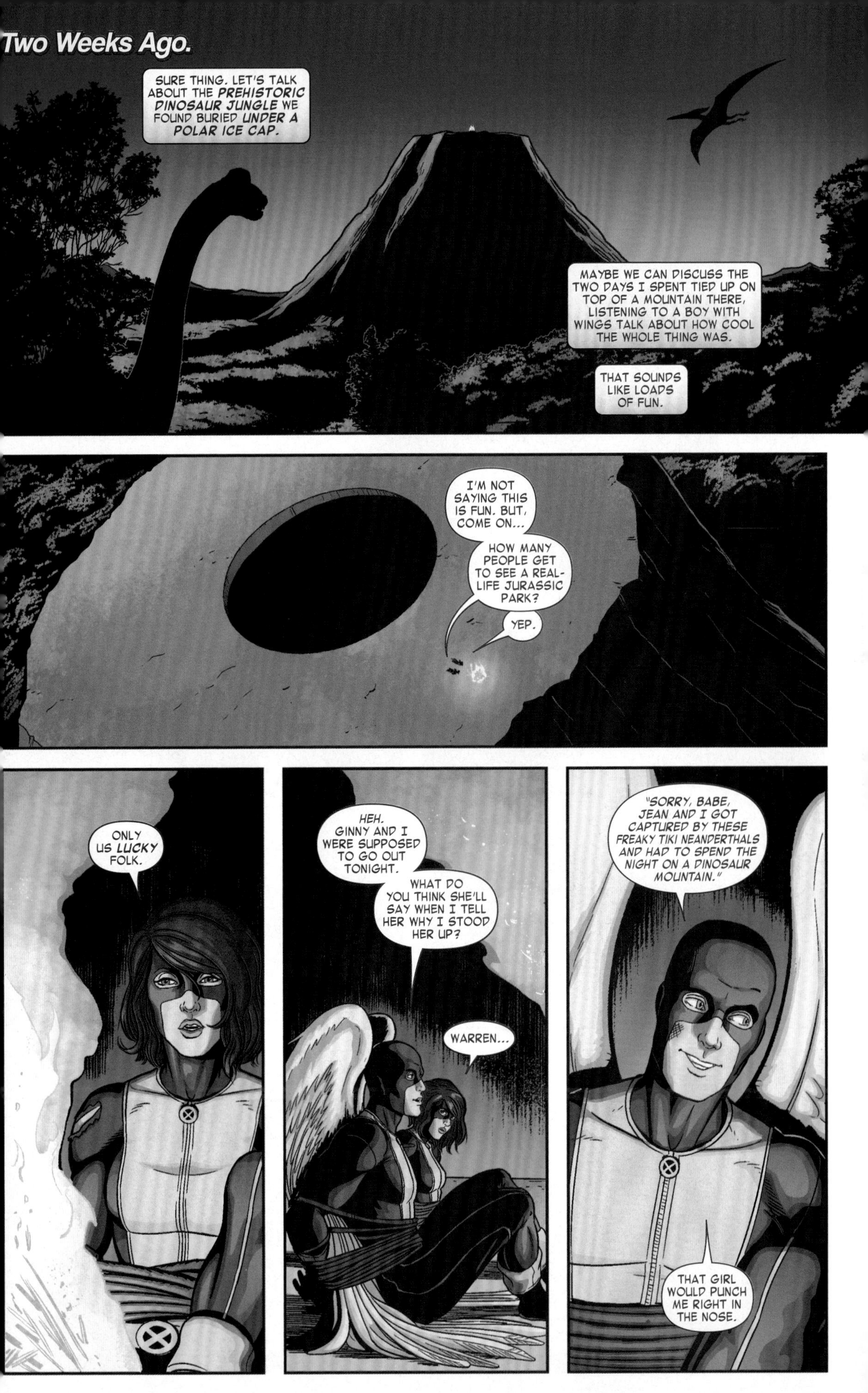
Two Weeks Ago.
SURE THING. LET'S TALK ABOUT THE PREHISTORIC DINOSAUR JUNGLE WE FOUND BURIED UNDER A POLAR ICE CAP.
MAYBE WE CAN DISCUSS THE TWO DAYS I SPENT TIED UP ON TOP OF A MOUNTAIN THERE, LISTENING TO A BOY WITH WINGS TALK ABOUT HOW COOL THE WHOLE THING WAS.
THAT SOUNDS LIKE LOADS OF FUN.
I'M NOT SAYING THIS IS FUN. BUT, COME ON...
HOW MANY PEOPLE GET TO SEE A REAL-LIFE JURASSIC PARK?
YEP.
ONLY US LUCKY FOLK.
HEH. GINNY AND I WERE SUPPOSED TO GO OUT TONIGHT.
WHAT DO YOU THINK SHE'LL SAY WHEN I TELL HER WHY I STOOD HER UP?
WARREN...
"SORRY, BABE, JEAN AND I GOT CAPTURED BY THESE FREAKY TIKI NEANDERTHALS AND HAD TO SPEND THE NIGHT ON A DINOSAUR MOUNTAIN."
THAT GIRL WOULD PUNCH ME RIGHT IN THE NOSE.

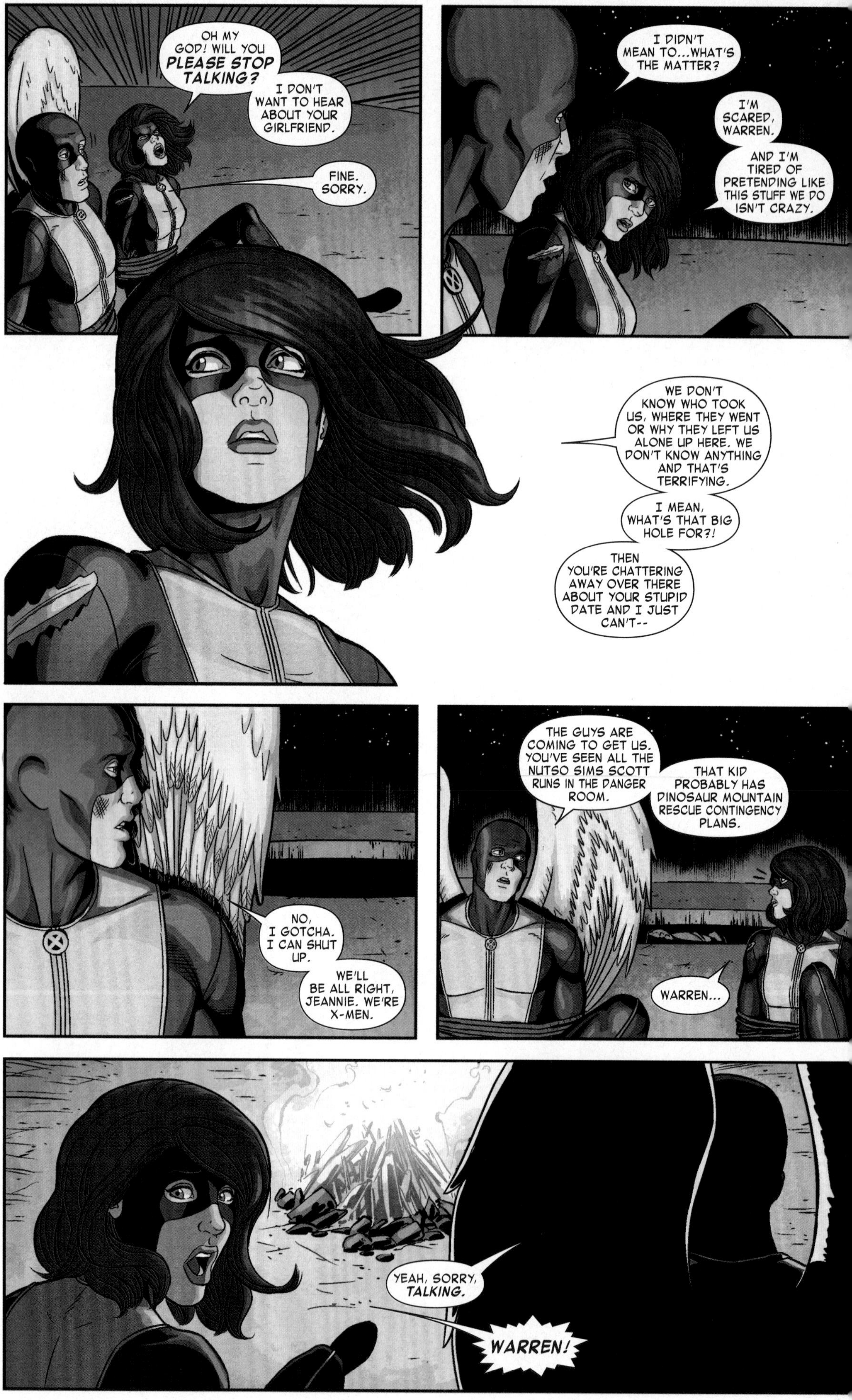
OH MY GOD! WILL YOU PLEASE STOP TALKING?
I DON'T WANT TO HEAR ABOUT YOUR GIRLFRIEND.
FINE. SORRY.
I DIDN'T MEAN TO...WHAT'S THE MATTER?
I'M SCARED, WARREN.
AND I'M TIRED OF PRETENDING LIKE THIS STUFF WE DO ISN'T CRAZY.
WE DON'T KNOW WHO TOOK US, WHERE THEY WENT OR WHY THEY LEFT US ALONE UP HERE. WE DON'T KNOW ANYTHING AND THAT'S TERRIFYING.
I MEAN, WHAT'S THAT BIG HOLE FOR?!
THEN YOU'RE CHATTERING AWAY OVER THERE ABOUT YOUR STUPID DATE AND I JUST CAN'T--
NO, I GOTCHA. I CAN SHUT UP.
WE'LL BE ALL RIGHT, JEANNIE. WE'RE X-MEN.
THE GUYS ARE COMING TO GET US. YOU'VE SEEN ALL THE NUTSO SIMS SCOTT RUNS IN THE DANGER ROOM.
THAT KID PROBABLY HAS DINOSAUR MOUNTAIN RESCUE CONTINGENCY PLANS.
WARREN...
YEAH, SORRY, TALKING.
WARREN!

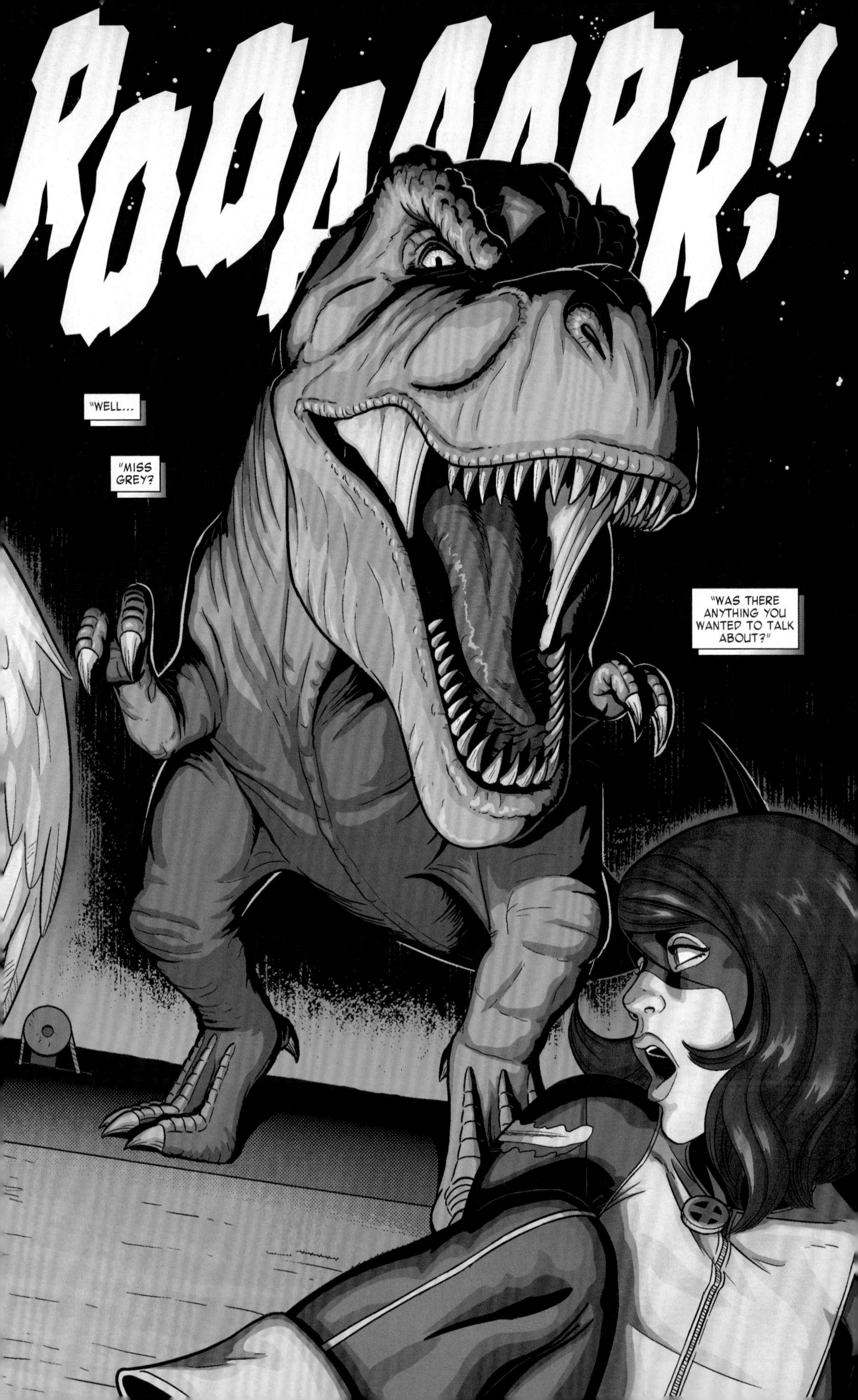
ROOAARR!
"WELL...
"MISS GREY?
"WAS THERE ANYTHING YOU WANTED TO TALK ABOUT?"

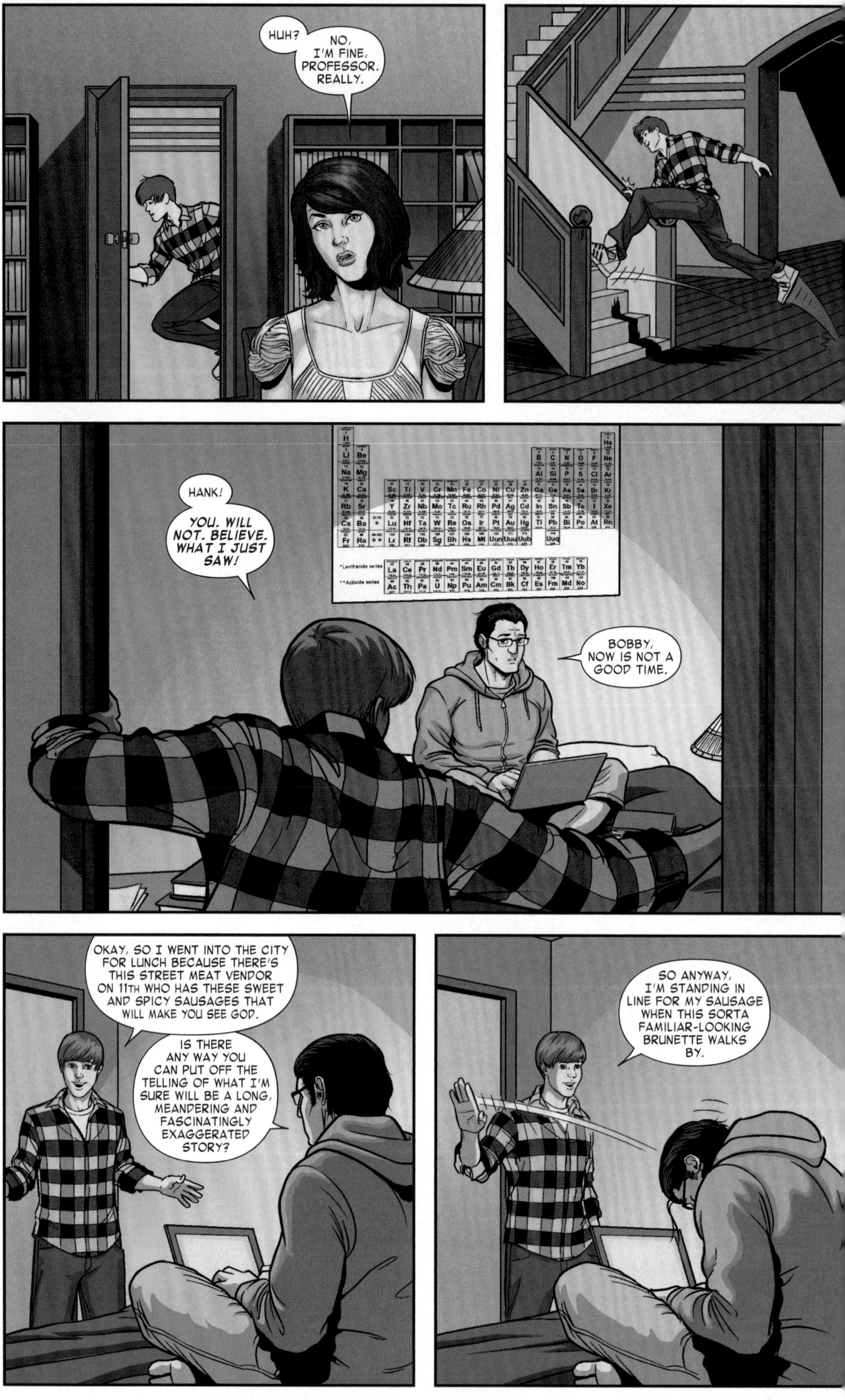
HUH?
NO, I'M FINE, PROFESSOR. REALLY.
HANK!
YOU. WILL NOT. BELIEVE. WHAT I JUST SAW!
BOBBY, NOW IS NOT A GOOD TIME.
OKAY, SO I WENT INTO THE CITY FOR LUNCH BECAUSE THERE'S THIS STREET MEAT VENDOR ON 11TH WHO HAS THESE SWEET AND SPICY SAUSAGES THAT WILL MAKE YOU SEE GOD.
IS THERE ANY WAY YOU CAN PUT OFF THE TELLING OF WHAT I'M SURE WILL BE A LONG, MEANDERING AND FASCINATINGLY EXAGGERATED STORY?
SO ANYWAY, I'M STANDING IN LINE FOR MY SAUSAGE WHEN THIS SORTA FAMILIAR-LOOKING BRUNETTE WALKS BY.

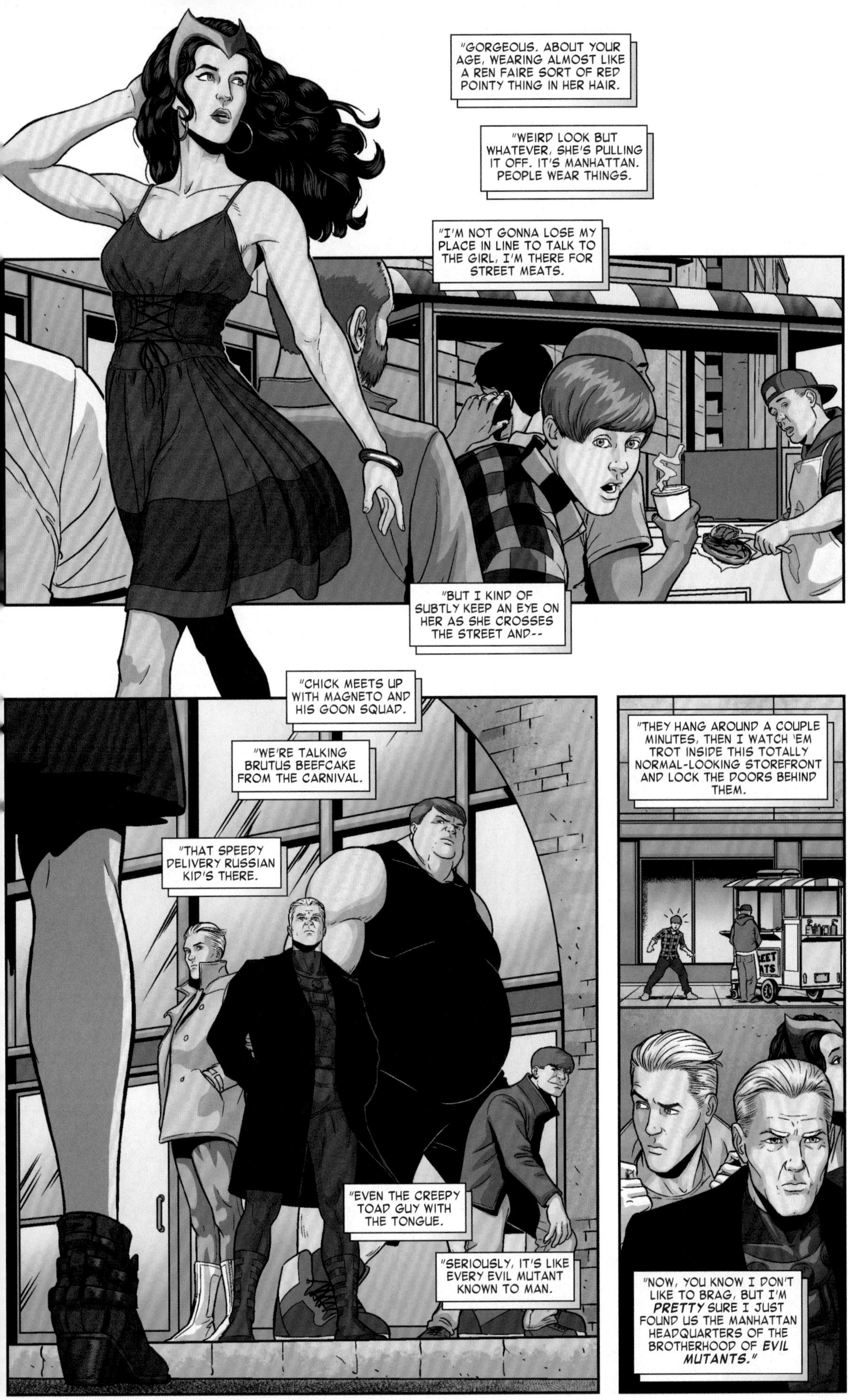
"GORGEOUS. ABOUT YOUR AGE, WEARING ALMOST LIKE A REN FAIRE SORT OF RED POINTY THING IN HER HAIR.
"WEIRD LOOK BUT WHATEVER, SHE'S PULLING IT OFF. IT'S MANHATTAN. PEOPLE WEAR THINGS.
"I'M NOT GONNA LOSE MY PLACE IN LINE TO TALK TO THE GIRL, I'M THERE FOR STREET MEATS.
"BUT I KIND OF SUBTLY KEEP AN EYE ON HER AS SHE CROSSES THE STREET AND--
"CHICK MEETS UP WITH MAGNETO AND HIS GOON SQUAD.
"WE'RE TALKING BRUTUS BEEFCAKE FROM THE CARNIVAL.
"THAT SPEEDY DELIVERY RUSSIAN KID'S THERE.
"EVEN THE CREEPY TOAD GUY WITH THE TONGUE.
"SERIOUSLY, IT'S LIKE EVERY EVIL MUTANT KNOWN TO MAN.
"THEY HANG AROUND A COUPLE MINUTES, THEN I WATCH 'EM TROT INSIDE THIS TOTALLY NORMAL-LOOKING STOREFRONT AND LOCK THE DOORS BEHIND THEM.
"NOW, YOU KNOW I DON'T LIKE TO BRAG, BUT I'M *PRETTY* SURE I JUST FOUND US THE MANHATTAN HEADQUARTERS OF THE BROTHERHOOD OF *EVIL MUTANTS.*"

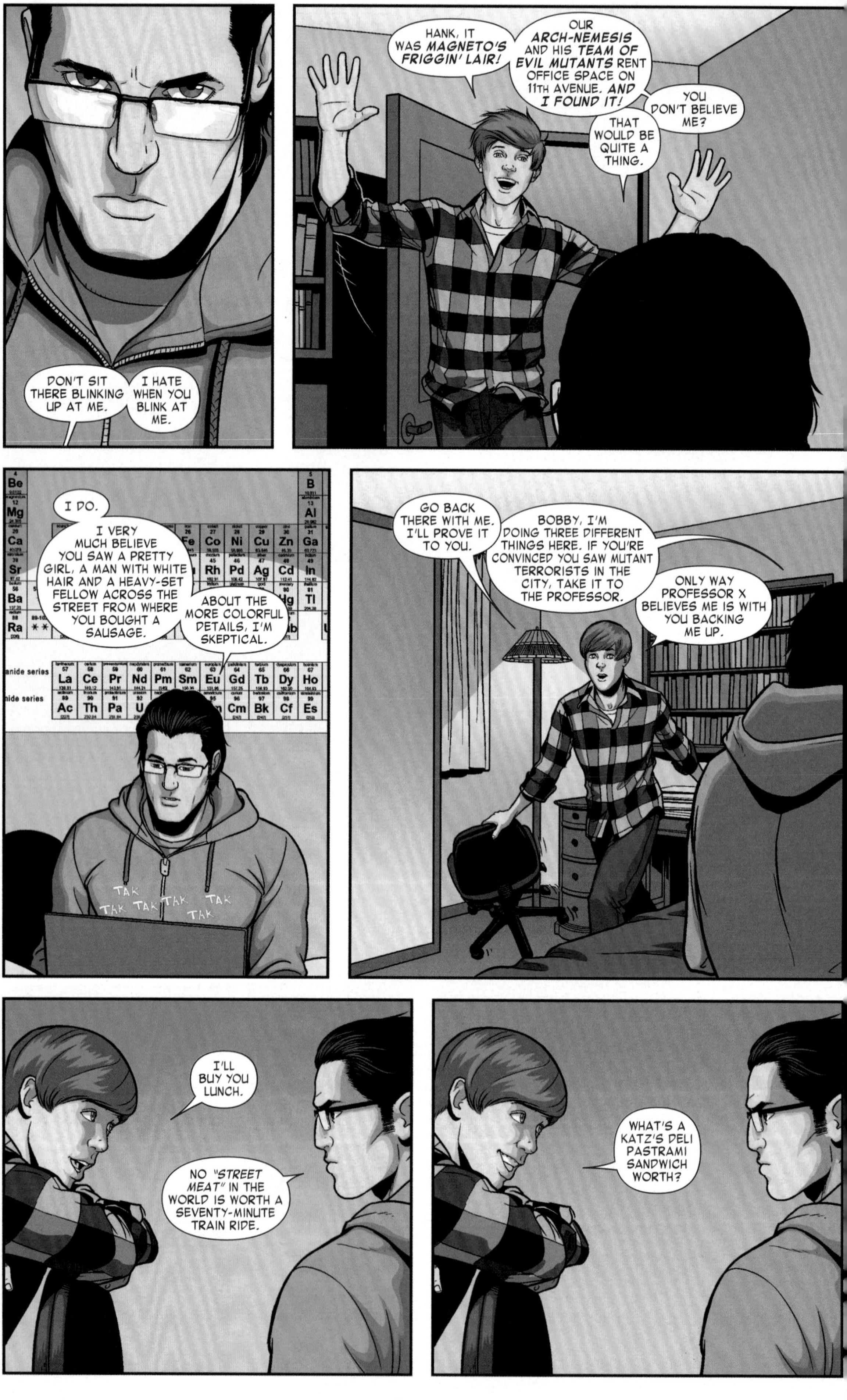
DON'T SIT THERE BLINKING UP AT ME.
I HATE WHEN YOU BLINK AT ME.
HANK, IT WAS MAGNETO'S FRIGGIN' LAIR!
OUR ARCH-NEMESIS AND HIS TEAM OF EVIL MUTANTS RENT OFFICE SPACE ON 11TH AVENUE. AND I FOUND IT!
THAT WOULD BE QUITE A THING.
YOU DON'T BELIEVE ME?
I DO.
I VERY MUCH BELIEVE YOU SAW A PRETTY GIRL, A MAN WITH WHITE HAIR AND A HEAVY-SET FELLOW ACROSS THE STREET FROM WHERE YOU BOUGHT A SAUSAGE.
ABOUT THE MORE COLORFUL DETAILS, I'M SKEPTICAL.
TAK TAK TAK TAK TAK TAK
GO BACK THERE WITH ME. I'LL PROVE IT TO YOU.
BOBBY, I'M DOING THREE DIFFERENT THINGS HERE. IF YOU'RE CONVINCED YOU SAW MUTANT TERRORISTS IN THE CITY, TAKE IT TO THE PROFESSOR.
ONLY WAY PROFESSOR X BELIEVES ME IS WITH YOU BACKING ME UP.
I'LL BUY YOU LUNCH.
NO "STREET MEAT" IN THE WORLD IS WORTH A SEVENTY-MINUTE TRAIN RIDE.
WHAT'S A KATZ'S DELI PASTRAMI SANDWICH WORTH?

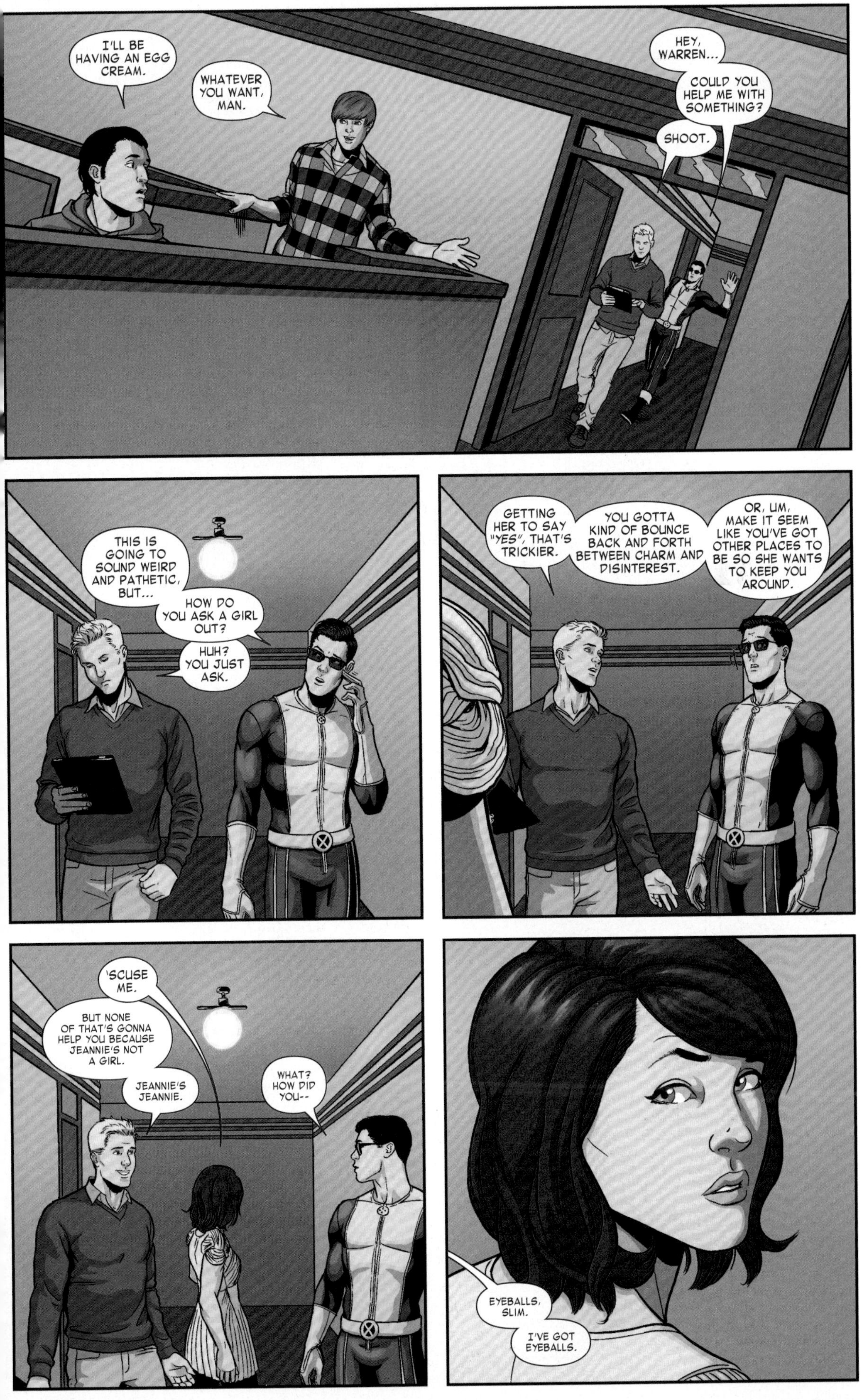
I'LL BE HAVING AN EGG CREAM.
WHATEVER YOU WANT, MAN.
HEY, WARREN...
COULD YOU HELP ME WITH SOMETHING?
SHOOT.
THIS IS GOING TO SOUND WEIRD AND PATHETIC, BUT...
HOW DO YOU ASK A GIRL OUT?
HUH? YOU JUST ASK.
GETTING HER TO SAY "YES", THAT'S TRICKIER.
YOU GOTTA KIND OF BOUNCE BACK AND FORTH BETWEEN CHARM AND DISINTEREST.
OR, UM, MAKE IT SEEM LIKE YOU'VE GOT OTHER PLACES TO BE SO SHE WANTS TO KEEP YOU AROUND.
'SCUSE ME.
BUT NONE OF THAT'S GONNA HELP YOU BECAUSE JEANNIE'S NOT A GIRL.
JEANNIE'S JEANNIE.
WHAT? HOW DID YOU--
EYEBALLS, SLIM.
I'VE GOT EYEBALLS.

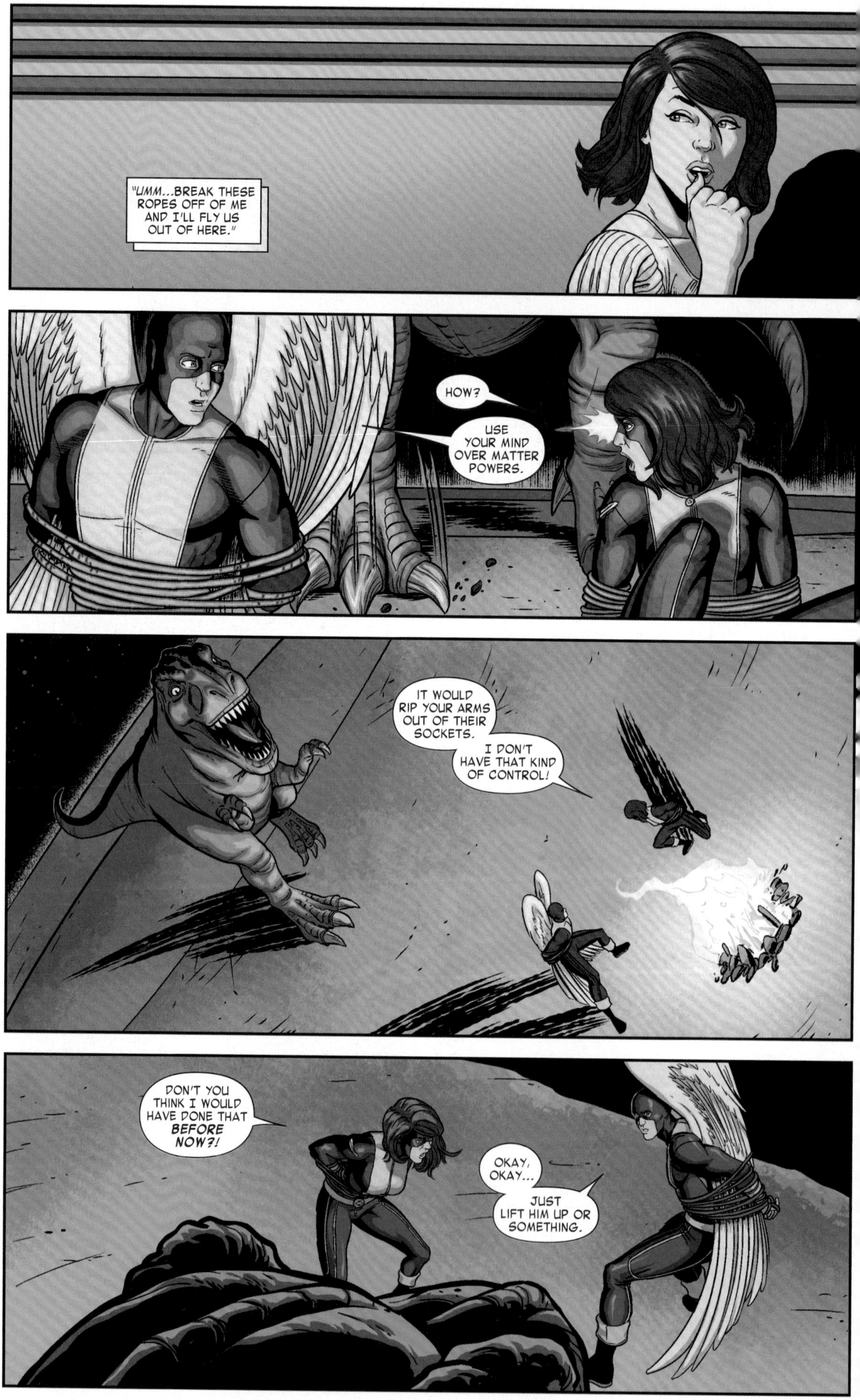
"UMM...BREAK THESE ROPES OFF OF ME AND I'LL FLY US OUT OF HERE."
HOW?
USE YOUR MIND OVER MATTER POWERS.
IT WOULD RIP YOUR ARMS OUT OF THEIR SOCKETS.
I DON'T HAVE THAT KIND OF CONTROL!
DON'T YOU THINK I WOULD HAVE DONE THAT *BEFORE NOW?!*
OKAY, OKAY...
JUST LIFT HIM UP OR SOMETHING.

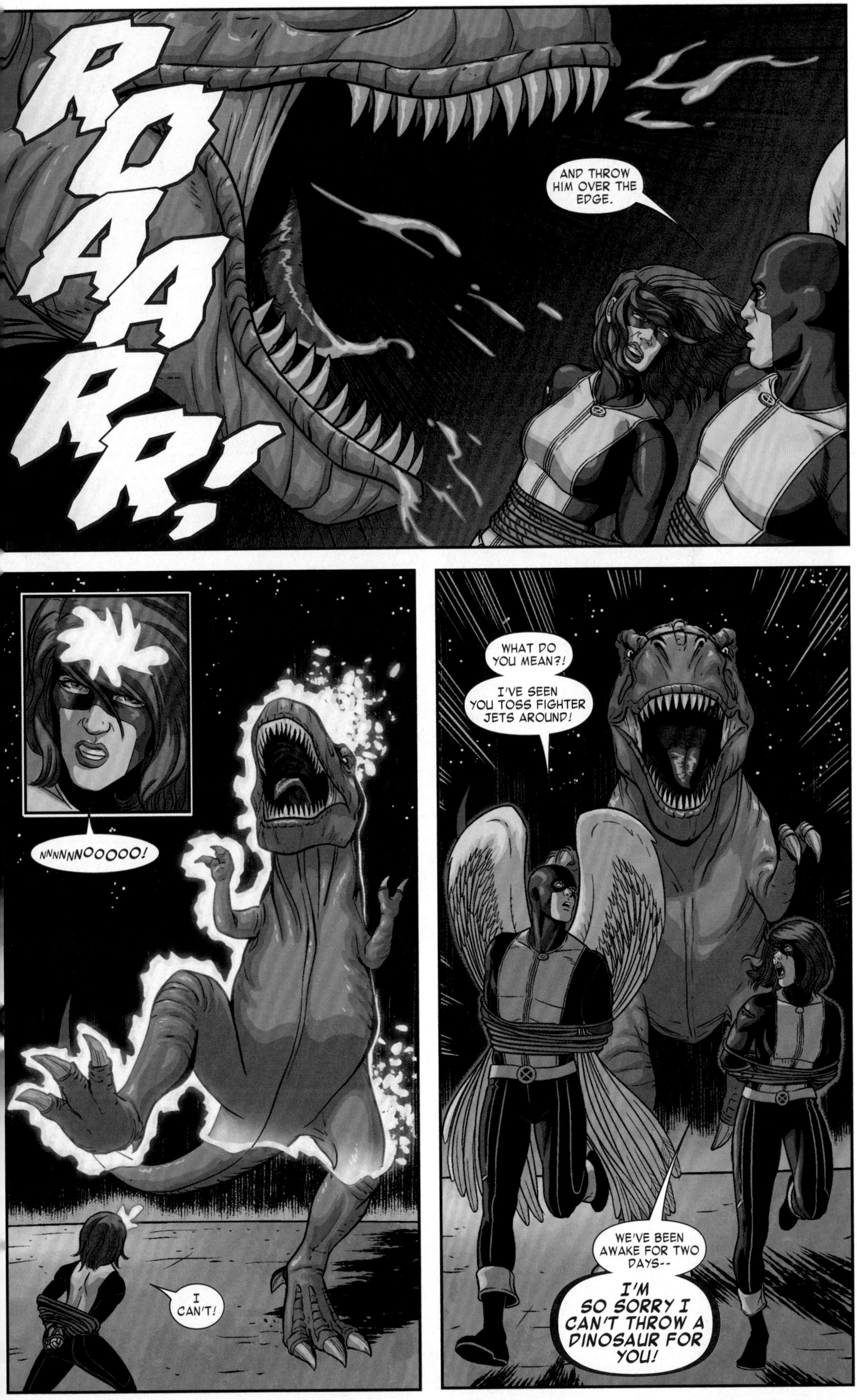
ROAARR!
AND THROW HIM OVER THE EDGE.
NNNNNNOOOOO!
I CAN'T!
WHAT DO YOU MEAN?!
I'VE SEEN YOU TOSS FIGHTER JETS AROUND!
WE'VE BEEN AWAKE FOR TWO DAYS--
I'M SO SORRY I CAN'T THROW A DINOSAUR FOR YOU!

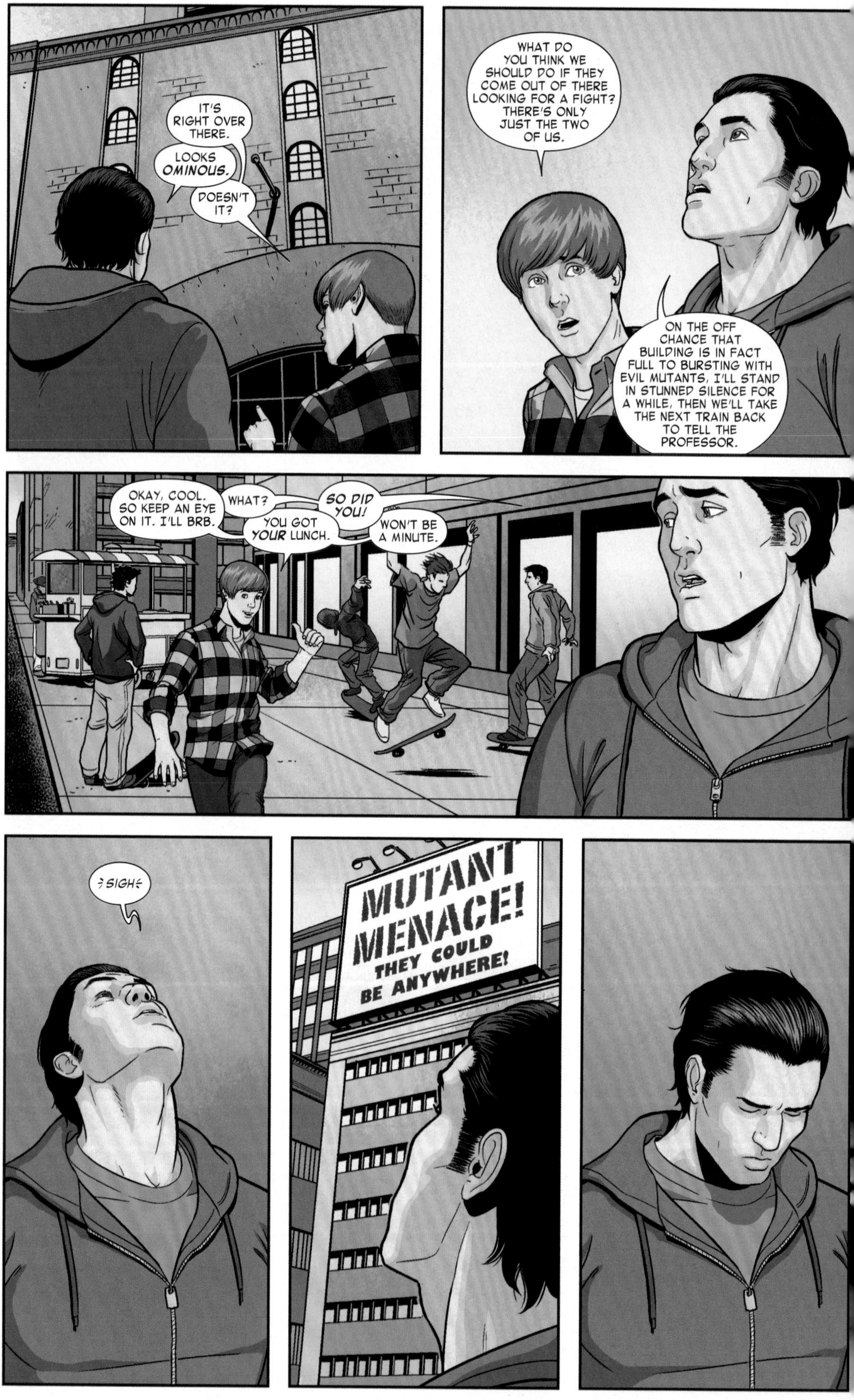
IT'S RIGHT OVER THERE.
LOOKS OMINOUS.
DOESN'T IT?
WHAT DO YOU THINK WE SHOULD DO IF THEY COME OUT OF THERE LOOKING FOR A FIGHT? THERE'S ONLY JUST THE TWO OF US.
ON THE OFF CHANCE THAT BUILDING IS IN FACT FULL TO BURSTING WITH EVIL MUTANTS, I'LL STAND IN STUNNED SILENCE FOR A WHILE, THEN WE'LL TAKE THE NEXT TRAIN BACK TO TELL THE PROFESSOR.
OKAY, COOL. SO KEEP AN EYE ON IT. I'LL BRB.
WHAT?
YOU GOT YOUR LUNCH.
SO DID YOU!
WON'T BE A MINUTE.
SIGH
MUTANT MENACE! THEY COULD BE ANYWHERE!

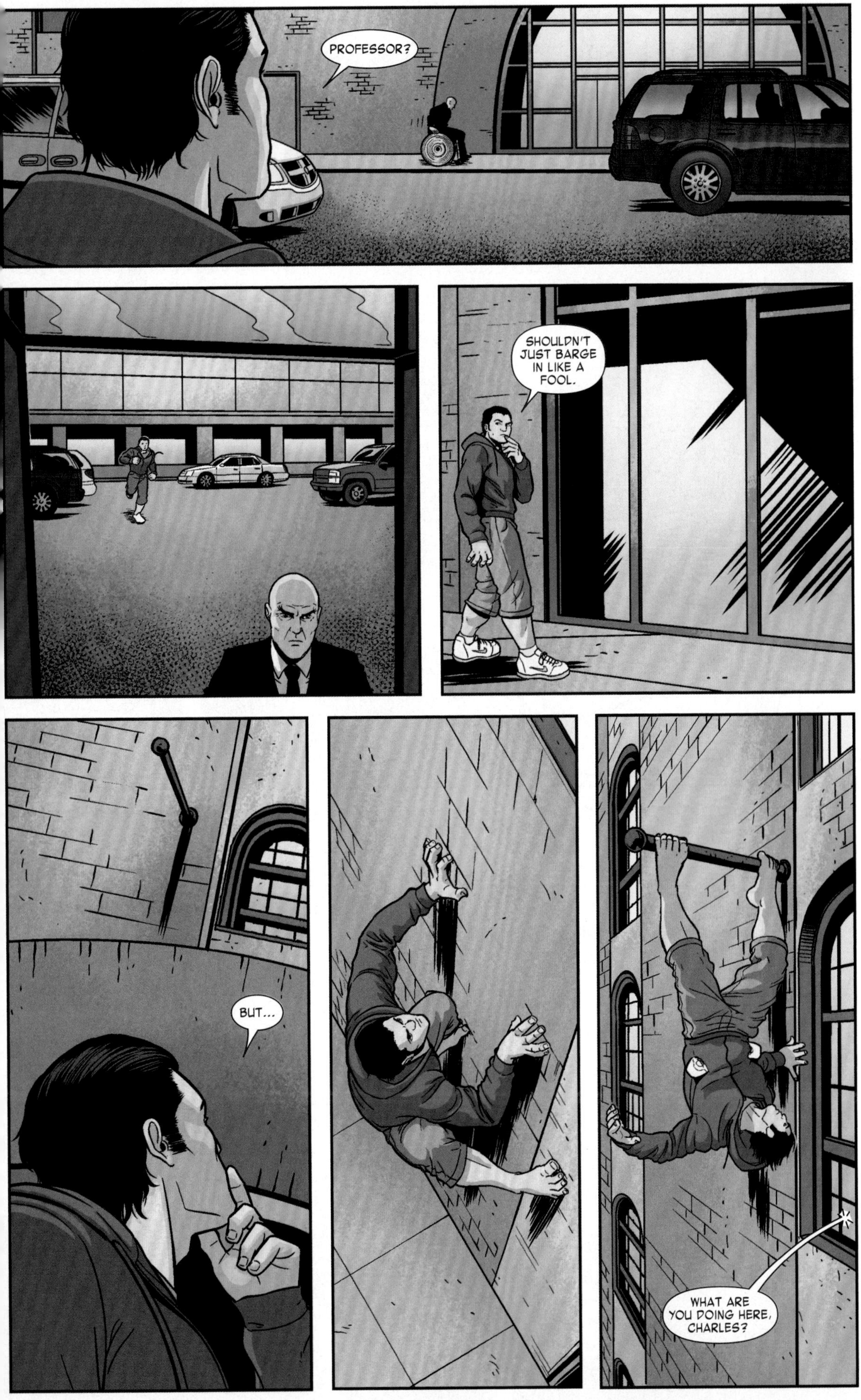
PROFESSOR?
SHOULDN'T JUST BARGE IN LIKE A FOOL.
BUT...
WHAT ARE YOU DOING HERE, CHARLES?

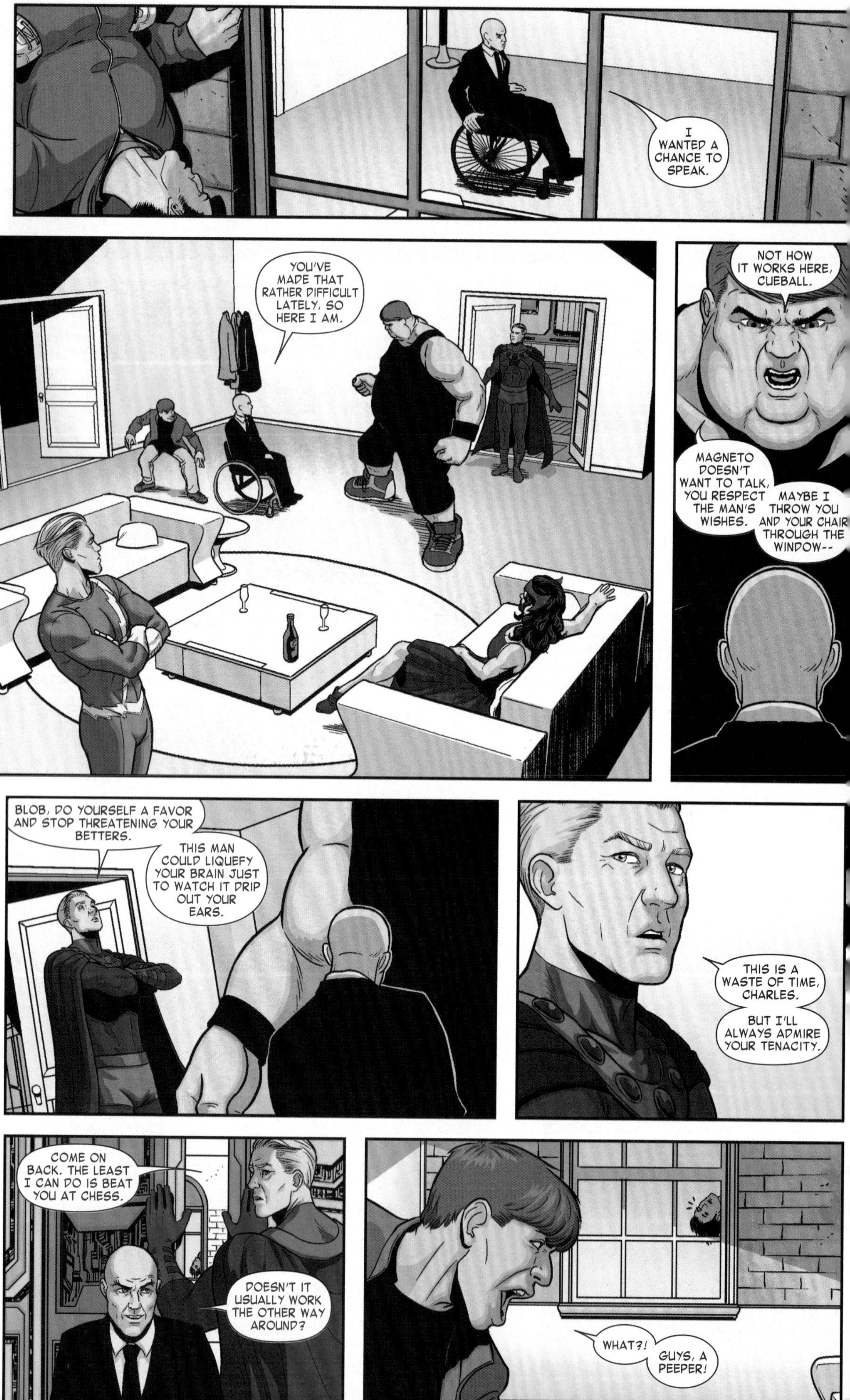
I WANTED A CHANCE TO SPEAK.
YOU'VE MADE THAT RATHER DIFFICULT LATELY, SO HERE I AM.
NOT HOW IT WORKS HERE, CUEBALL.
MAGNETO DOESN'T WANT TO TALK, YOU RESPECT THE MAN'S WISHES.
MAYBE I THROW YOU AND YOUR CHAIR THROUGH THE WINDOW--
BLOB, DO YOURSELF A FAVOR AND STOP THREATENING YOUR BETTERS.
THIS MAN COULD LIQUEFY YOUR BRAIN JUST TO WATCH IT DRIP OUT YOUR EARS.
THIS IS A WASTE OF TIME, CHARLES.
BUT I'LL ALWAYS ADMIRE YOUR TENACITY.
COME ON BACK. THE LEAST I CAN DO IS BEAT YOU AT CHESS.
DOESN'T IT USUALLY WORK THE OTHER WAY AROUND?
WHAT?!
GUYS, A PEEPER!

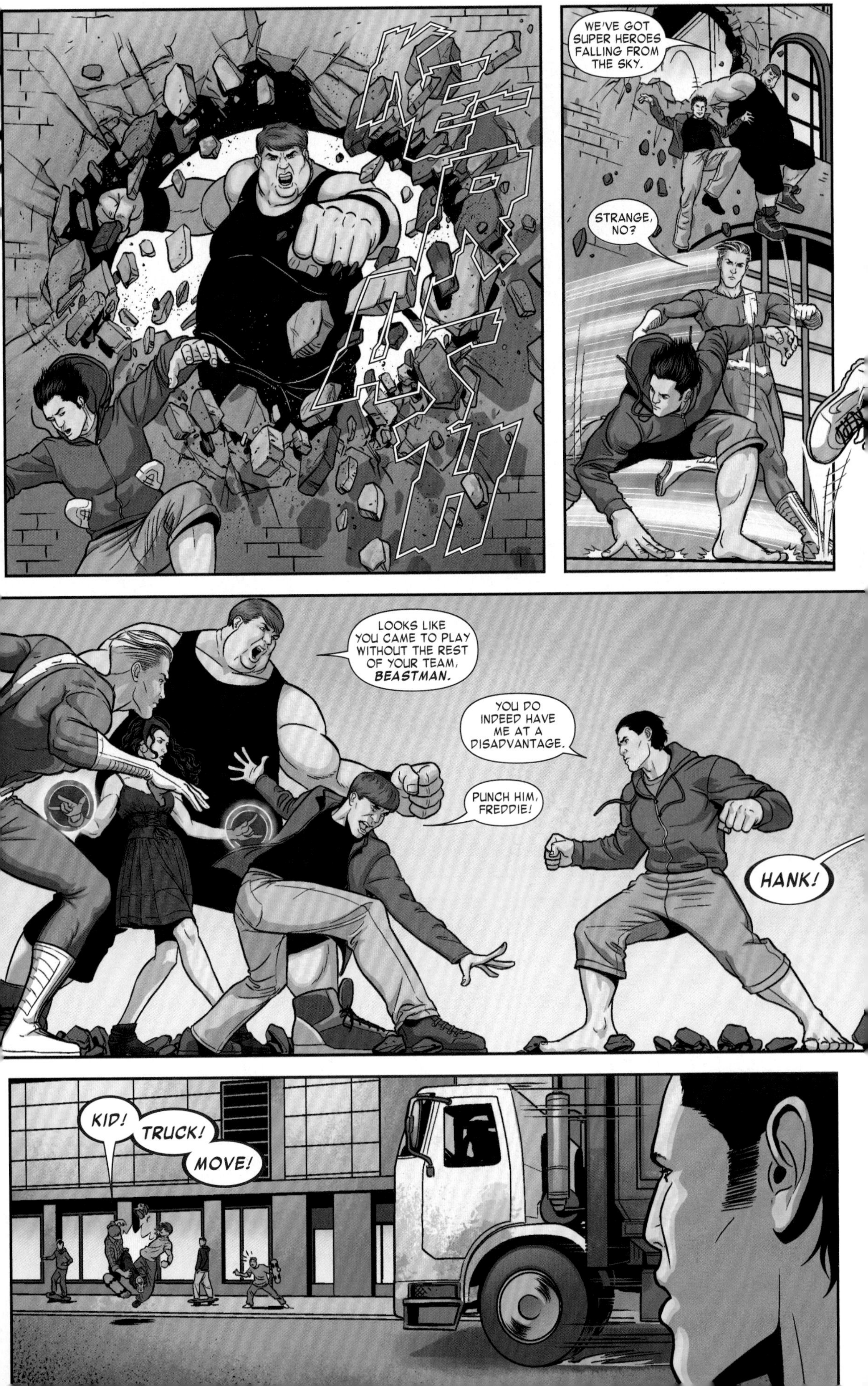
WE'VE GOT SUPER HEROES FALLING FROM THE SKY.
STRANGE, NO?
LOOKS LIKE YOU CAME TO PLAY WITHOUT THE REST OF YOUR TEAM, BEASTMAN.
YOU DO INDEED HAVE ME AT A DISADVANTAGE.
PUNCH HIM, FREDDIE!
HANK!
KID!
TRUCK!
MOVE!

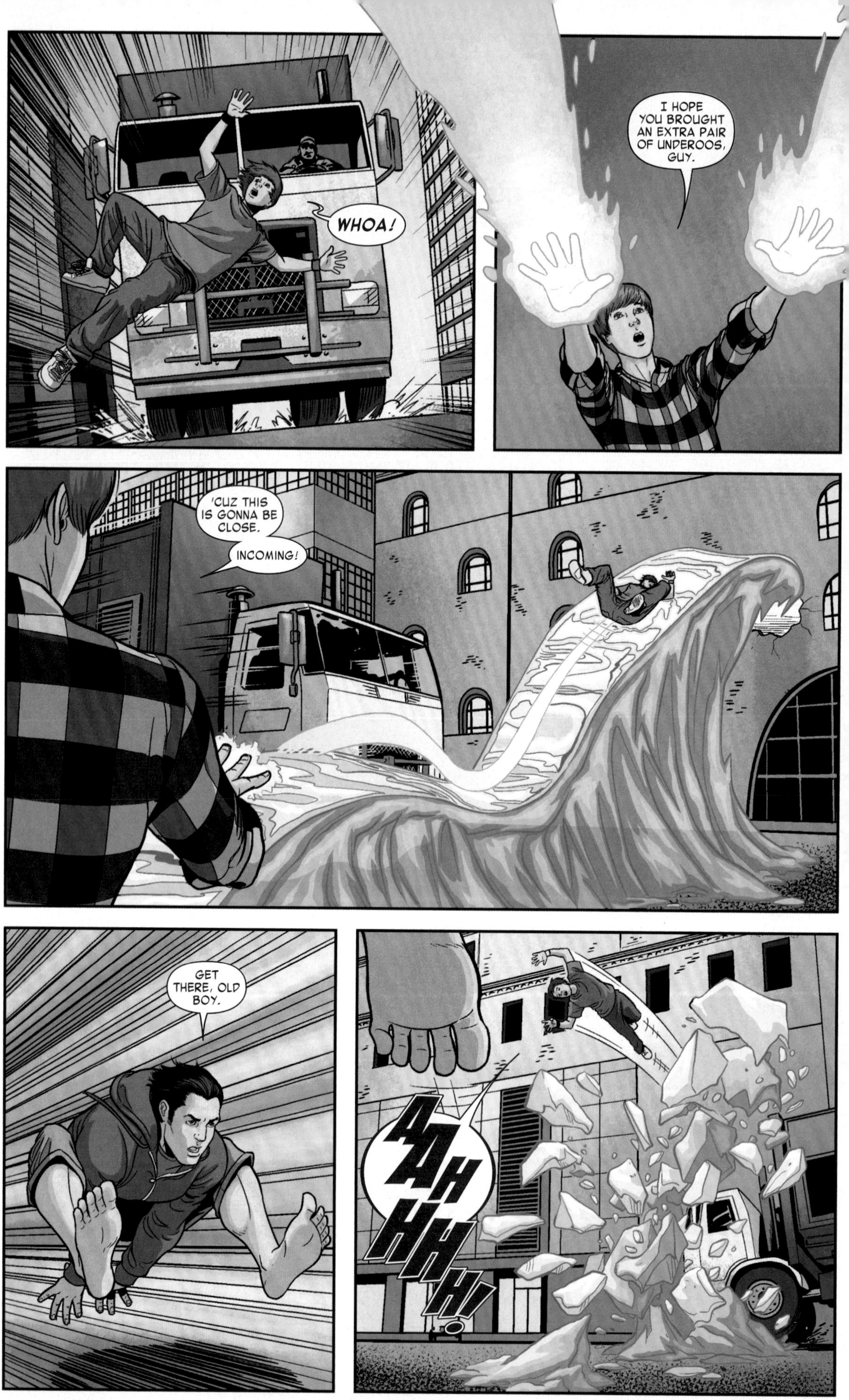
WHOA!
I HOPE YOU BROUGHT AN EXTRA PAIR OF UNDEROOS, GUY.
'CUZ THIS IS GONNA BE CLOSE.
INCOMING!
GET THERE, OLD BOY.
AAHHHH!

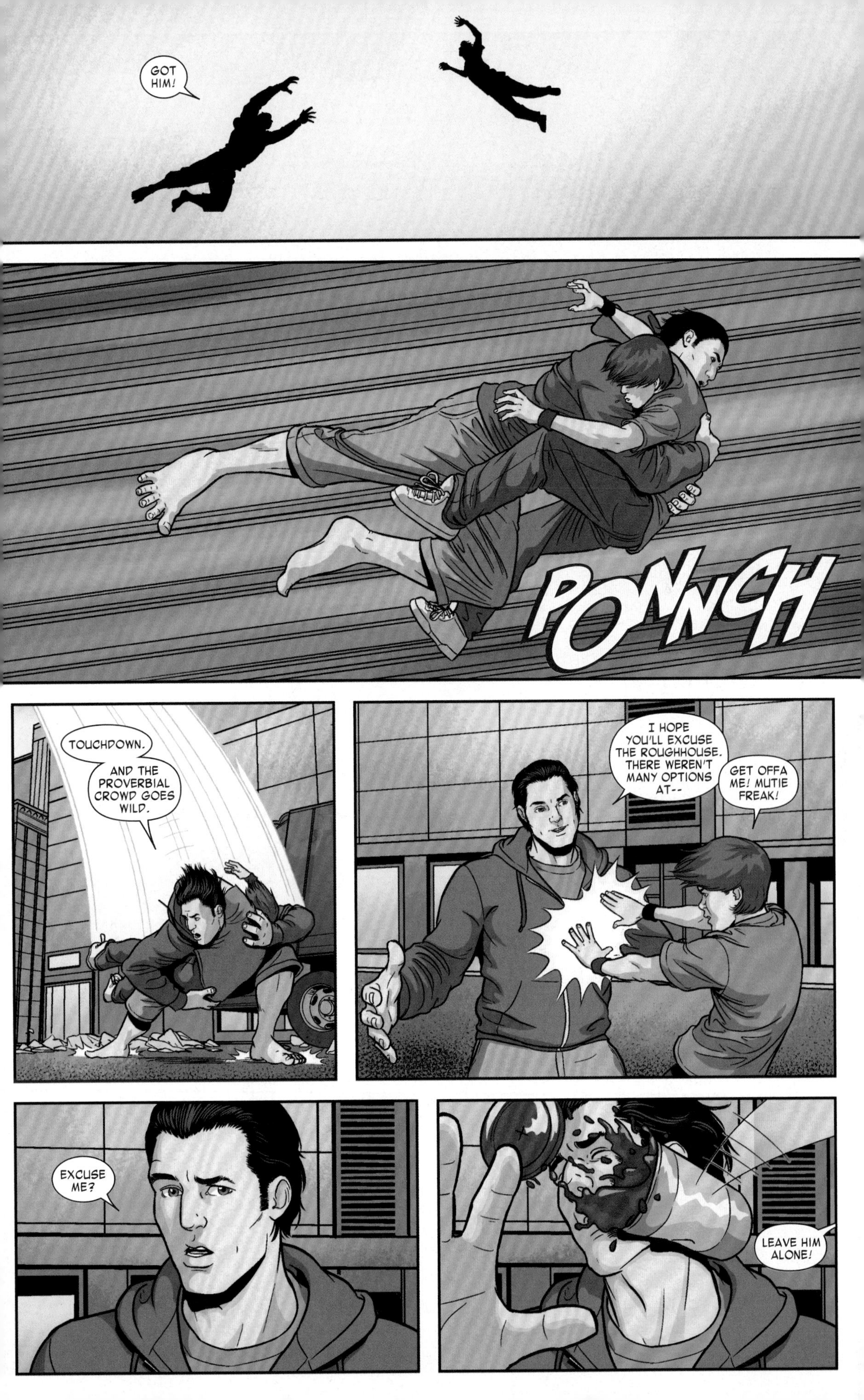

GOT HIM!
PONNCH
TOUCHDOWN.
AND THE PROVERBIAL CROWD GOES WILD.
I HOPE YOU'LL EXCUSE THE ROUGHHOUSE. THERE WEREN'T MANY OPTIONS AT--
GET OFFA ME! MUTIE FREAK!
EXCUSE ME?
LEAVE HIM ALONE!

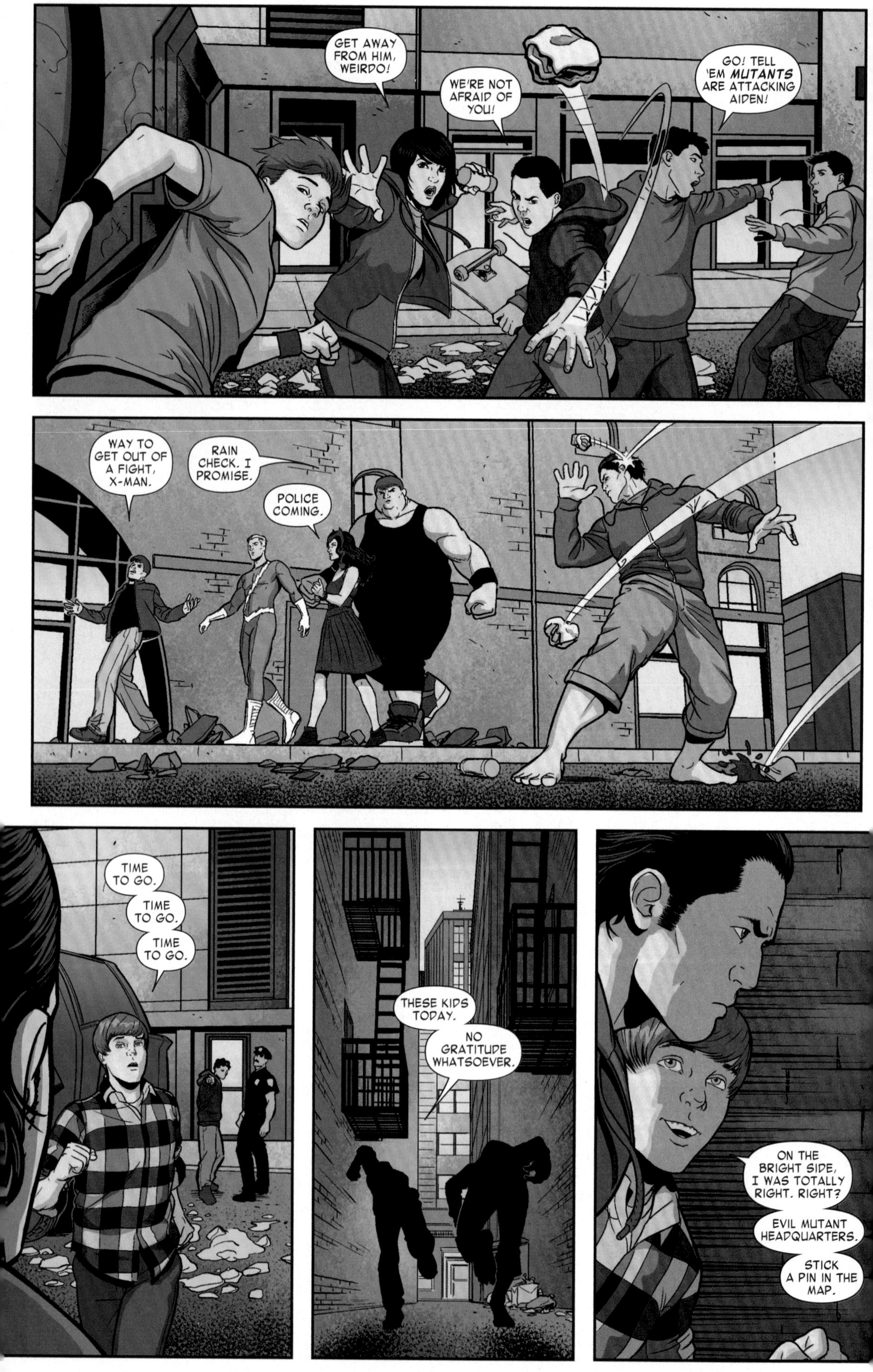

GET AWAY FROM HIM, WEIRDO!
WE'RE NOT AFRAID OF YOU!
GO! TELL 'EM MUTANTS ARE ATTACKING AIDEN!
WAY TO GET OUT OF A FIGHT, X-MAN.
RAIN CHECK. I PROMISE.
POLICE COMING.
TIME TO GO.
TIME TO GO.
TIME TO GO.
THESE KIDS TODAY.
NO GRATITUDE WHATSOEVER.
ON THE BRIGHT SIDE, I WAS TOTALLY RIGHT. RIGHT?
EVIL MUTANT HEADQUARTERS.
STICK A PIN IN THE MAP.

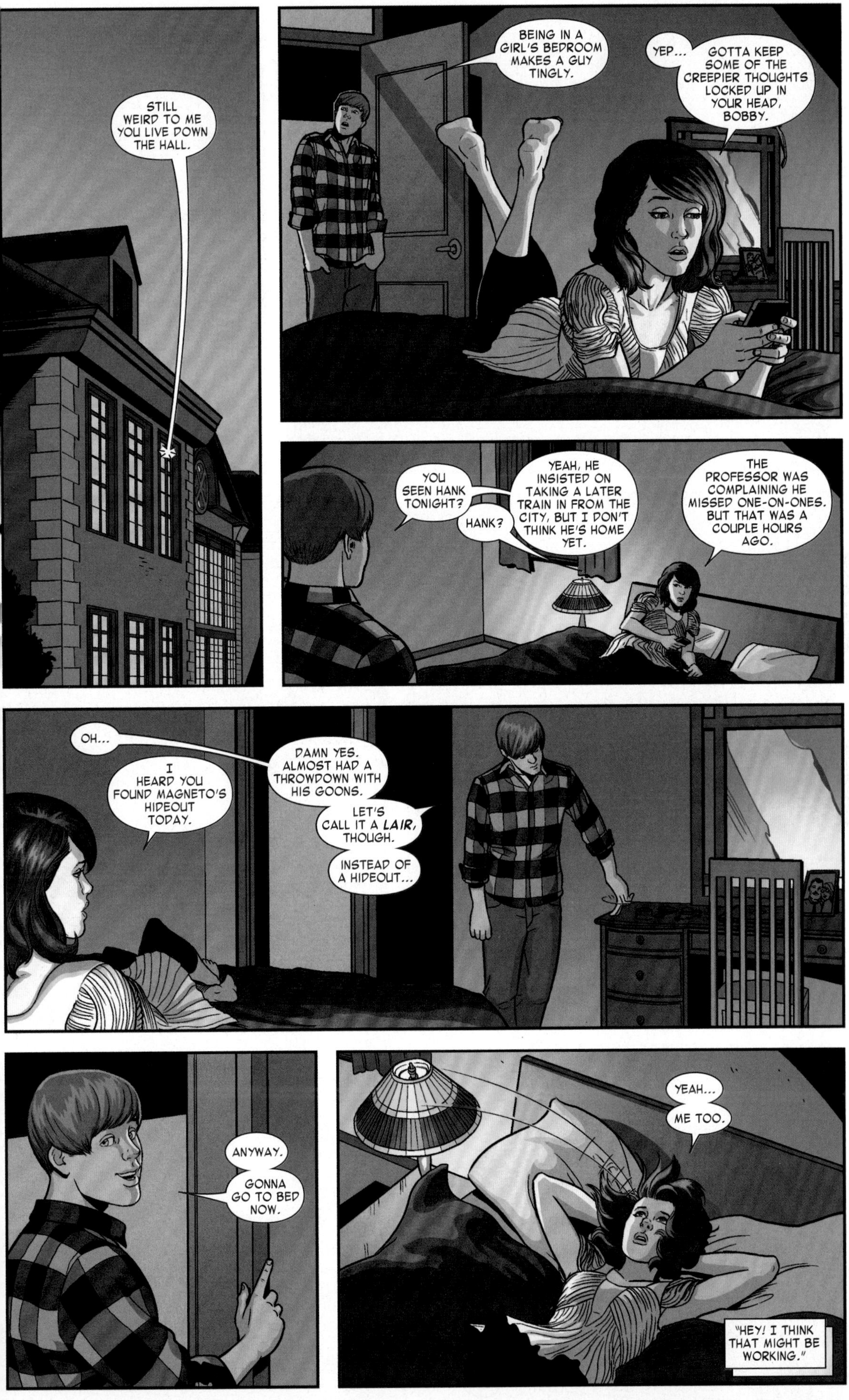
STILL WEIRD TO ME YOU LIVE DOWN THE HALL.
BEING IN A GIRL'S BEDROOM MAKES A GUY TINGLY.
YEP...
GOTTA KEEP SOME OF THE CREEPIER THOUGHTS LOCKED UP IN YOUR HEAD, BOBBY.
YOU SEEN HANK TONIGHT?
HANK?
YEAH, HE INSISTED ON TAKING A LATER TRAIN IN FROM THE CITY, BUT I DON'T THINK HE'S HOME YET.
THE PROFESSOR WAS COMPLAINING HE MISSED ONE-ON-ONES. BUT THAT WAS A COUPLE HOURS AGO.
OH...
I HEARD YOU FOUND MAGNETO'S HIDEOUT TODAY.
DAMN YES. ALMOST HAD A THROWDOWN WITH HIS GOONS.
LET'S CALL IT A LAIR, THOUGH.
INSTEAD OF A HIDEOUT...
ANYWAY.
GONNA GO TO BED NOW.
YEAH...
ME TOO.
"HEY! I THINK THAT MIGHT BE WORKING."

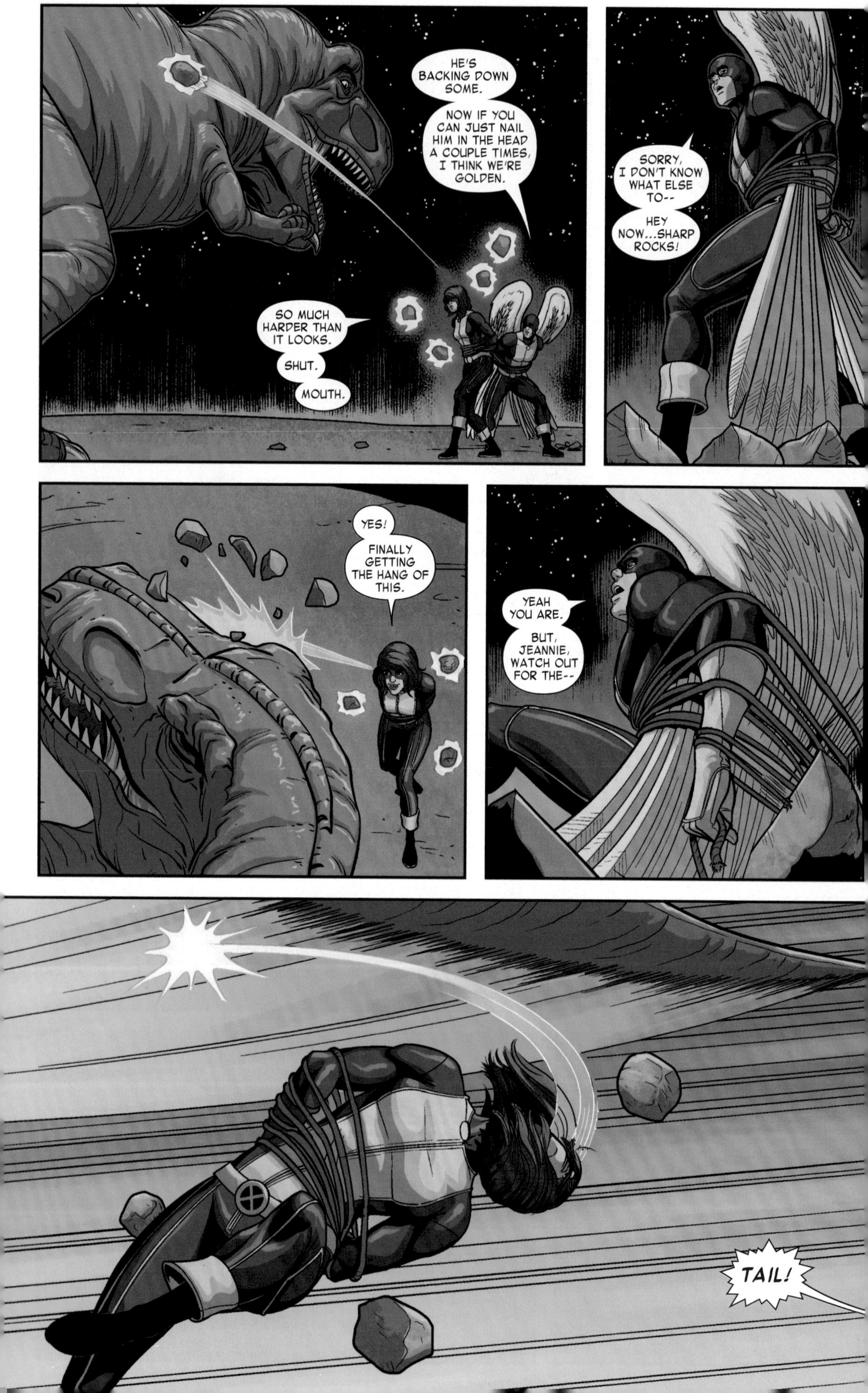
HE'S BACKING DOWN SOME.
NOW IF YOU CAN JUST NAIL HIM IN THE HEAD A COUPLE TIMES, I THINK WE'RE GOLDEN.
SO MUCH HARDER THAN IT LOOKS.
SHUT.
MOUTH.
SORRY, I DON'T KNOW WHAT ELSE TO--
HEY NOW...SHARP ROCKS!
YES!
FINALLY GETTING THE HANG OF THIS.
YEAH YOU ARE.
BUT, JEANNIE, WATCH OUT FOR THE--
TAIL!

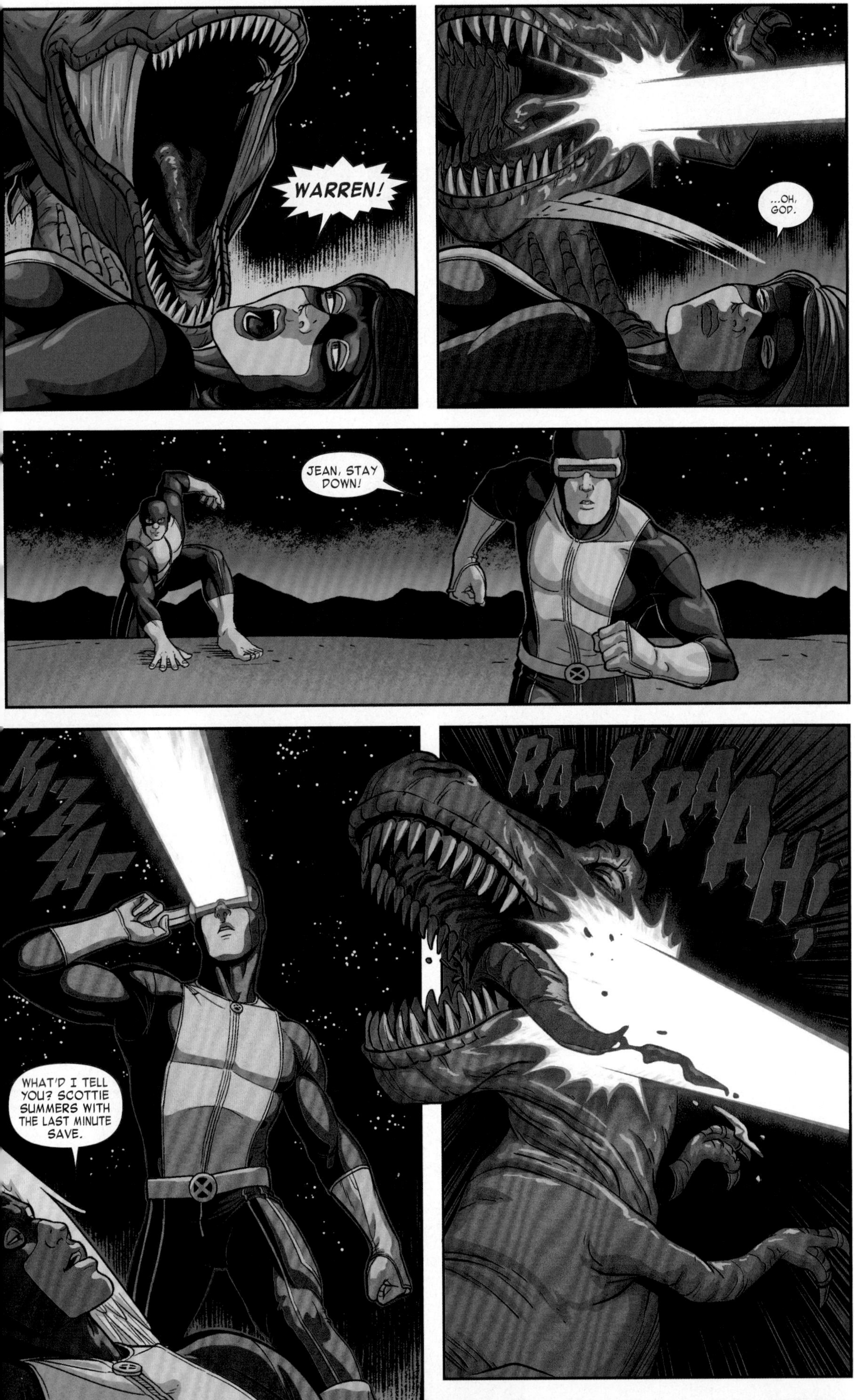
WARREN!
...OH, GOD.
JEAN, STAY DOWN!
KA-ZZAT
RA-KRAAH!
WHAT'D I TELL YOU? SCOTTIE SUMMERS WITH THE LAST MINUTE SAVE.

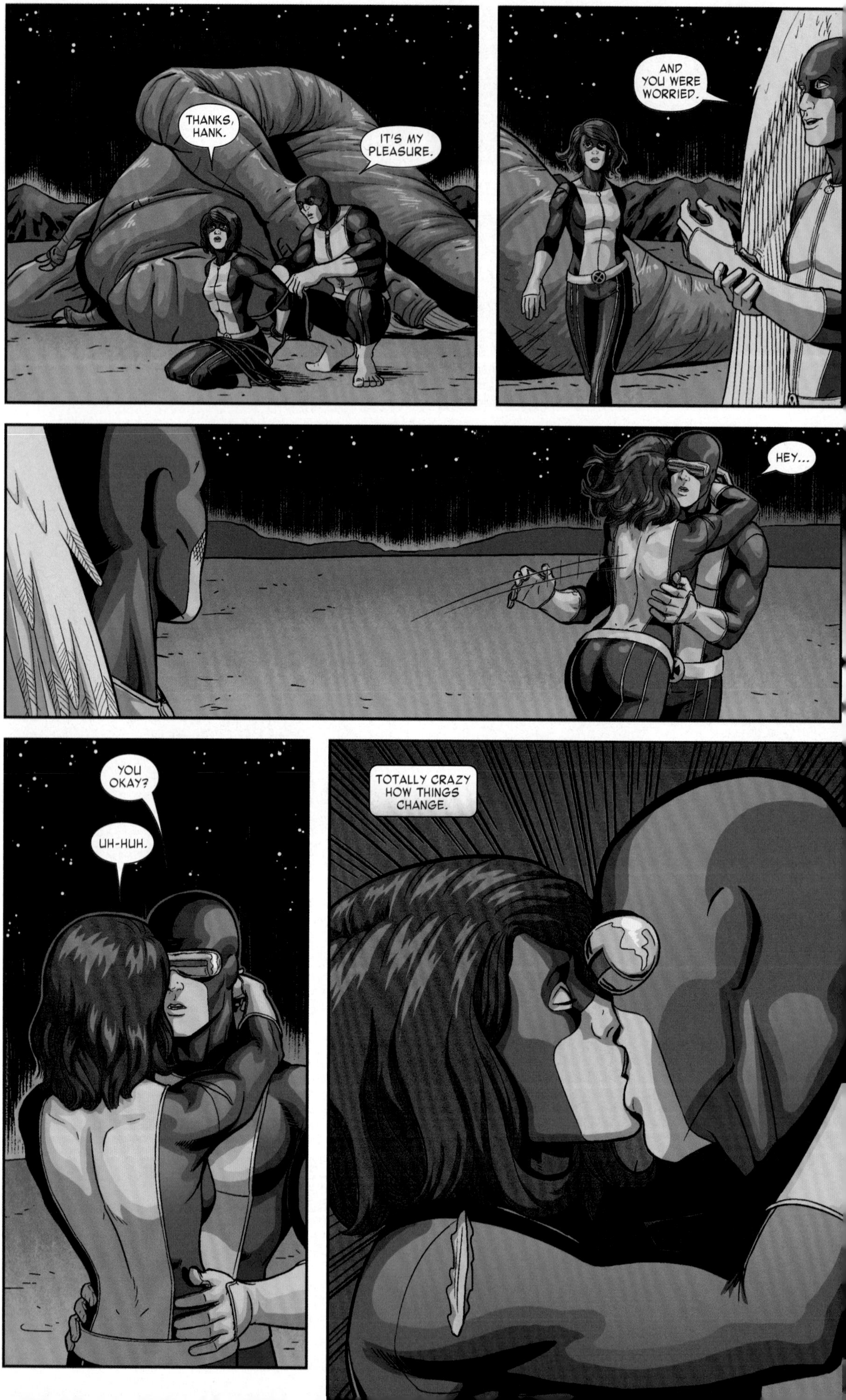
THANKS, HANK.
IT'S MY PLEASURE.
AND YOU WERE WORRIED.
HEY...
YOU OKAY?
UH-HUH.
TOTALLY CRAZY HOW THINGS CHANGE.

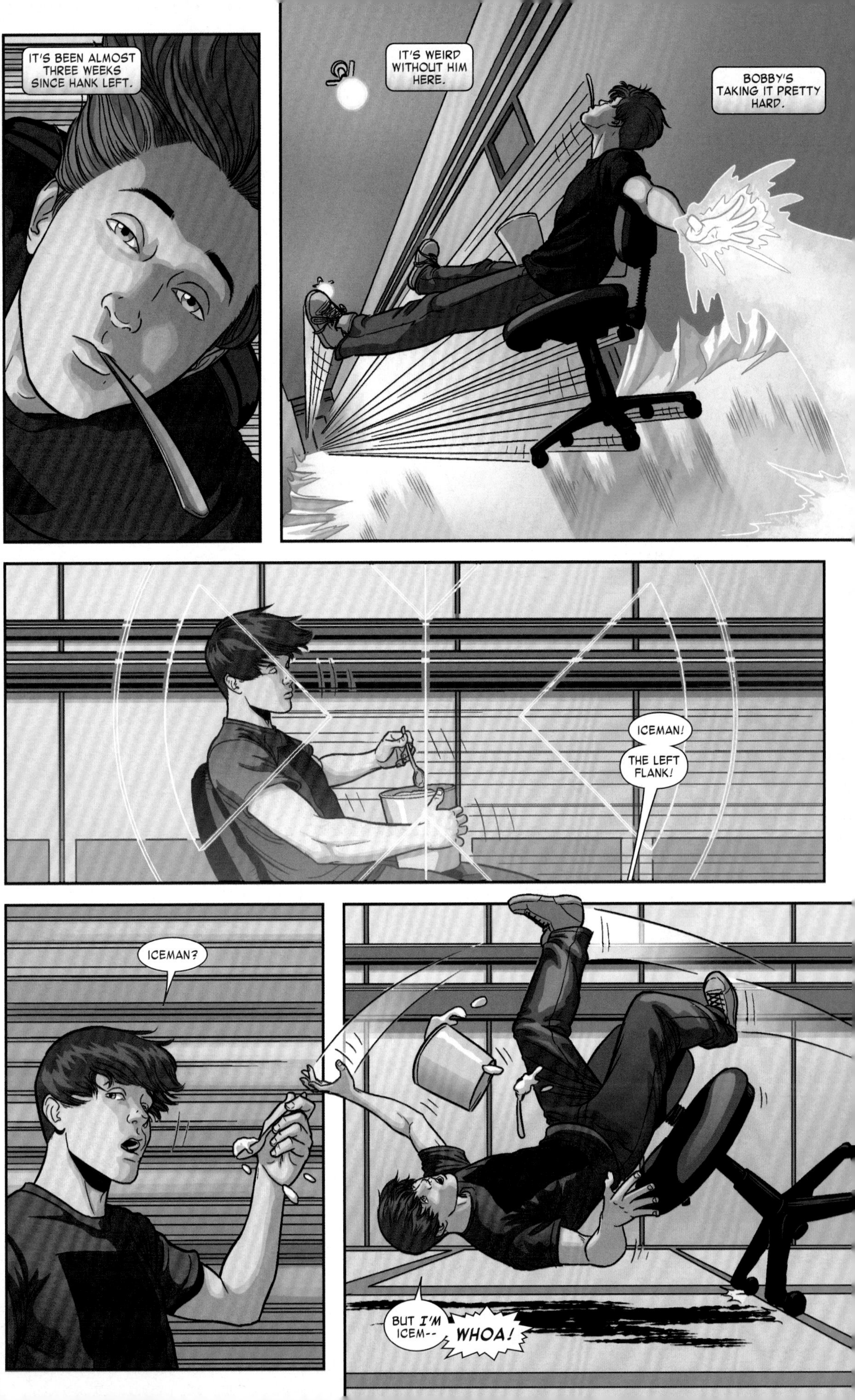
IT'S BEEN ALMOST THREE WEEKS SINCE HANK LEFT.
IT'S WEIRD WITHOUT HIM HERE.
BOBBY'S TAKING IT PRETTY HARD.
ICEMAN!
THE LEFT FLANK!
ICEMAN?
BUT I'M ICEM--
WHOA!

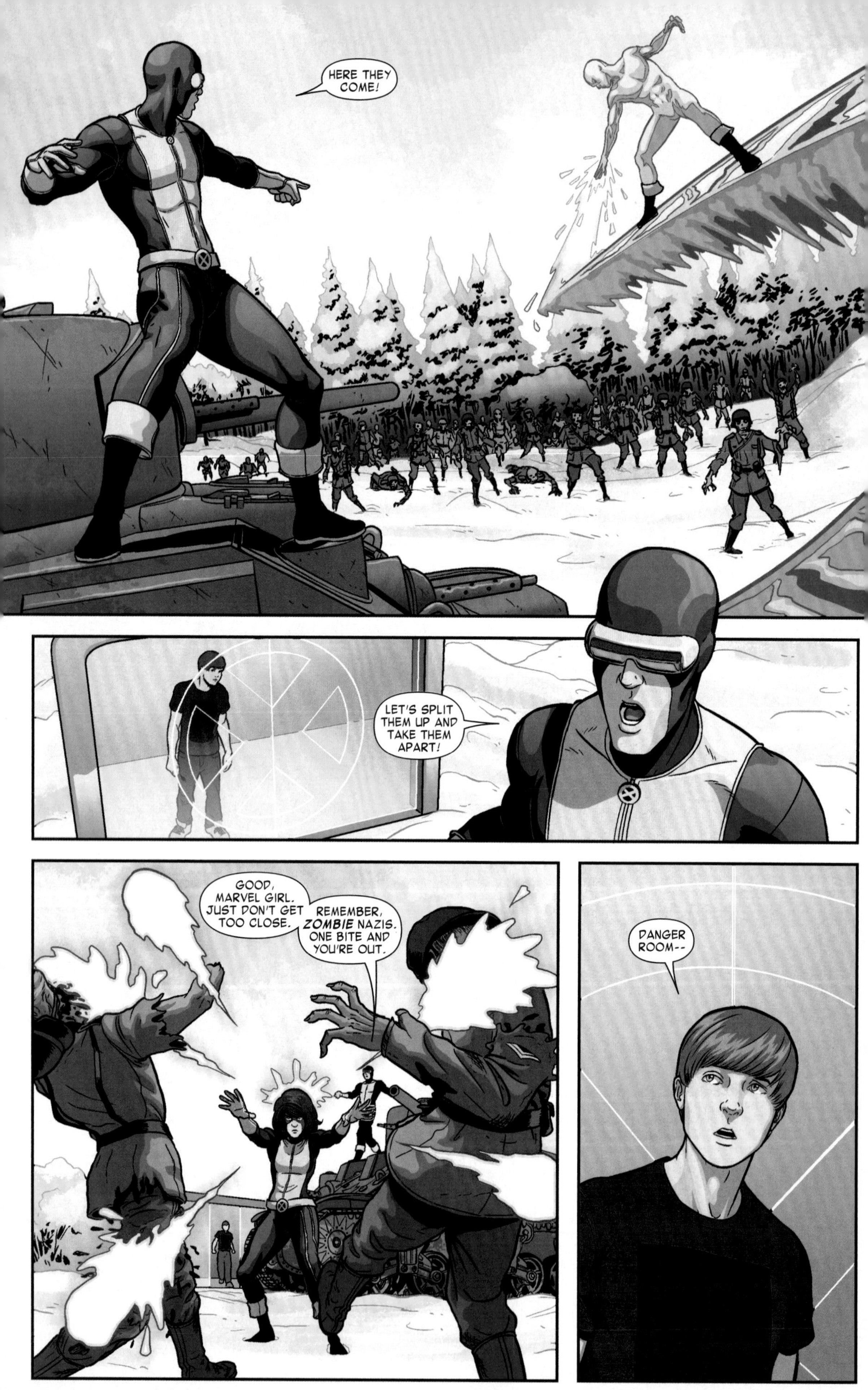
HERE THEY COME!
LET'S SPLIT THEM UP AND TAKE THEM APART!
GOOD, MARVEL GIRL. JUST DON'T GET TOO CLOSE.
REMEMBER, ZOMBIE NAZIS. ONE BITE AND YOU'RE OUT.
DANGER ROOM--

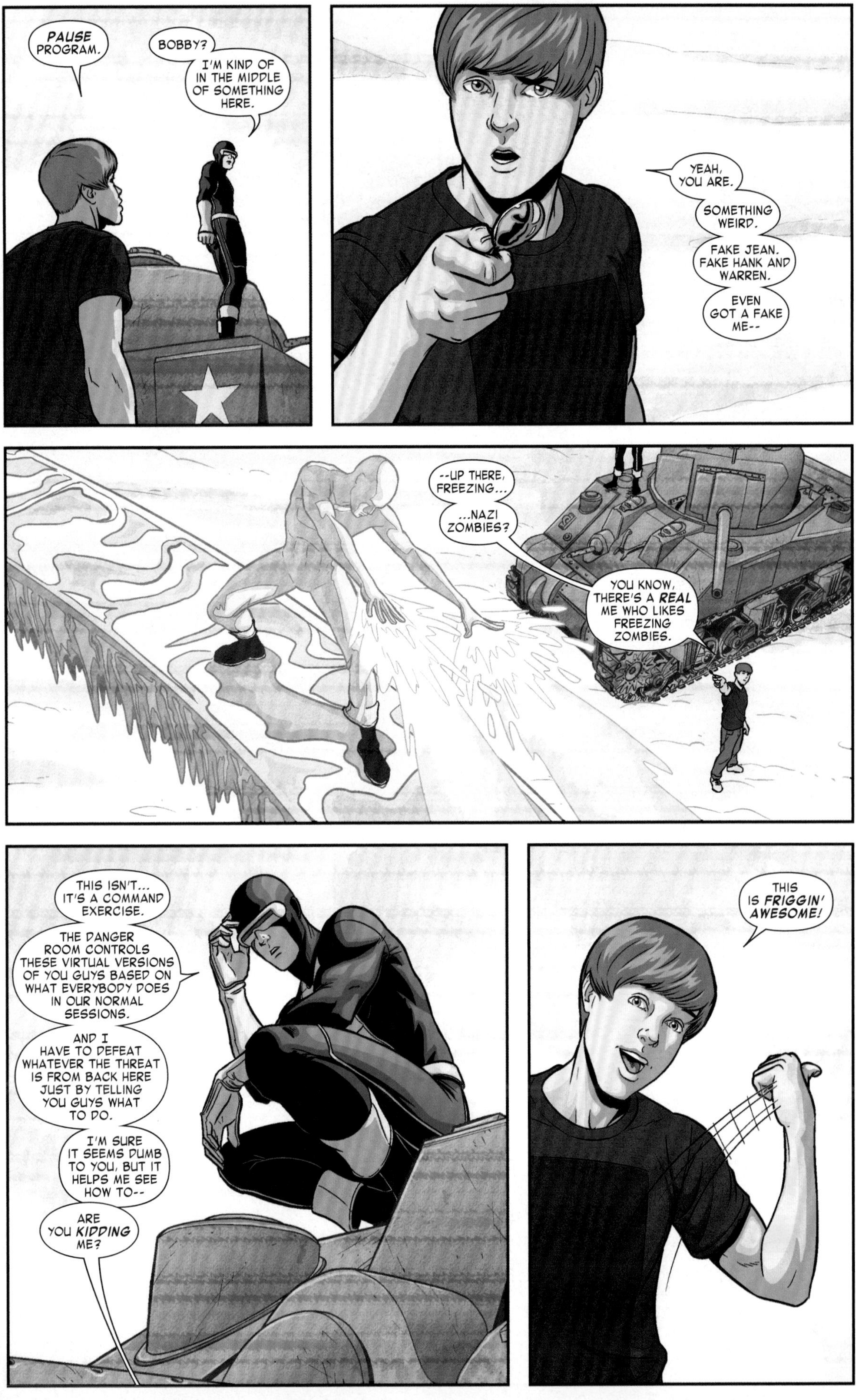
PAUSE PROGRAM.
BOBBY?
I'M KIND OF IN THE MIDDLE OF SOMETHING HERE.
YEAH, YOU ARE.
SOMETHING WEIRD.
FAKE JEAN. FAKE HANK AND WARREN.
EVEN GOT A FAKE ME--
--UP THERE, FREEZING...
...NAZI ZOMBIES?
YOU KNOW, THERE'S A REAL ME WHO LIKES FREEZING ZOMBIES.
THIS ISN'T... IT'S A COMMAND EXERCISE.
THE DANGER ROOM CONTROLS THESE VIRTUAL VERSIONS OF YOU GUYS BASED ON WHAT EVERYBODY DOES IN OUR NORMAL SESSIONS.
AND I HAVE TO DEFEAT WHATEVER THE THREAT IS FROM BACK HERE JUST BY TELLING YOU GUYS WHAT TO DO.
I'M SURE IT SEEMS DUMB TO YOU, BUT IT HELPS ME SEE HOW TO--
ARE YOU KIDDING ME?
THIS IS FRIGGIN' AWESOME!

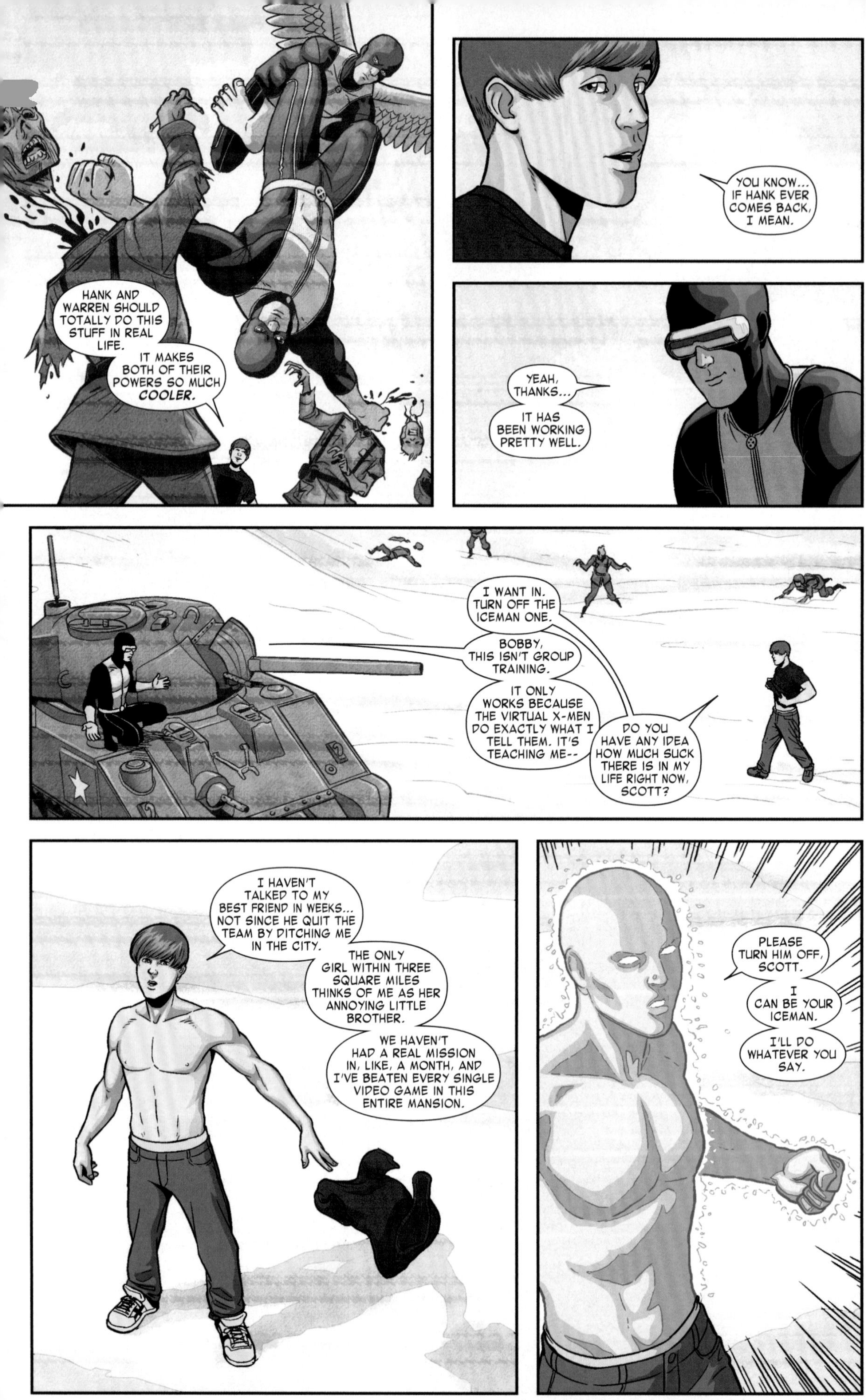
HANK AND WARREN SHOULD TOTALLY DO THIS STUFF IN REAL LIFE.
IT MAKES BOTH OF THEIR POWERS SO MUCH COOLER.
YOU KNOW... IF HANK EVER COMES BACK, I MEAN.
YEAH, THANKS...
IT HAS BEEN WORKING PRETTY WELL.
I WANT IN. TURN OFF THE ICEMAN ONE.
BOBBY, THIS ISN'T GROUP TRAINING.
IT ONLY WORKS BECAUSE THE VIRTUAL X-MEN DO EXACTLY WHAT I TELL THEM. IT'S TEACHING ME--
DO YOU HAVE ANY IDEA HOW MUCH SUCK THERE IS IN MY LIFE RIGHT NOW, SCOTT?
I HAVEN'T TALKED TO MY BEST FRIEND IN WEEKS... NOT SINCE HE QUIT THE TEAM BY DITCHING ME IN THE CITY.
THE ONLY GIRL WITHIN THREE SQUARE MILES THINKS OF ME AS HER ANNOYING LITTLE BROTHER.
WE HAVEN'T HAD A REAL MISSION IN, LIKE, A MONTH, AND I'VE BEATEN EVERY SINGLE VIDEO GAME IN THIS ENTIRE MANSION.
PLEASE TURN HIM OFF, SCOTT.
I CAN BE YOUR ICEMAN.
I'LL DO WHATEVER YOU SAY.

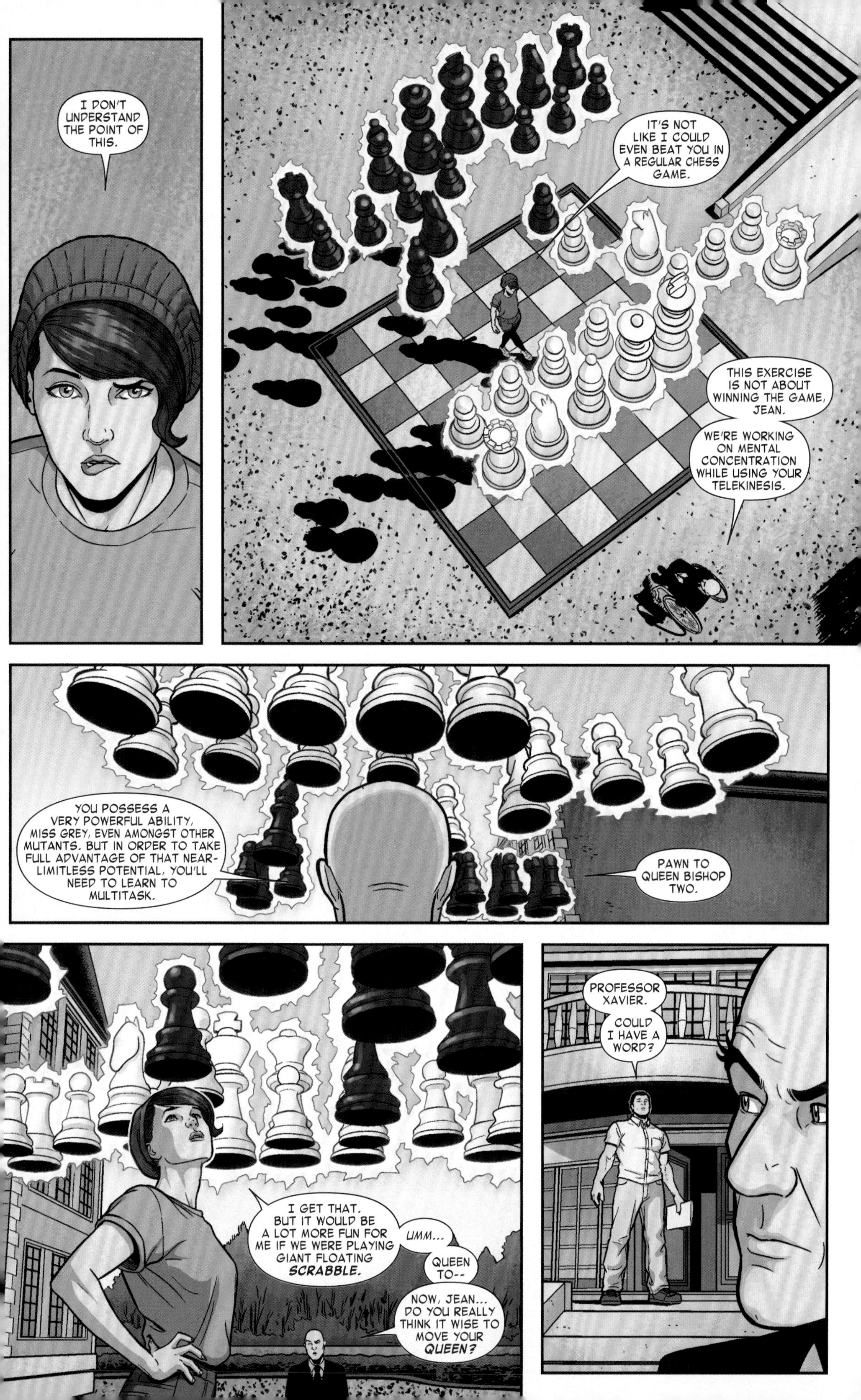
I DON'T UNDERSTAND THE POINT OF THIS.
IT'S NOT LIKE I COULD EVEN BEAT YOU IN A REGULAR CHESS GAME.
THIS EXERCISE IS NOT ABOUT WINNING THE GAME, JEAN.
WE'RE WORKING ON MENTAL CONCENTRATION WHILE USING YOUR TELEKINESIS.
YOU POSSESS A VERY POWERFUL ABILITY, MISS GREY, EVEN AMONGST OTHER MUTANTS. BUT IN ORDER TO TAKE FULL ADVANTAGE OF THAT NEAR-LIMITLESS POTENTIAL, YOU'LL NEED TO LEARN TO MULTITASK.
PAWN TO QUEEN BISHOP TWO.
I GET THAT. BUT IT WOULD BE A LOT MORE FUN FOR ME IF WE WERE PLAYING GIANT FLOATING *SCRABBLE.*
UMM...
QUEEN TO--
NOW, JEAN... DO YOU REALLY THINK IT WISE TO MOVE YOUR *QUEEN?*
PROFESSOR XAVIER.
COULD I HAVE A WORD?

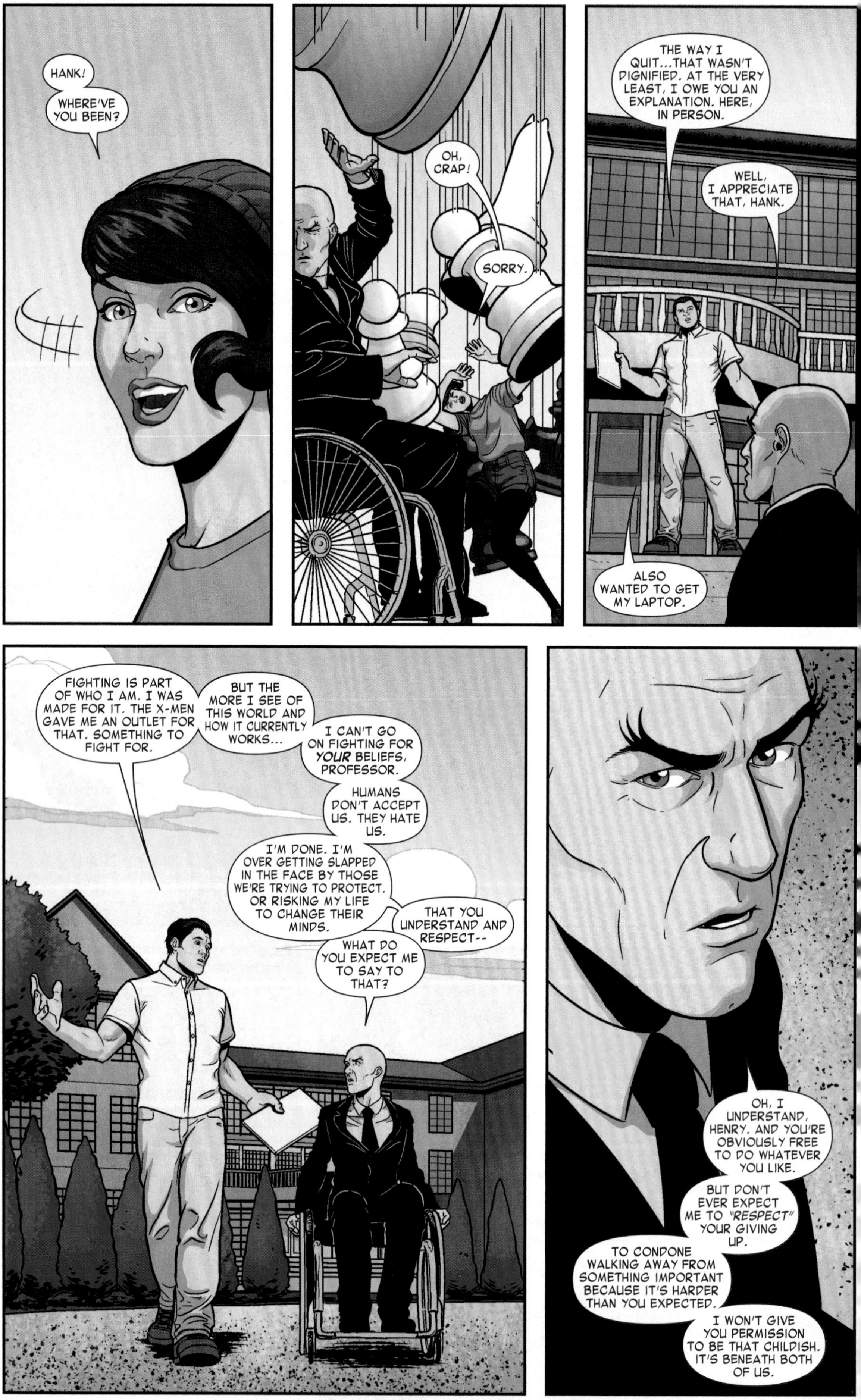
HANK!
WHERE'VE YOU BEEN?
OH, CRAP!
SORRY.
THE WAY I QUIT...THAT WASN'T DIGNIFIED. AT THE VERY LEAST, I OWE YOU AN EXPLANATION. HERE, IN PERSON.
WELL, I APPRECIATE THAT, HANK.
ALSO WANTED TO GET MY LAPTOP.
FIGHTING IS PART OF WHO I AM. I WAS MADE FOR IT. THE X-MEN GAVE ME AN OUTLET FOR THAT. SOMETHING TO FIGHT FOR.
BUT THE MORE I SEE OF THIS WORLD AND HOW IT CURRENTLY WORKS...
I CAN'T GO ON FIGHTING FOR YOUR BELIEFS, PROFESSOR.
HUMANS DON'T ACCEPT US. THEY HATE US.
I'M DONE. I'M OVER GETTING SLAPPED IN THE FACE BY THOSE WE'RE TRYING TO PROTECT. OR RISKING MY LIFE TO CHANGE THEIR MINDS.
THAT YOU UNDERSTAND AND RESPECT--
WHAT DO YOU EXPECT ME TO SAY TO THAT?
OH, I UNDERSTAND, HENRY. AND YOU'RE OBVIOUSLY FREE TO DO WHATEVER YOU LIKE.
BUT DON'T EVER EXPECT ME TO "RESPECT" YOUR GIVING UP.
TO CONDONE WALKING AWAY FROM SOMETHING IMPORTANT BECAUSE IT'S HARDER THAN YOU EXPECTED.
I WON'T GIVE YOU PERMISSION TO BE THAT CHILDISH. IT'S BENEATH BOTH OF US.

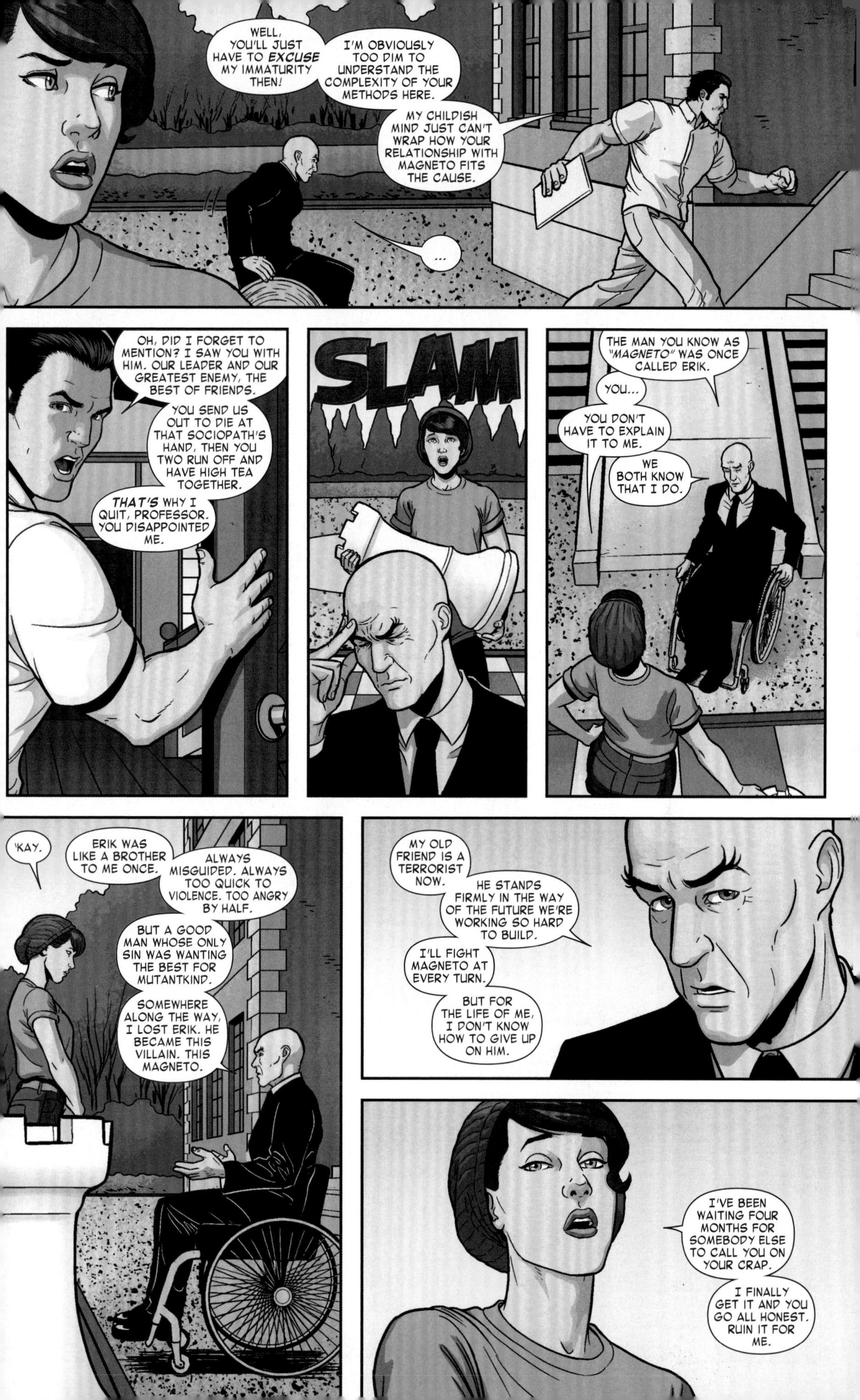
WELL, YOU'LL JUST HAVE TO *EXCUSE* MY IMMATURITY THEN!
I'M OBVIOUSLY TOO DIM TO UNDERSTAND THE COMPLEXITY OF YOUR METHODS HERE.
MY CHILDISH MIND JUST CAN'T WRAP HOW YOUR RELATIONSHIP WITH MAGNETO FITS THE CAUSE.
...
OH, DID I FORGET TO MENTION? I SAW YOU WITH HIM. OUR LEADER AND OUR GREATEST ENEMY, THE BEST OF FRIENDS.
YOU SEND US OUT TO DIE AT THAT SOCIOPATH'S HAND, THEN YOU TWO RUN OFF AND HAVE HIGH TEA TOGETHER.
THAT'S WHY I QUIT, PROFESSOR. YOU DISAPPOINTED ME.
SLAM
THE MAN YOU KNOW AS "*MAGNETO*" WAS ONCE CALLED ERIK.
YOU...
YOU DON'T HAVE TO EXPLAIN IT TO ME.
WE BOTH KNOW THAT I DO.
'KAY.
ERIK WAS LIKE A BROTHER TO ME ONCE.
ALWAYS MISGUIDED. ALWAYS TOO QUICK TO VIOLENCE. TOO ANGRY BY HALF.
BUT A GOOD MAN WHOSE ONLY SIN WAS WANTING THE BEST FOR MUTANTKIND.
SOMEWHERE ALONG THE WAY, I LOST ERIK. HE BECAME THIS VILLAIN. THIS MAGNETO.
MY OLD FRIEND IS A TERRORIST NOW.
HE STANDS FIRMLY IN THE WAY OF THE FUTURE WE'RE WORKING SO HARD TO BUILD.
I'LL FIGHT MAGNETO AT EVERY TURN.
BUT FOR THE LIFE OF ME, I DON'T KNOW HOW TO GIVE UP ON HIM.
I'VE BEEN WAITING FOUR MONTHS FOR SOMEBODY ELSE TO CALL YOU ON YOUR CRAP.
I FINALLY GET IT AND YOU GO ALL HONEST. RUIN IT FOR ME.

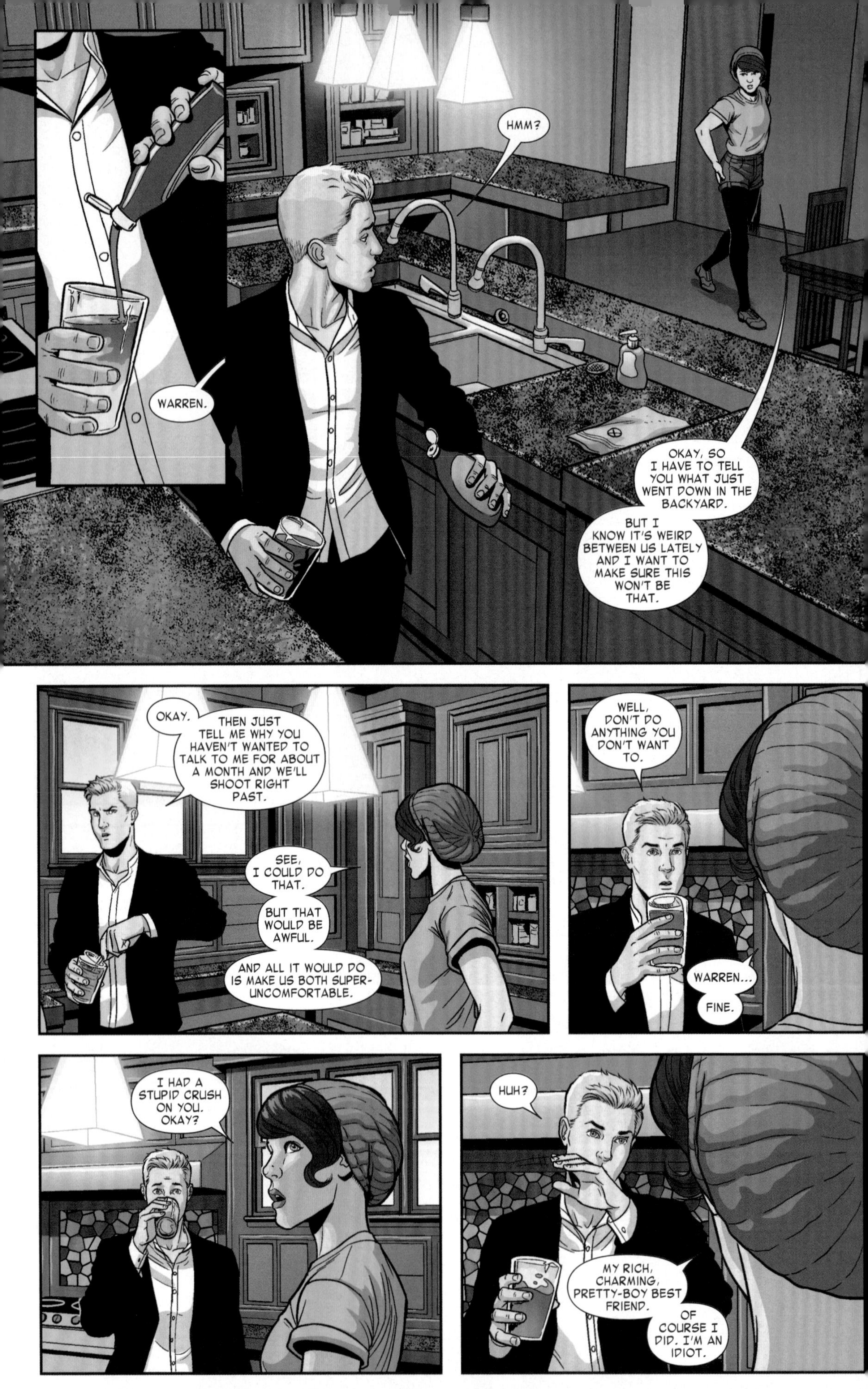
WARREN.
HMM?
OKAY, SO I HAVE TO TELL YOU WHAT JUST WENT DOWN IN THE BACKYARD.
BUT I KNOW IT'S WEIRD BETWEEN US LATELY AND I WANT TO MAKE SURE THIS WON'T BE THAT.
OKAY.
THEN JUST TELL ME WHY YOU HAVEN'T WANTED TO TALK TO ME FOR ABOUT A MONTH AND WE'LL SHOOT RIGHT PAST.
SEE, I COULD DO THAT.
BUT THAT WOULD BE AWFUL.
AND ALL IT WOULD DO IS MAKE US BOTH SUPER-UNCOMFORTABLE.
WELL, DON'T DO ANYTHING YOU DON'T WANT TO.
WARREN...
FINE.
I HAD A STUPID CRUSH ON YOU. OKAY?
HUH?
MY RICH, CHARMING, PRETTY-BOY BEST FRIEND.
OF COURSE I DID. I'M AN IDIOT.

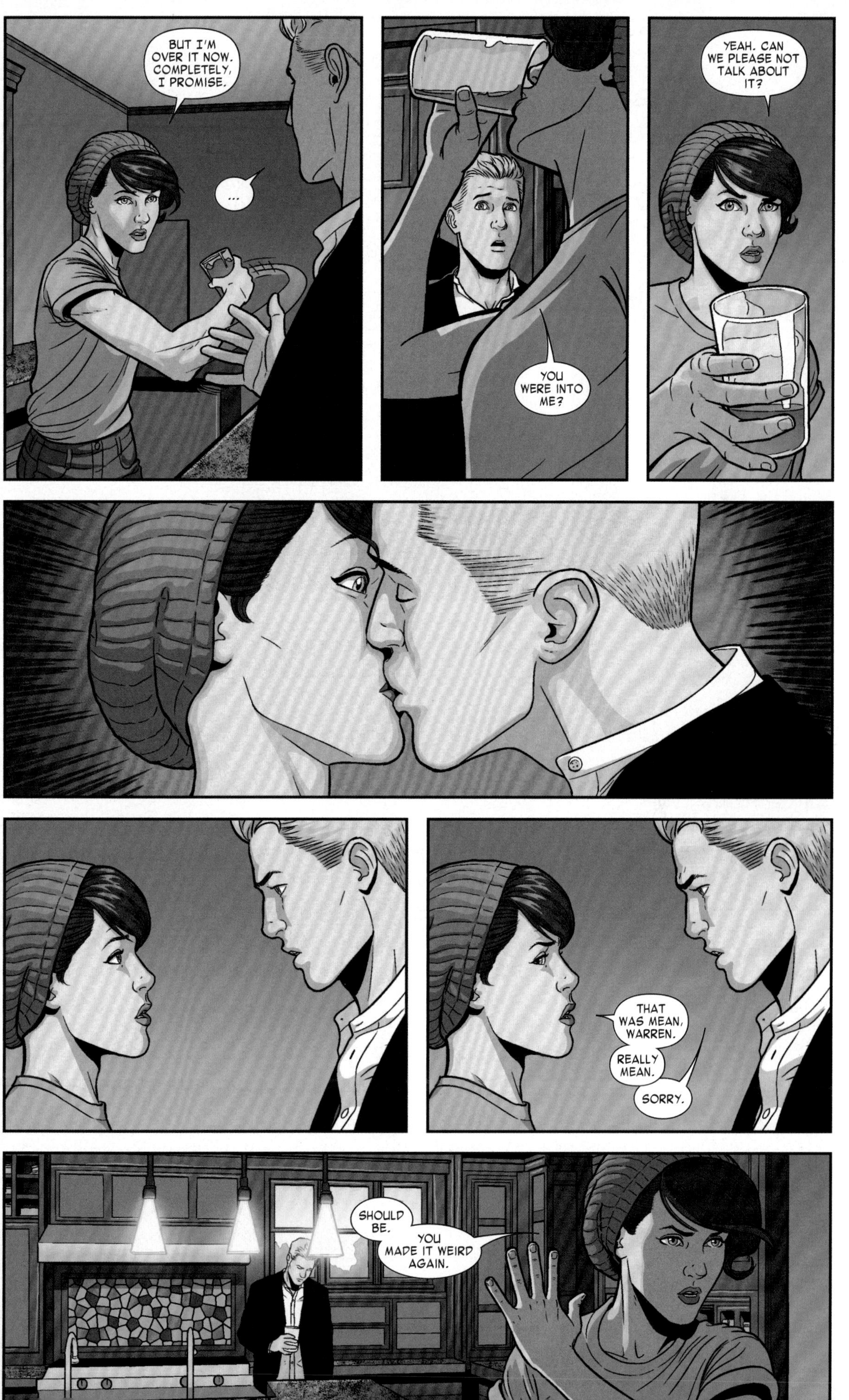

BUT I'M OVER IT NOW. COMPLETELY, I PROMISE.
...
YOU WERE INTO ME?
YEAH. CAN WE PLEASE NOT TALK ABOUT IT?
THAT WAS MEAN, WARREN.
REALLY MEAN.
SORRY.
SHOULD BE.
YOU MADE IT WEIRD AGAIN.

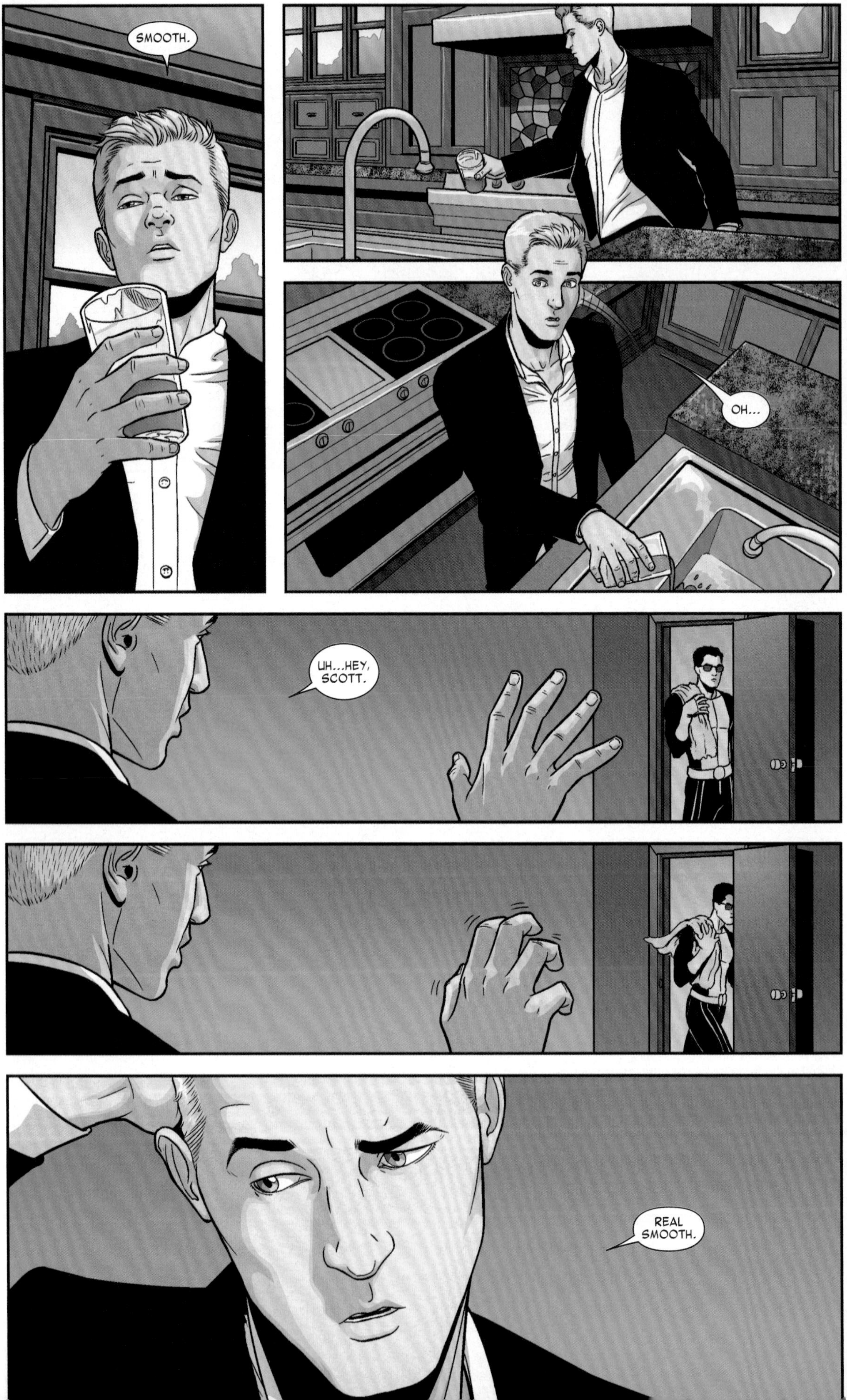
SMOOTH.
OH...
UH...HEY, SCOTT.
REAL SMOOTH.

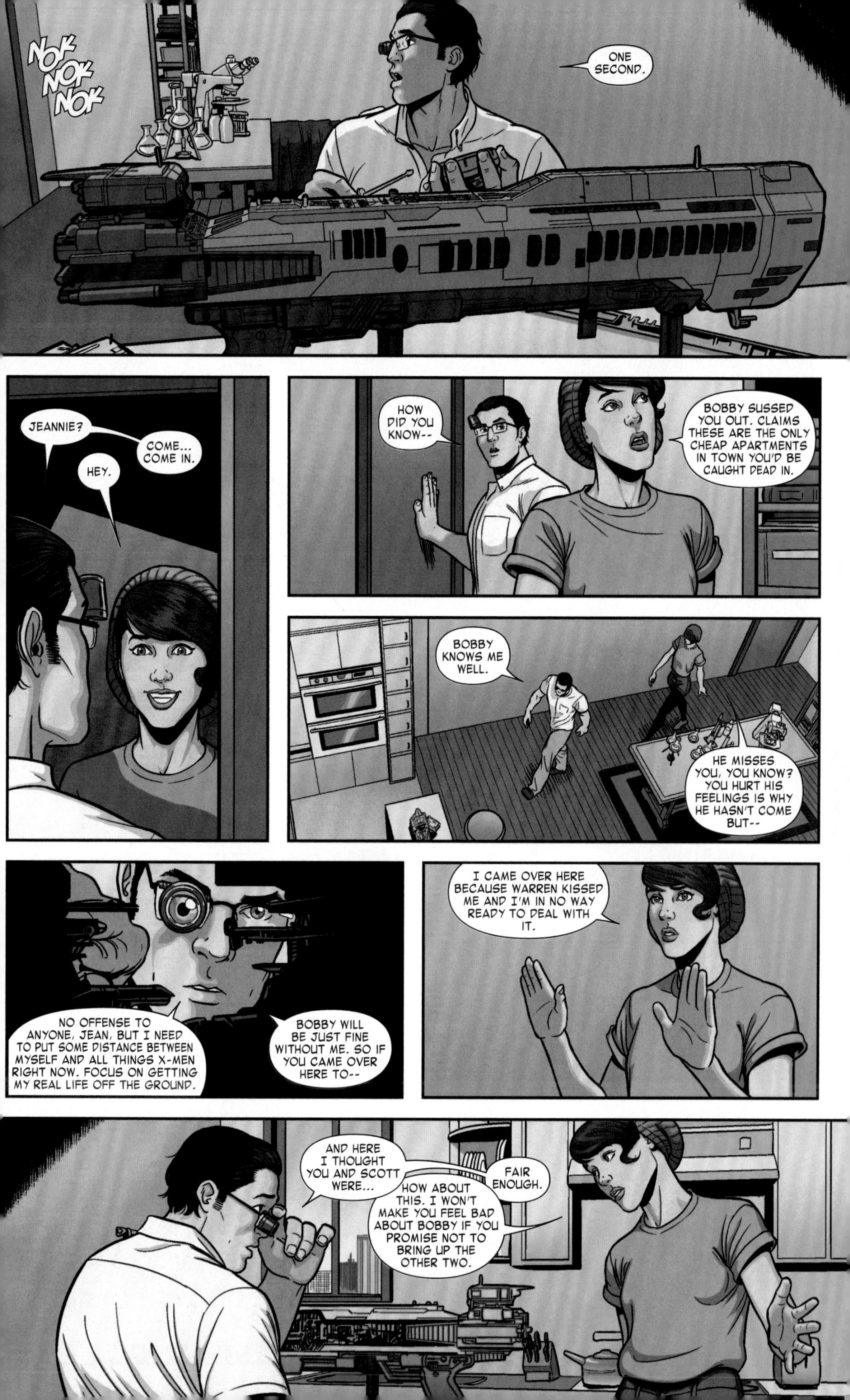
NOK NOK NOK
ONE SECOND.
JEANNIE?
COME... COME IN.
HEY.
HOW DID YOU KNOW--
BOBBY SUSSED YOU OUT. CLAIMS THESE ARE THE ONLY CHEAP APARTMENTS IN TOWN YOU'D BE CAUGHT DEAD IN.
BOBBY KNOWS ME WELL.
HE MISSES YOU, YOU KNOW? YOU HURT HIS FEELINGS IS WHY HE HASN'T COME BUT--
NO OFFENSE TO ANYONE, JEAN, BUT I NEED TO PUT SOME DISTANCE BETWEEN MYSELF AND ALL THINGS X-MEN RIGHT NOW. FOCUS ON GETTING MY REAL LIFE OFF THE GROUND.
BOBBY WILL BE JUST FINE WITHOUT ME. SO IF YOU CAME OVER HERE TO--
I CAME OVER HERE BECAUSE WARREN KISSED ME AND I'M IN NO WAY READY TO DEAL WITH IT.
AND HERE I THOUGHT YOU AND SCOTT WERE...
FAIR ENOUGH.
HOW ABOUT THIS. I WON'T MAKE YOU FEEL BAD ABOUT BOBBY IF YOU PROMISE NOT TO BRING UP THE OTHER TWO.

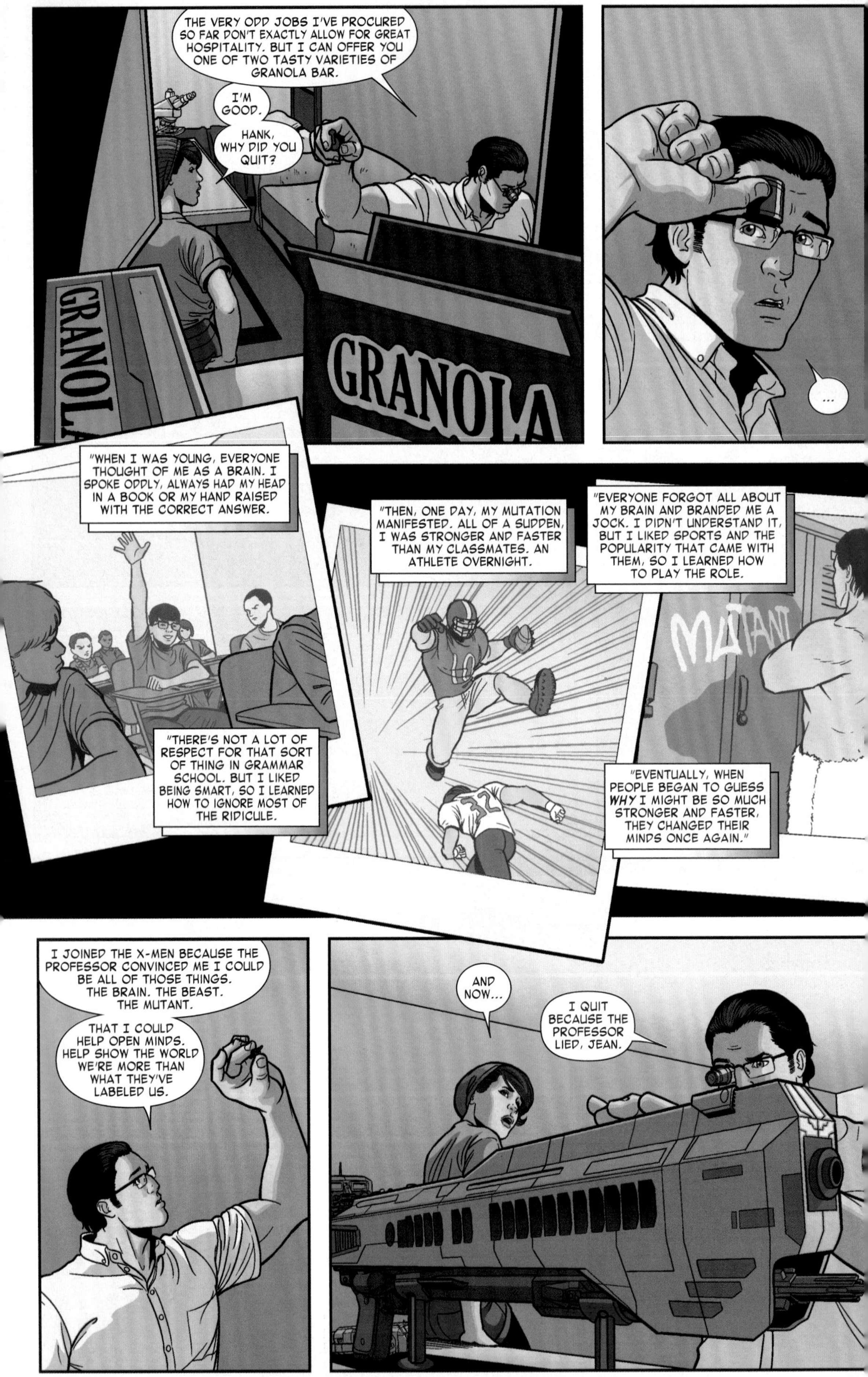

THE VERY ODD JOBS I'VE PROCURED SO FAR DON'T EXACTLY ALLOW FOR GREAT HOSPITALITY. BUT I CAN OFFER YOU ONE OF TWO TASTY VARIETIES OF GRANOLA BAR.
I'M GOOD.
HANK, WHY DID YOU QUIT?
GRANOLA
GRANOLA
...
"WHEN I WAS YOUNG, EVERYONE THOUGHT OF ME AS A BRAIN. I SPOKE ODDLY, ALWAYS HAD MY HEAD IN A BOOK OR MY HAND RAISED WITH THE CORRECT ANSWER.
"THERE'S NOT A LOT OF RESPECT FOR THAT SORT OF THING IN GRAMMAR SCHOOL. BUT I LIKED BEING SMART, SO I LEARNED HOW TO IGNORE MOST OF THE RIDICULE.
"THEN, ONE DAY, MY MUTATION MANIFESTED. ALL OF A SUDDEN, I WAS STRONGER AND FASTER THAN MY CLASSMATES. AN ATHLETE OVERNIGHT.
"EVERYONE FORGOT ALL ABOUT MY BRAIN AND BRANDED ME A JOCK. I DIDN'T UNDERSTAND IT, BUT I LIKED SPORTS AND THE POPULARITY THAT CAME WITH THEM, SO I LEARNED HOW TO PLAY THE ROLE.
MUTANT
"EVENTUALLY, WHEN PEOPLE BEGAN TO GUESS *WHY* I MIGHT BE SO MUCH STRONGER AND FASTER, THEY CHANGED THEIR MINDS ONCE AGAIN."
I JOINED THE X-MEN BECAUSE THE PROFESSOR CONVINCED ME I COULD BE ALL OF THOSE THINGS. THE BRAIN. THE BEAST. THE MUTANT.
THAT I COULD HELP OPEN MINDS. HELP SHOW THE WORLD WE'RE MORE THAN WHAT THEY'VE LABELED US.
AND NOW...
I QUIT BECAUSE THE PROFESSOR LIED, JEAN.

EVERYBODY KNOWS THE PROFESSOR DRIVES ME NUTS. HE'S A MANIPULATIVE AND SNOBBY FAKE. HE LOVES HEARING HIMSELF TALK. AND I'M PRETTY SURE HE READS OUR MINDS WAY MORE THAN HE SAYS. BUT...

THAT MAGNETO THING. HE TALKED ABOUT IT AFTER YOU LEFT. THEY USED TO BE FRIENDS.

HE'S NOT, LIKE, WORKING WITH THE ENEMY. HE JUST DOESN'T WANNA--

YES, I'M SURE HE HAD HIS REASONS FOR COLLUDING WITH A KNOWN TERRORIST. BUT THAT'S NOT THE LIE TO WHICH I WAS REFERRING.

THE PROFESSOR LIES, TO US AND LIKELY HIMSELF, EVERY TIME HE TALKS ABOUT HOW THE X-MEN WILL CHANGE THE WORLD.

IT'S A GROUP OF NAÏVE KIDS DRESSED UP LIKE SUPER HEROES AND PUNCHING THINGS. IF ANYTHING, WE'VE PROVEN TO THE ALREADY FRIGHTENED MASSES THAT MUTANTS TRULY ARE *DIFFERENT* AND *SCARY.*

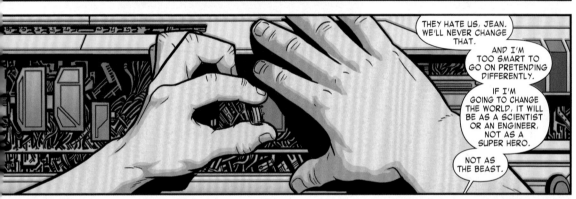

THEY HATE US, JEAN. WE'LL NEVER CHANGE THAT.

AND I'M TOO SMART TO GO ON PRETENDING DIFFERENTLY.

IF I'M GOING TO CHANGE THE WORLD, IT WILL BE AS A SCIENTIST OR AN ENGINEER, NOT AS A SUPER HERO.

NOT AS THE BEAST.

I'M DONE WASTING MY POTENTIAL ON A LOST CAUSE.

THIS IS AN ARGUMENT BETWEEN TWO PEOPLE WAY SMARTER THAN ME. IT'D BE SILLY TO JUMP IN THE MIDDLE.

BUT ONE OF THOSE GUYS TOLD ME TODAY THAT, NO MATTER WHAT, HE'LL NEVER GIVE UP ON HIS FRIEND.

THE OTHER ONE SAID HIS BEST FRIEND CAN DO WITHOUT HIM. THAT IT'S TIME TO FOCUS ON BEING SELFISH. AND HE'S PRETTY MUCH GIVEN UP ON THE WHOLE WORLD.

I CAN HARDLY BELIEVE IT, HANK. BUT I THINK YOU JUST MADE ME PROUD TO BE AN X-MAN.

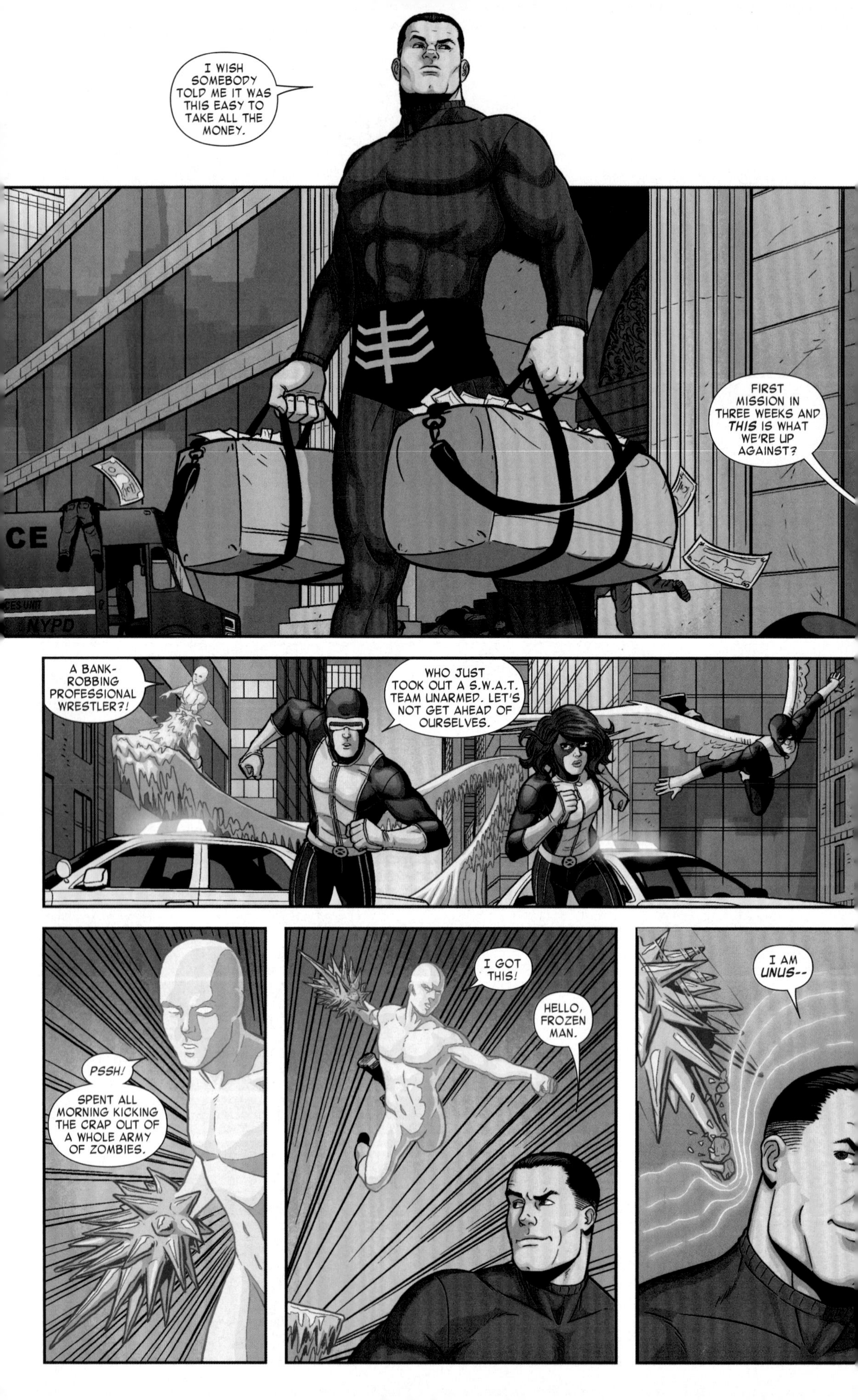
I WISH SOMEBODY TOLD ME IT WAS THIS EASY TO TAKE ALL THE MONEY.
CE
NYPD
FIRST MISSION IN THREE WEEKS AND *THIS* IS WHAT WE'RE UP AGAINST?
A BANK-ROBBING PROFESSIONAL WRESTLER?!
WHO JUST TOOK OUT A S.W.A.T. TEAM UNARMED. LET'S NOT GET AHEAD OF OURSELVES.
PSSH!
SPENT ALL MORNING KICKING THE CRAP OUT OF A WHOLE ARMY OF ZOMBIES.
I GOT *THIS!*
HELLO, FROZEN MAN.
I AM *UNUS--*

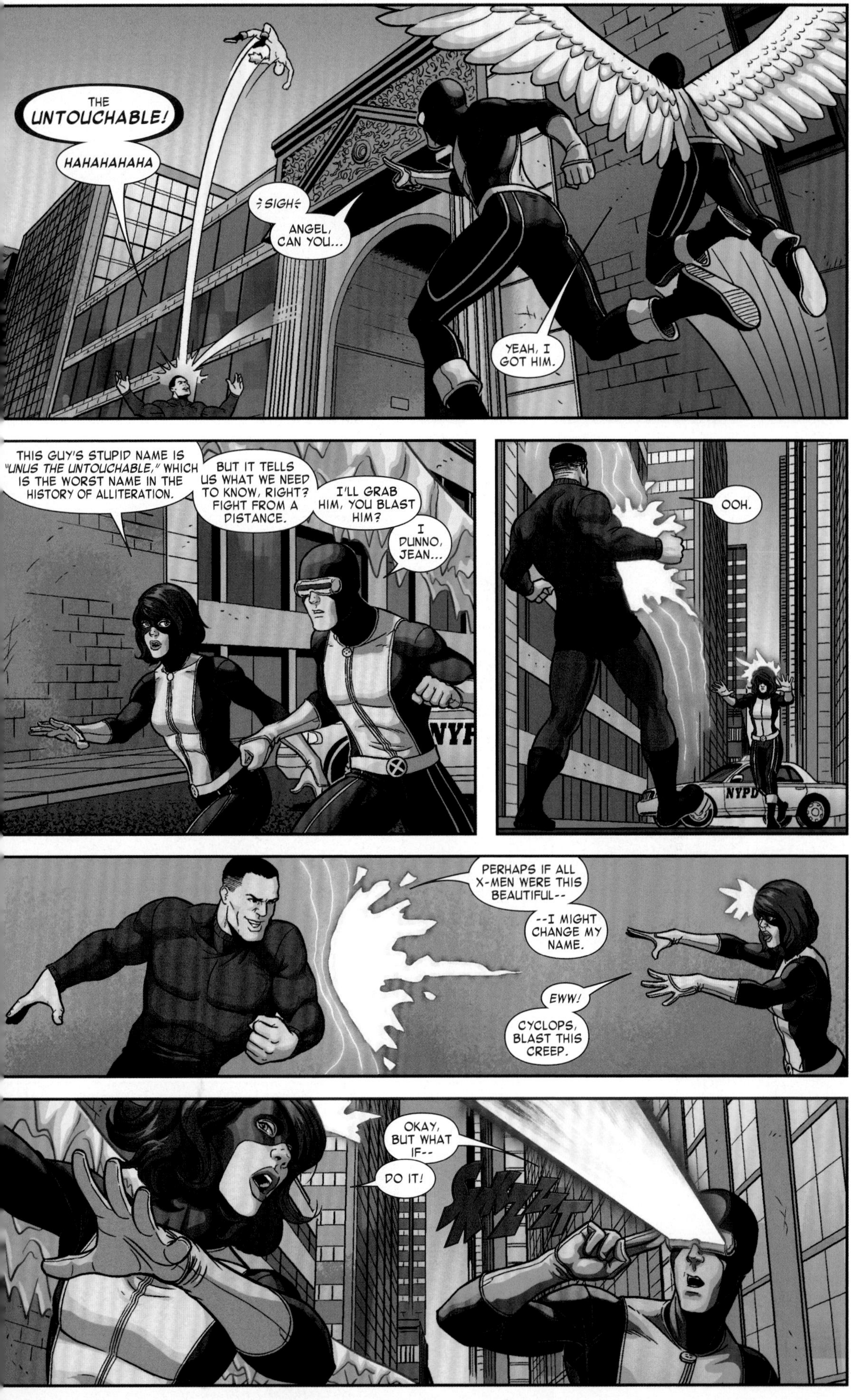
THE UNTOUCHABLE!
HAHAHAHAHA
SIGH
ANGEL, CAN YOU...
YEAH, I GOT HIM.
THIS GUY'S STUPID NAME IS "UNUS THE UNTOUCHABLE," WHICH IS THE WORST NAME IN THE HISTORY OF ALLITERATION.
BUT IT TELLS US WHAT WE NEED TO KNOW, RIGHT? FIGHT FROM A DISTANCE.
I'LL GRAB HIM, YOU BLAST HIM?
I DUNNO, JEAN...
OOH.
NYPD
PERHAPS IF ALL X-MEN WERE THIS BEAUTIFUL--
--I MIGHT CHANGE MY NAME.
EWW!
CYCLOPS, BLAST THIS CREEP.
OKAY, BUT WHAT IF--
DO IT!

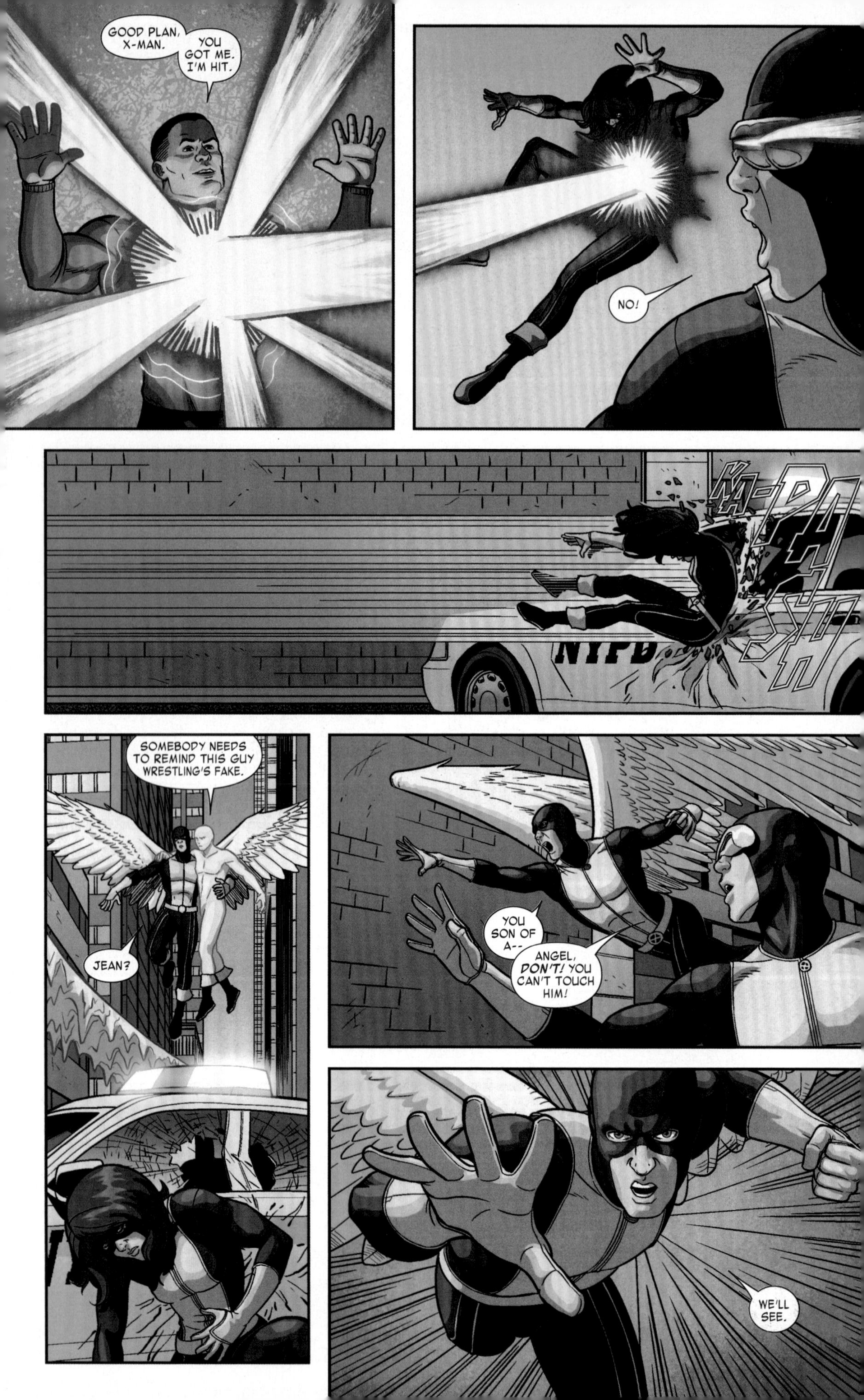
GOOD PLAN, X-MAN.
YOU GOT ME. I'M HIT.
NO!
KA-PASH
NYPD
SOMEBODY NEEDS TO REMIND THIS GUY WRESTLING'S FAKE.
JEAN?
YOU SON OF A--
ANGEL, *DON'T!* YOU CAN'T TOUCH HIM!
WE'LL SEE.

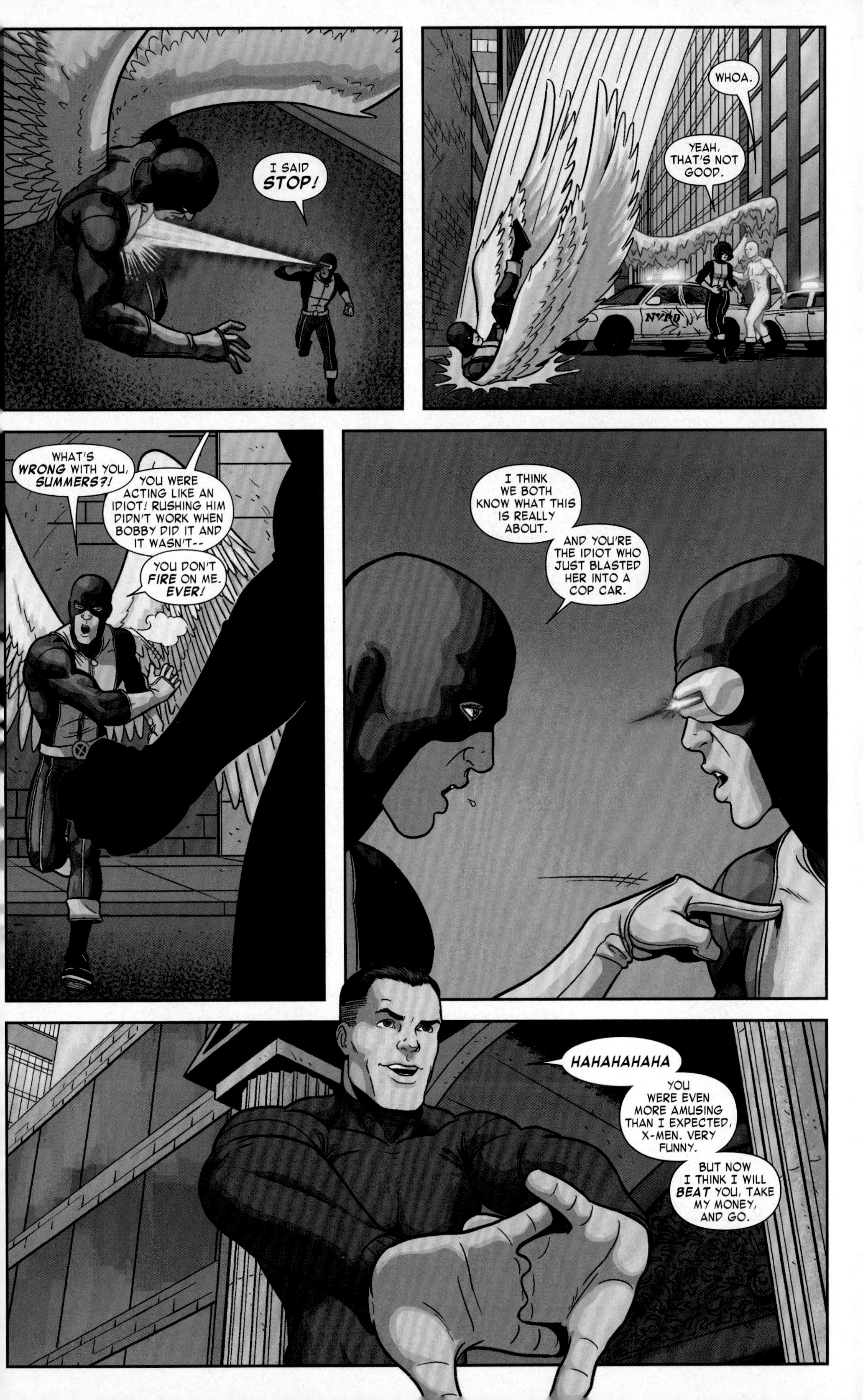
I SAID **STOP!**
WHOA.
YEAH, THAT'S NOT GOOD.
WHAT'S **WRONG** WITH YOU, **SUMMERS?!**
YOU WERE ACTING LIKE AN IDIOT! RUSHING HIM DIDN'T WORK WHEN BOBBY DID IT AND IT WASN'T--
YOU DON'T **FIRE** ON ME. **EVER!**
I THINK WE BOTH KNOW WHAT THIS IS REALLY ABOUT.
AND YOU'RE THE IDIOT WHO JUST BLASTED HER INTO A COP CAR.
HAHAHAHAHA
YOU WERE EVEN MORE AMUSING THAN I EXPECTED, X-MEN. VERY FUNNY.
BUT NOW I THINK I WILL **BEAT** YOU, TAKE MY MONEY, AND GO.

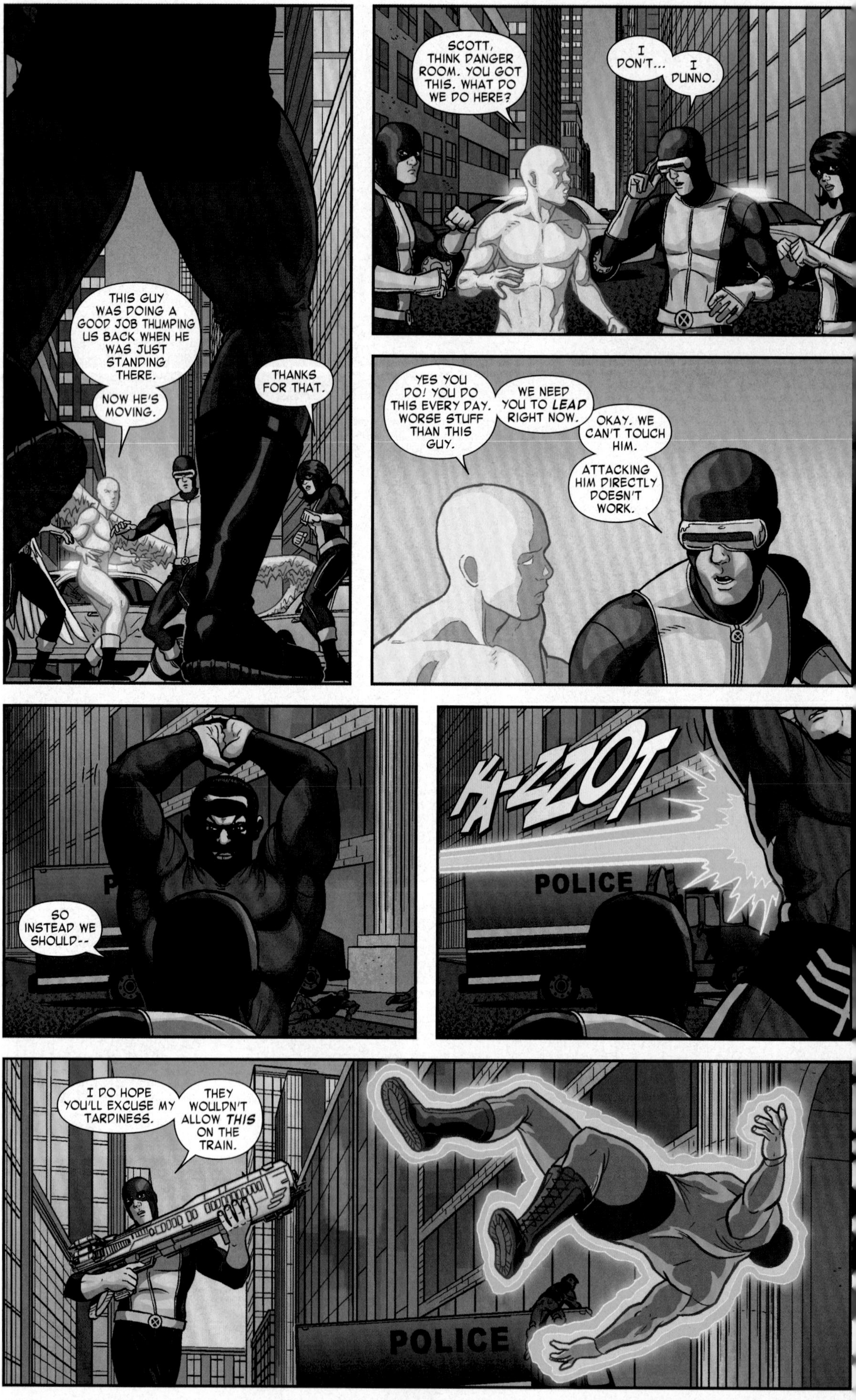
THIS GUY WAS DOING A GOOD JOB THUMPING US BACK WHEN HE WAS JUST STANDING THERE.
NOW HE'S MOVING.
THANKS FOR THAT.
SCOTT, THINK DANGER ROOM. YOU GOT THIS. WHAT DO WE DO HERE?
I DON'T...
I DUNNO.
YES YOU DO! YOU DO THIS EVERY DAY. WORSE STUFF THAN THIS GUY.
WE NEED YOU TO LEAD RIGHT NOW.
OKAY. WE CAN'T TOUCH HIM.
ATTACKING HIM DIRECTLY DOESN'T WORK.
SO INSTEAD WE SHOULD--
KA-ZZOT
POLICE
I DO HOPE YOU'LL EXCUSE MY TARDINESS.
THEY WOULDN'T ALLOW THIS ON THE TRAIN.
POLICE

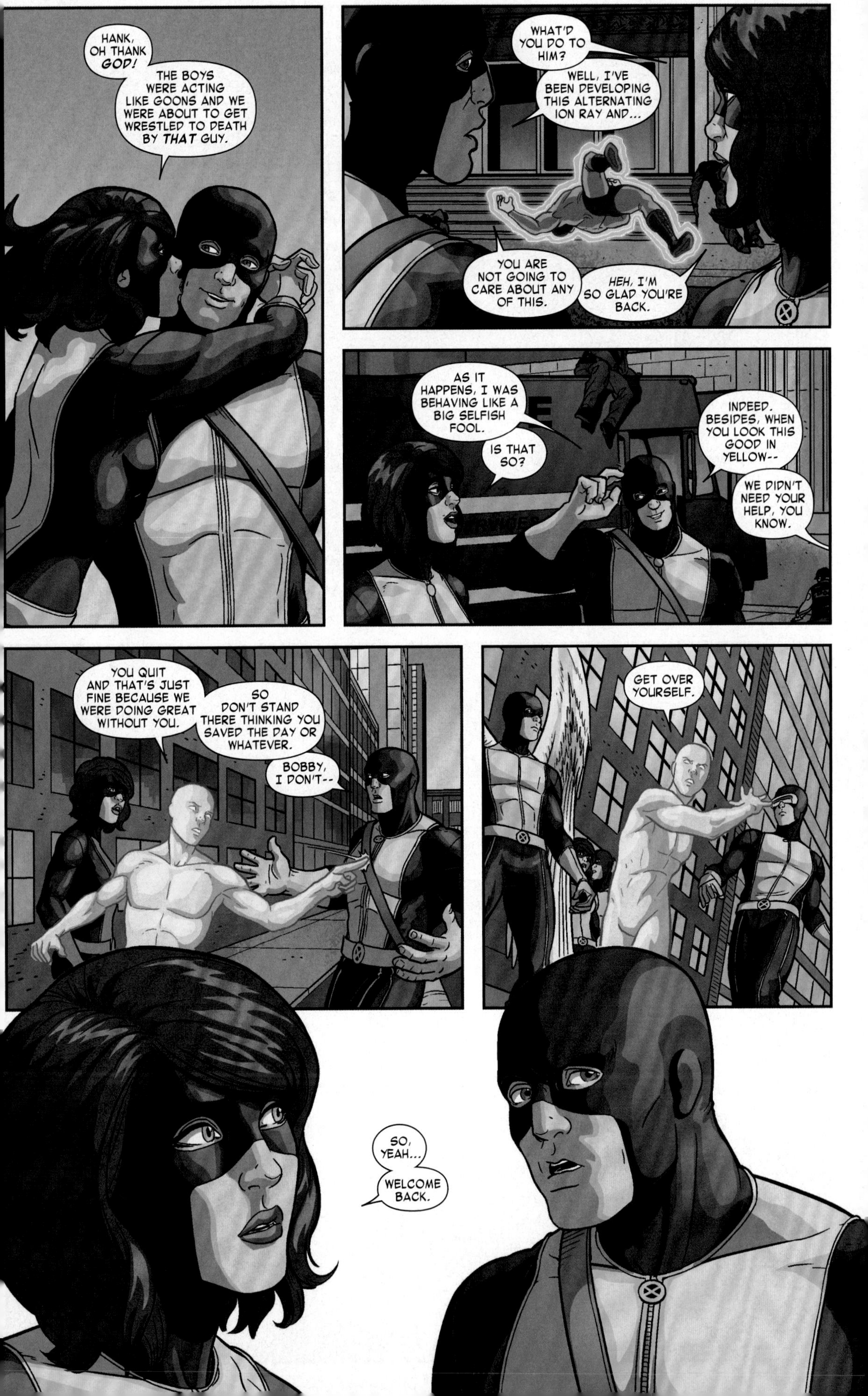
HANK, OH THANK *GOD!*
THE BOYS WERE ACTING LIKE GOONS AND WE WERE ABOUT TO GET WRESTLED TO DEATH BY *THAT* GUY.
WHAT'D YOU DO TO HIM?
WELL, I'VE BEEN DEVELOPING THIS ALTERNATING ION RAY AND...
YOU ARE NOT GOING TO CARE ABOUT ANY OF THIS.
HEH, I'M SO GLAD YOU'RE BACK.
AS IT HAPPENS, I WAS BEHAVING LIKE A BIG SELFISH FOOL.
IS THAT SO?
INDEED. BESIDES, WHEN YOU LOOK THIS GOOD IN YELLOW--
WE DIDN'T NEED YOUR HELP, YOU KNOW.
YOU QUIT AND THAT'S JUST FINE BECAUSE WE WERE DOING GREAT WITHOUT YOU.
SO DON'T STAND THERE THINKING YOU SAVED THE DAY OR WHATEVER.
BOBBY, I DON'T--
GET OVER YOURSELF.
SO, YEAH...
WELCOME BACK.

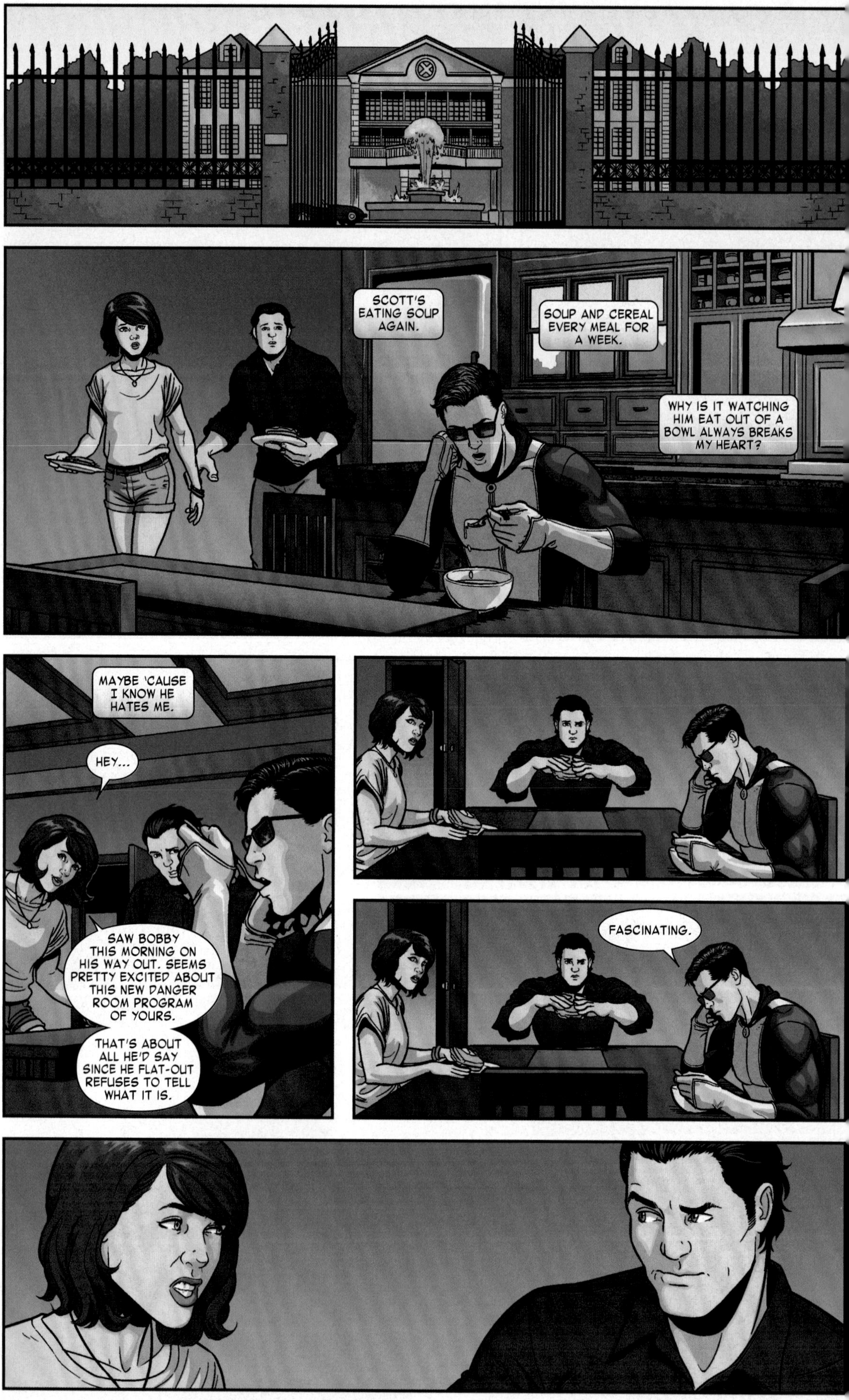
SCOTT'S EATING SOUP AGAIN.
SOUP AND CEREAL EVERY MEAL FOR A WEEK.
WHY IS IT WATCHING HIM EAT OUT OF A BOWL ALWAYS BREAKS MY HEART?
MAYBE 'CAUSE I KNOW HE HATES ME.
HEY...
SAW BOBBY THIS MORNING ON HIS WAY OUT. SEEMS PRETTY EXCITED ABOUT THIS NEW DANGER ROOM PROGRAM OF YOURS.
THAT'S ABOUT ALL HE'D SAY SINCE HE FLAT-OUT REFUSES TO TELL WHAT IT IS.
FASCINATING.

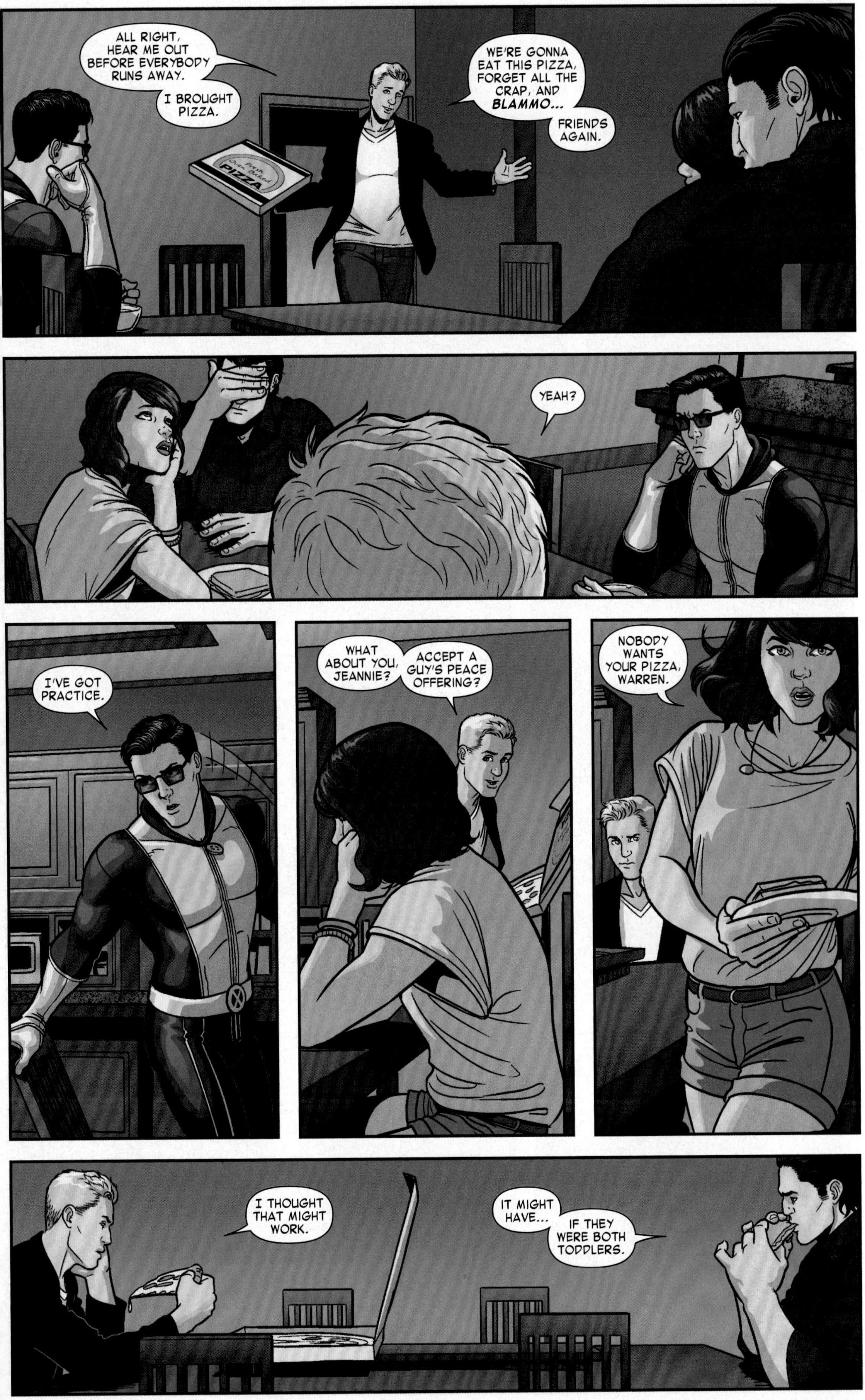
ALL RIGHT, HEAR ME OUT BEFORE EVERYBODY RUNS AWAY.
I BROUGHT PIZZA.
Fresh Oven Baked PIZZA
WE'RE GONNA EAT THIS PIZZA, FORGET ALL THE CRAP, AND BLAMMO...
FRIENDS AGAIN.
YEAH?
I'VE GOT PRACTICE.
WHAT ABOUT YOU, JEANNIE?
ACCEPT A GUY'S PEACE OFFERING?
NOBODY WANTS YOUR PIZZA, WARREN.
I THOUGHT THAT MIGHT WORK.
IT MIGHT HAVE...
IF THEY WERE BOTH TODDLERS.

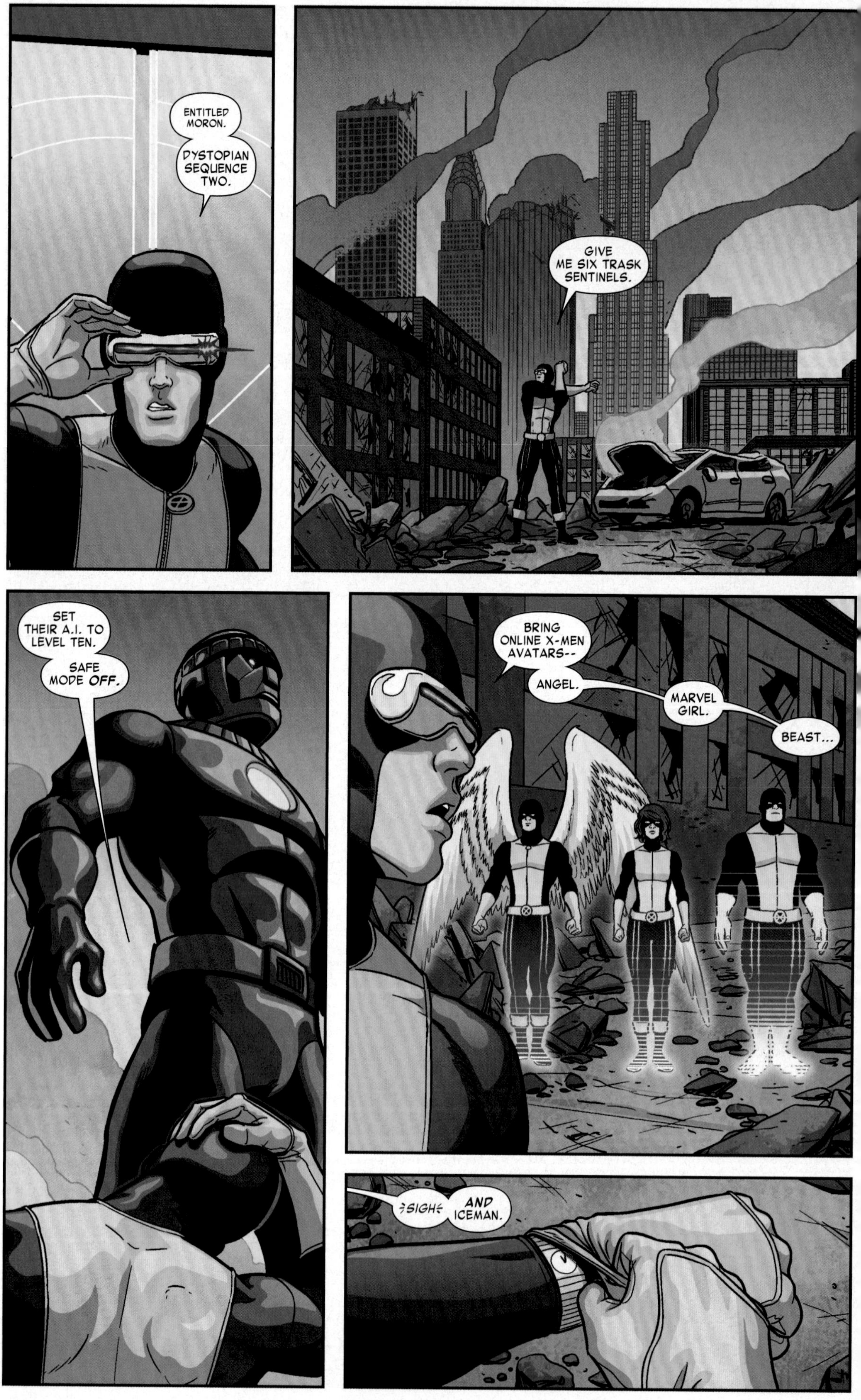
ENTITLED MORON.
DYSTOPIAN SEQUENCE TWO.
GIVE ME SIX TRASK SENTINELS.
SET THEIR A.I. TO LEVEL TEN.
SAFE MODE OFF.
BRING ONLINE X-MEN AVATARS--
ANGEL.
MARVEL GIRL.
BEAST...
SIGH
AND ICEMAN.

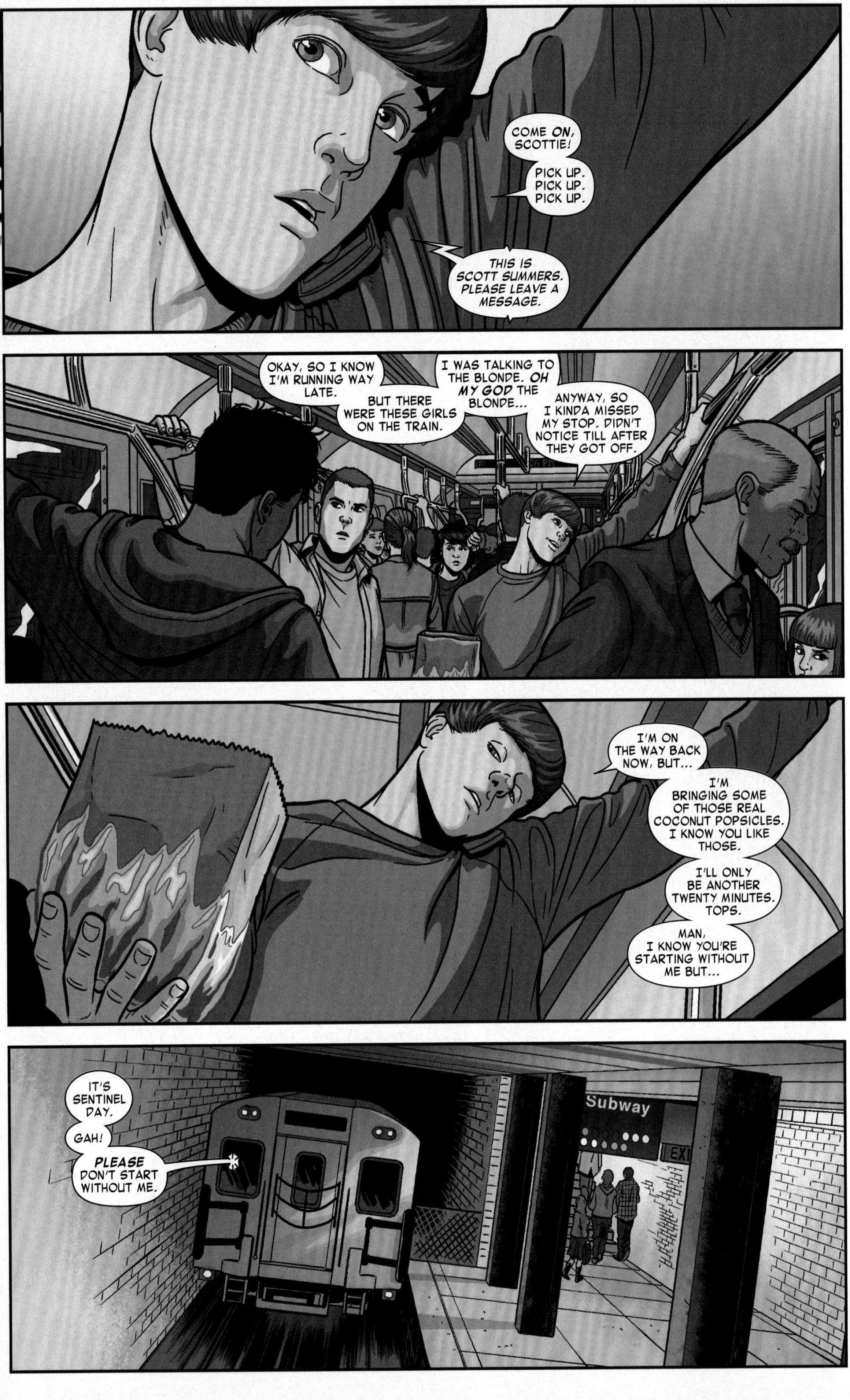
COME *ON*, SCOTTIE!
PICK UP. PICK UP. PICK UP.
THIS IS SCOTT SUMMERS. PLEASE LEAVE A MESSAGE.
OKAY, SO I KNOW I'M RUNNING WAY LATE.
BUT THERE WERE THESE GIRLS ON THE TRAIN.
I WAS TALKING TO THE BLONDE. *OH MY GOD* THE BLONDE...
ANYWAY, SO I KINDA MISSED MY STOP. DIDN'T NOTICE TILL AFTER THEY GOT OFF.
I'M ON THE WAY BACK NOW, BUT...
I'M BRINGING SOME OF THOSE REAL COCONUT POPSICLES. I KNOW YOU LIKE THOSE.
I'LL ONLY BE ANOTHER TWENTY MINUTES. TOPS.
MAN, I KNOW YOU'RE STARTING WITHOUT ME BUT...
IT'S SENTINEL DAY.
GAH!
PLEASE DON'T START WITHOUT ME.
Subway

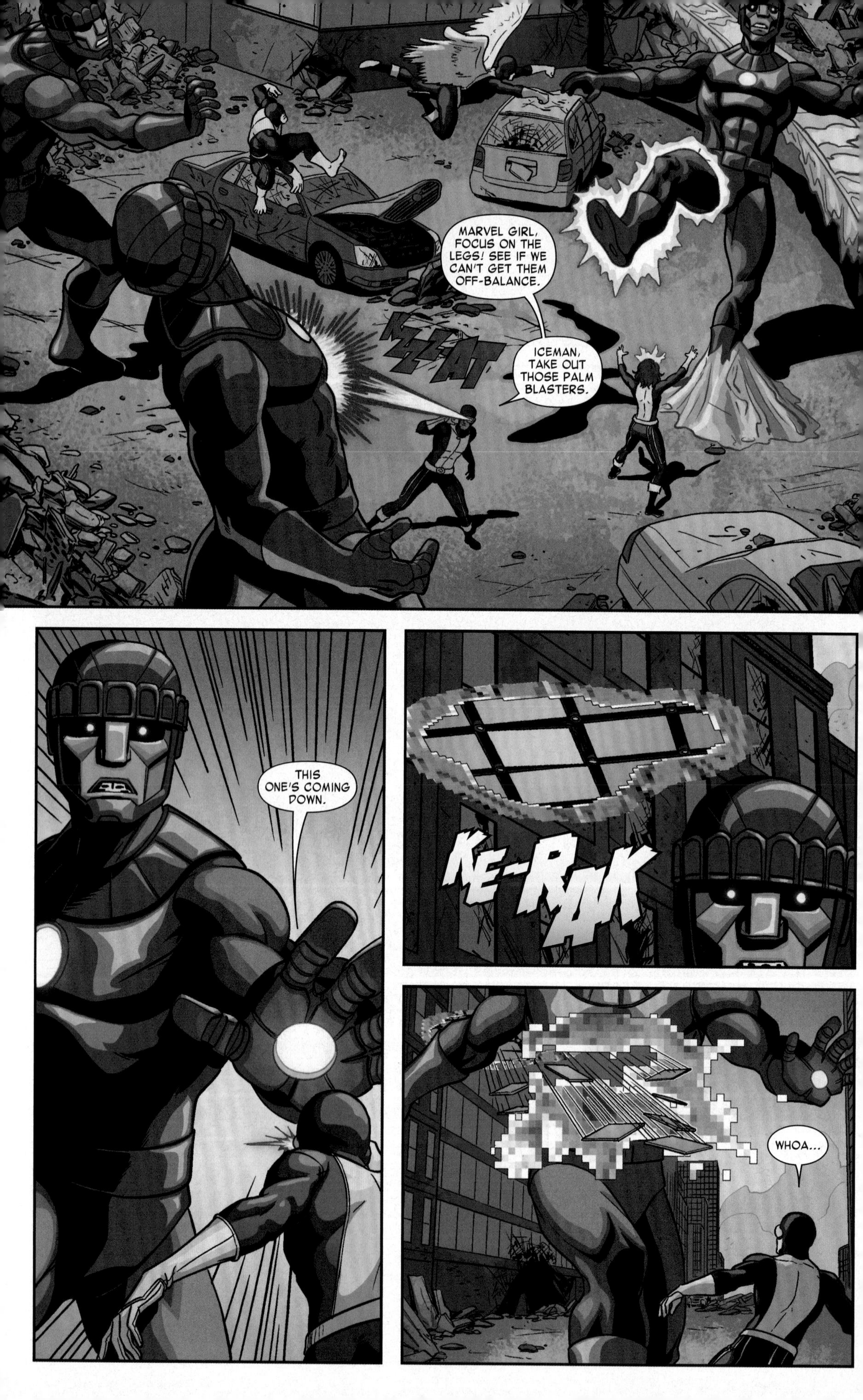
MARVEL GIRL, FOCUS ON THE LEGS! SEE IF WE CAN'T GET THEM OFF-BALANCE.
KZZEAT
ICEMAN, TAKE OUT THOSE PALM BLASTERS.
THIS ONE'S COMING DOWN.
KE-RAK
WHOA...

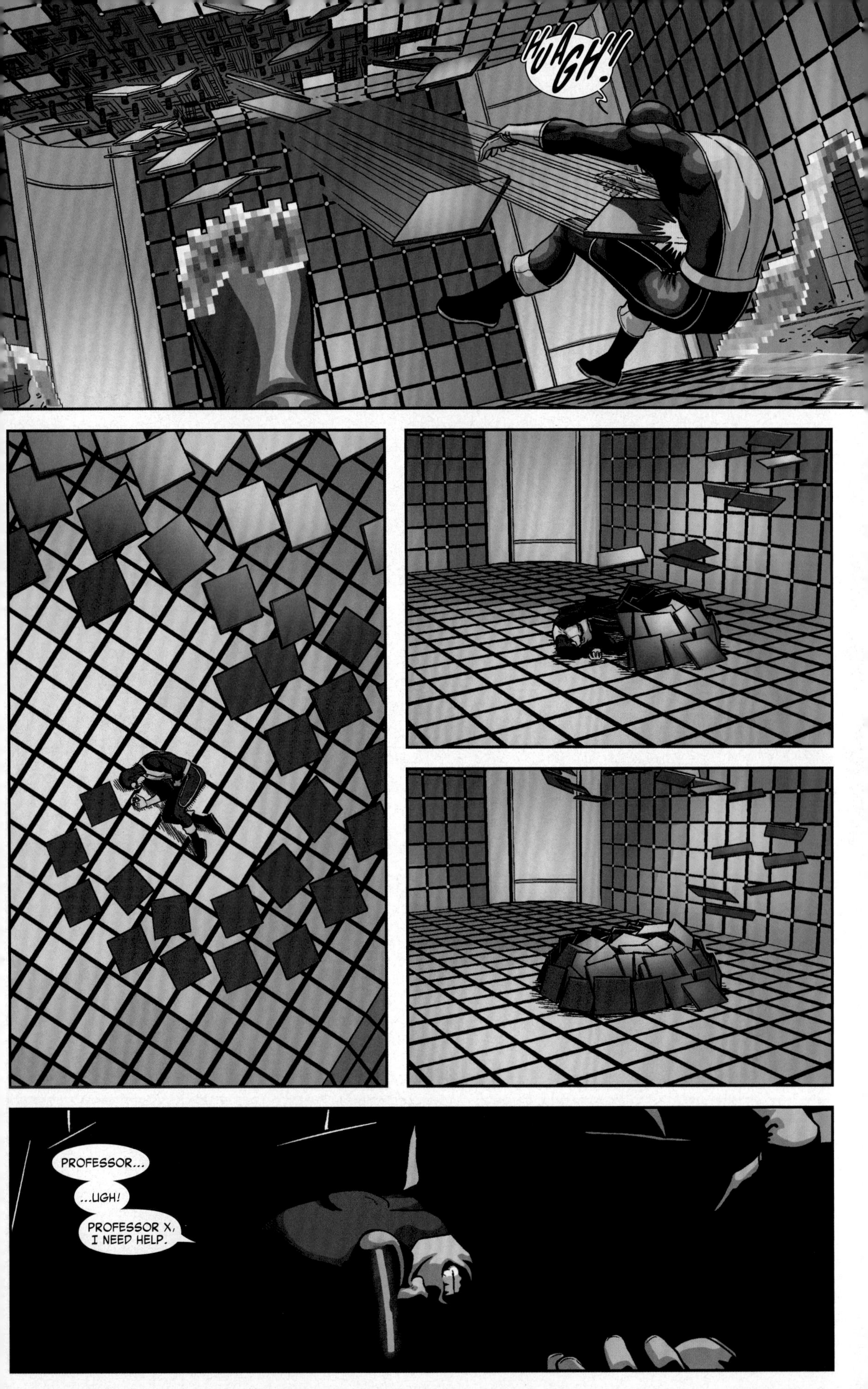
HUAGH!
PROFESSOR...
...UGH!
PROFESSOR X, I NEED HELP.

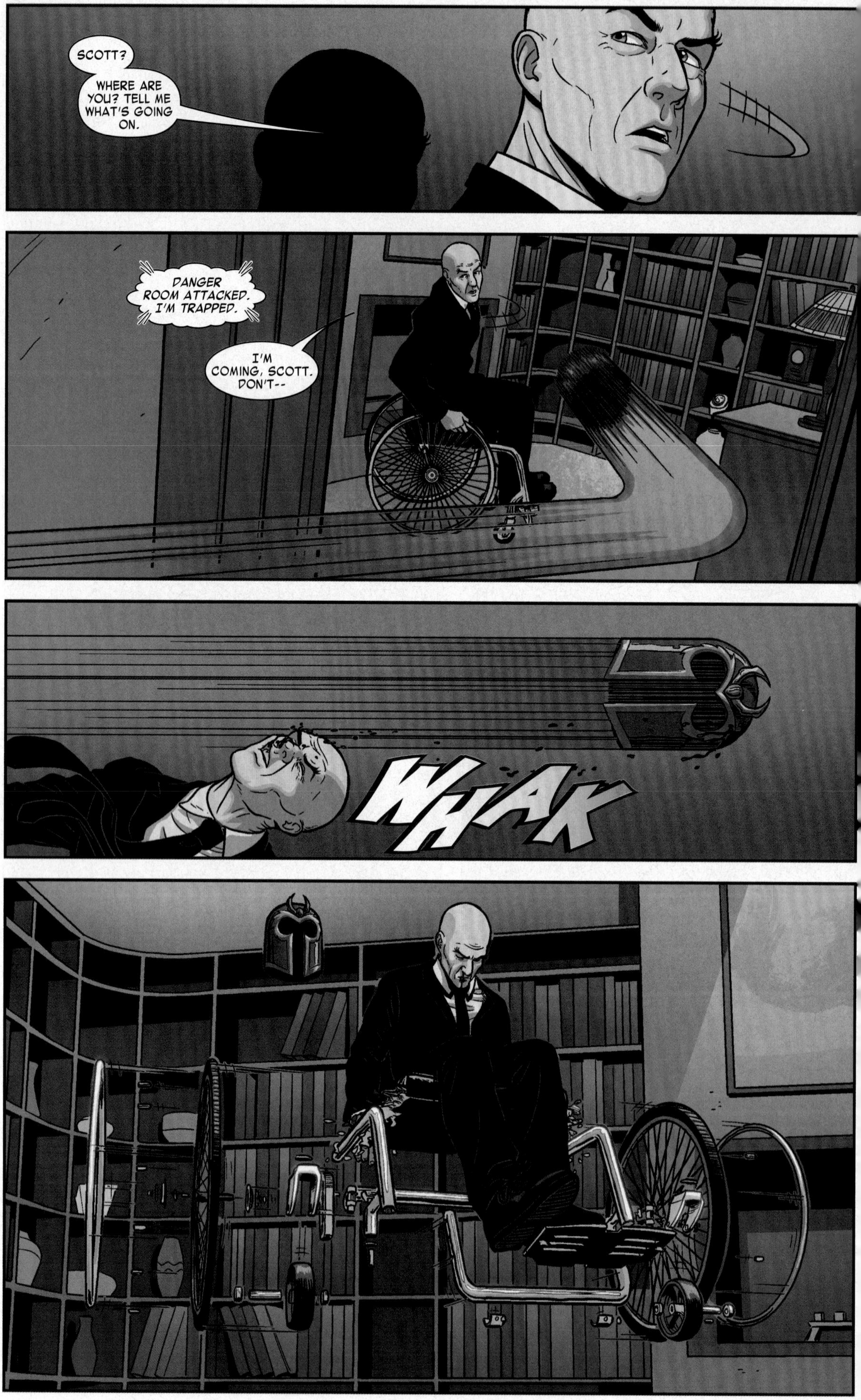
SCOTT?
WHERE ARE YOU? TELL ME WHAT'S GOING ON.
DANGER ROOM ATTACKED. I'M TRAPPED.
I'M COMING, SCOTT. DON'T--
WHAK

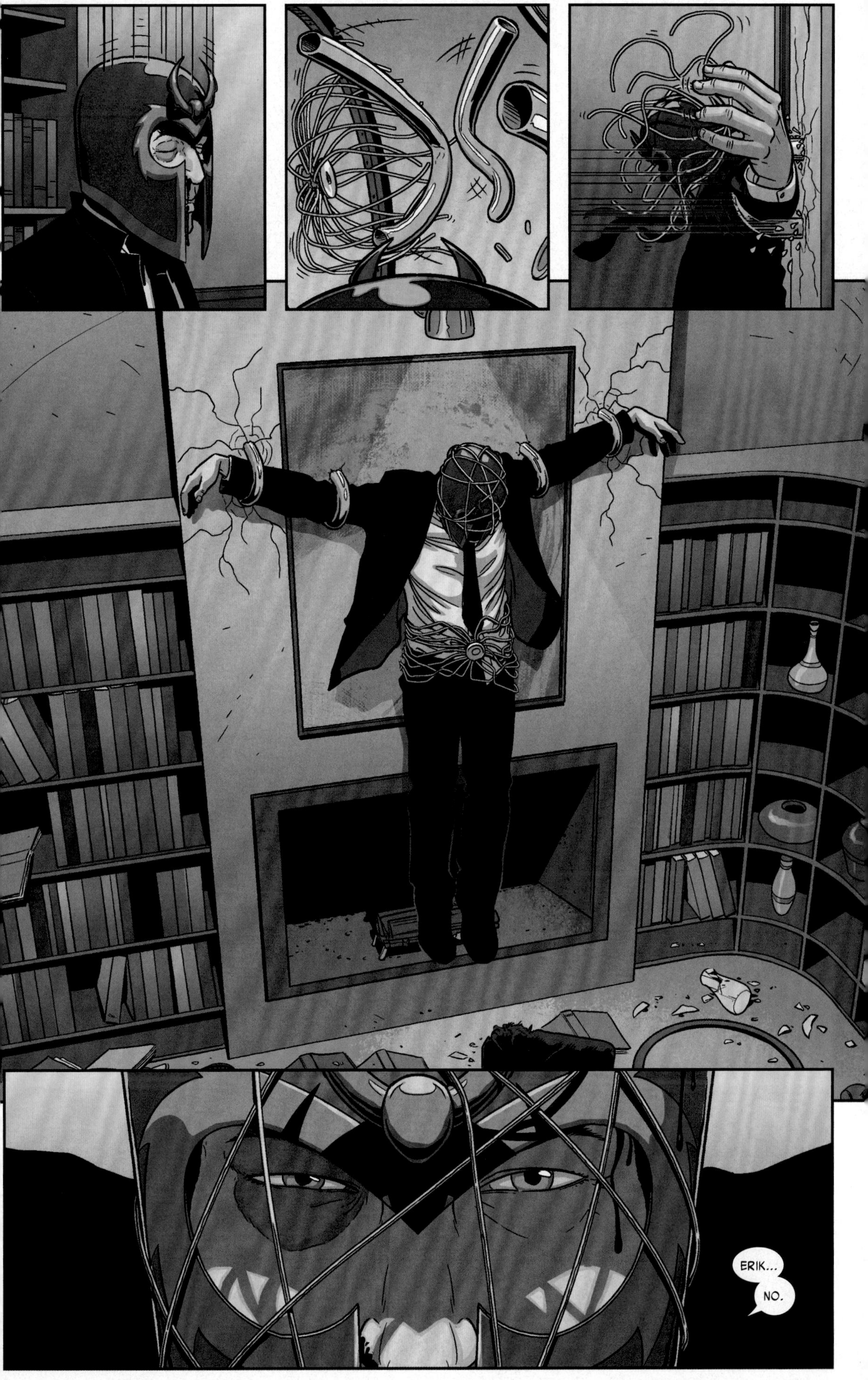
ERIK...
NO.

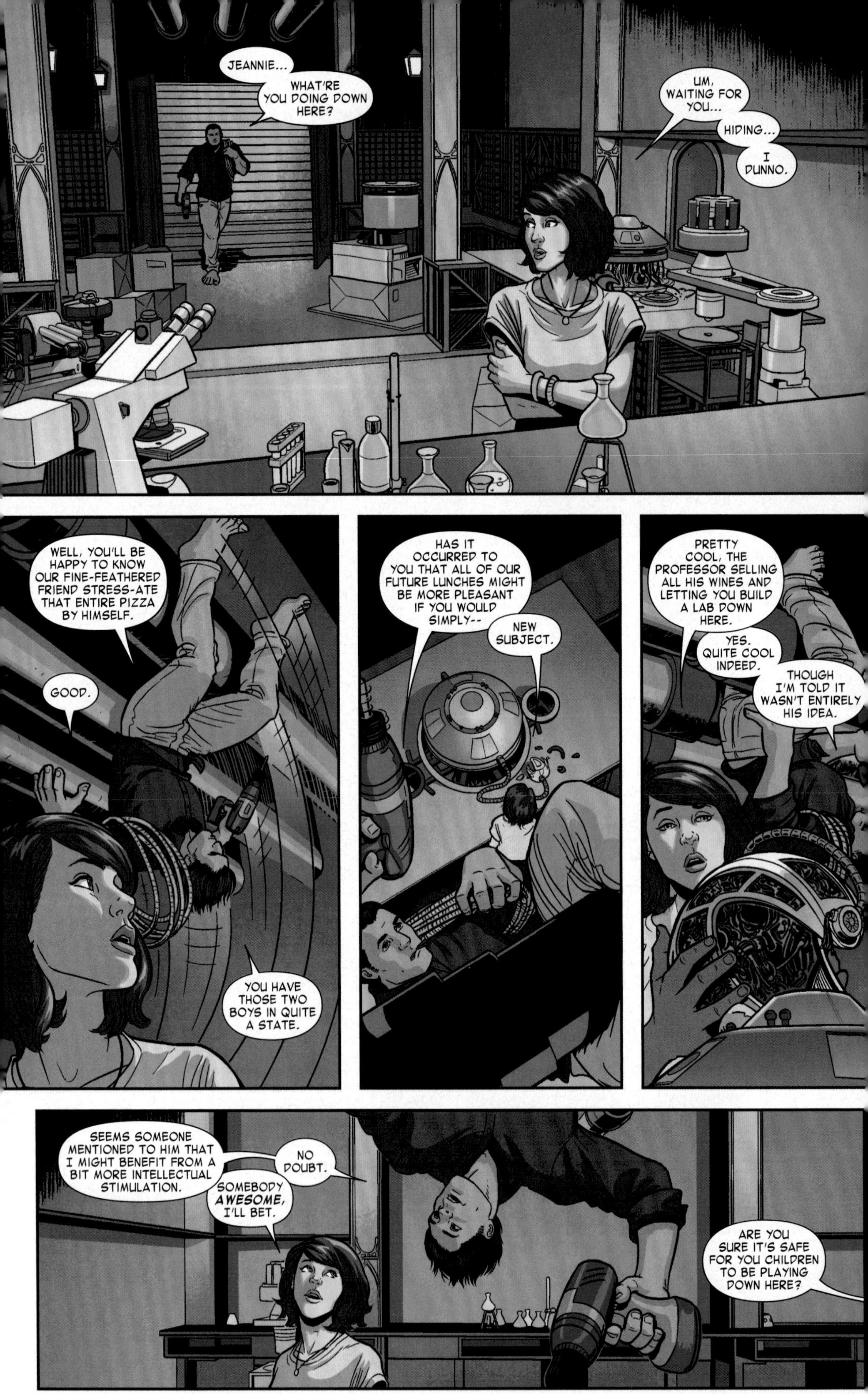
JEANNIE...
WHAT'RE YOU DOING DOWN HERE?
UM, WAITING FOR YOU...
HIDING...
I DUNNO.
WELL, YOU'LL BE HAPPY TO KNOW OUR FINE-FEATHERED FRIEND STRESS-ATE THAT ENTIRE PIZZA BY HIMSELF.
GOOD.
YOU HAVE THOSE TWO BOYS IN QUITE A STATE.
HAS IT OCCURRED TO YOU THAT ALL OF OUR FUTURE LUNCHES MIGHT BE MORE PLEASANT IF YOU WOULD SIMPLY--
NEW SUBJECT.
PRETTY COOL, THE PROFESSOR SELLING ALL HIS WINES AND LETTING YOU BUILD A LAB DOWN HERE.
YES. QUITE COOL INDEED.
THOUGH I'M TOLD IT WASN'T ENTIRELY HIS IDEA.
SEEMS SOMEONE MENTIONED TO HIM THAT I MIGHT BENEFIT FROM A BIT MORE INTELLECTUAL STIMULATION.
NO DOUBT.
SOMEBODY *AWESOME*, I'LL BET.
ARE YOU SURE IT'S SAFE FOR YOU CHILDREN TO BE PLAYING DOWN HERE?

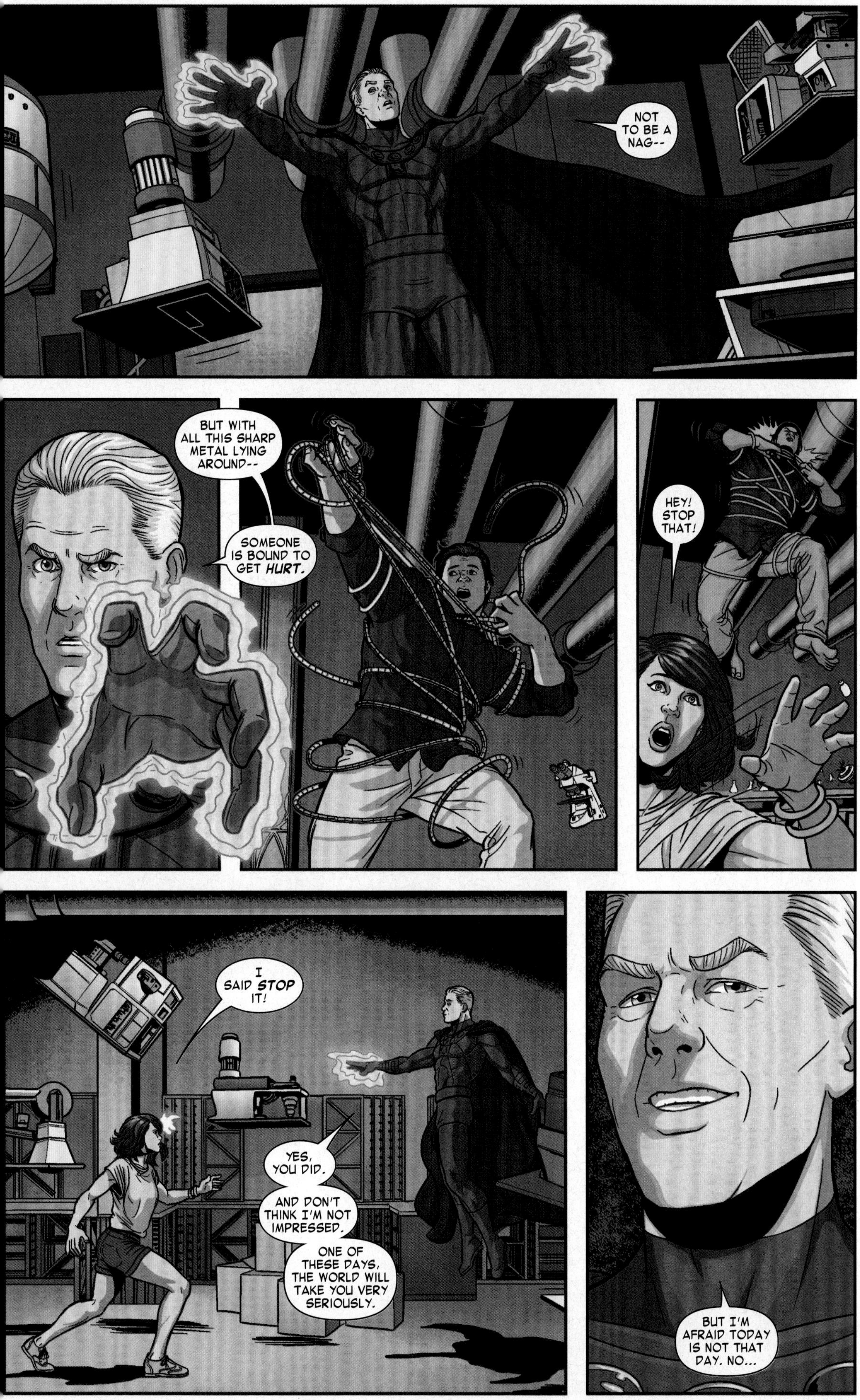
NOT TO BE A NAG--
BUT WITH ALL THIS SHARP METAL LYING AROUND--
SOMEONE IS BOUND TO GET HURT.
HEY! STOP THAT!
I SAID STOP IT!
YES, YOU DID.
AND DON'T THINK I'M NOT IMPRESSED.
ONE OF THESE DAYS, THE WORLD WILL TAKE YOU VERY SERIOUSLY.
BUT I'M AFRAID TODAY IS NOT THAT DAY. NO...

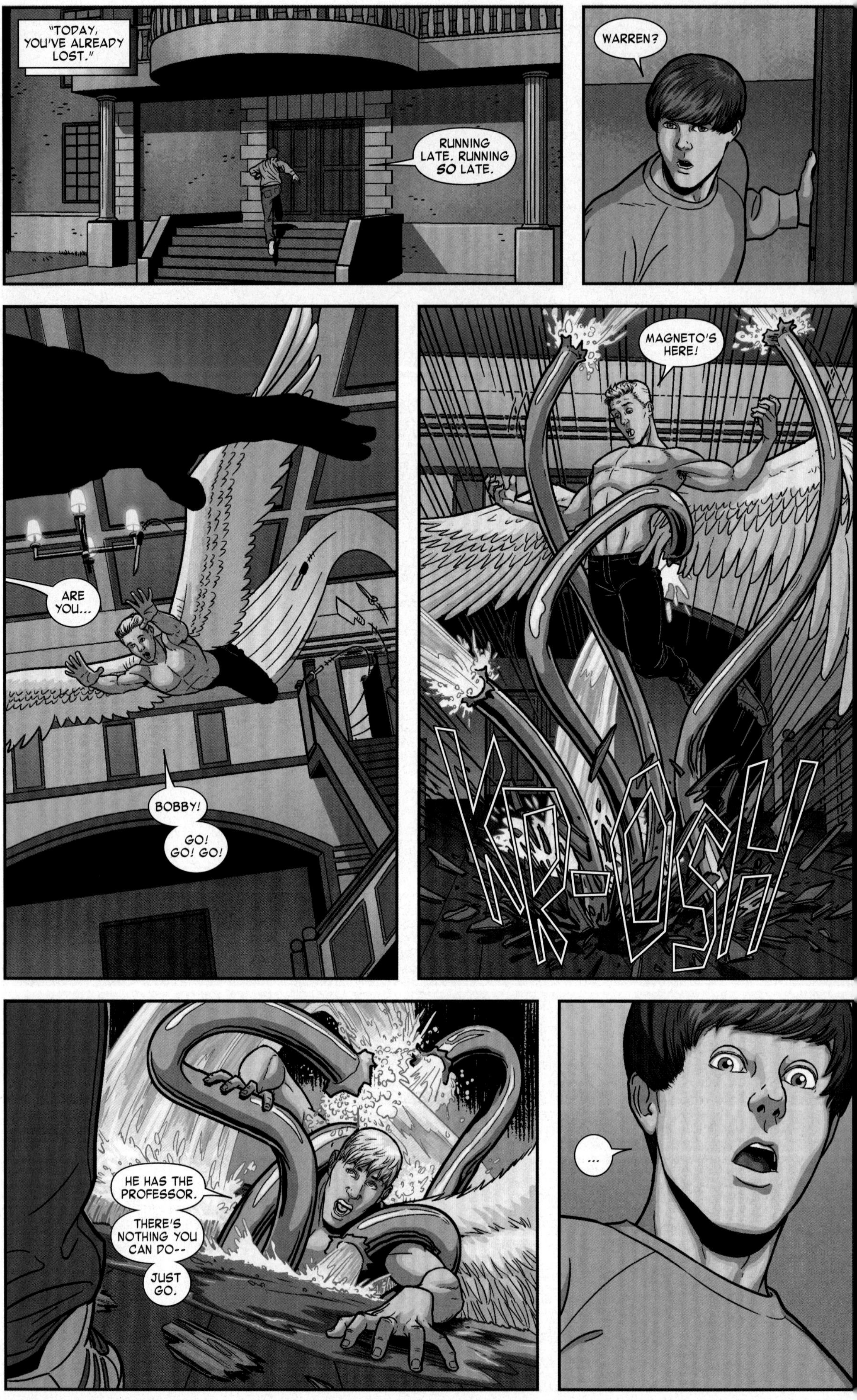
"TODAY, YOU'VE ALREADY LOST."
RUNNING LATE. RUNNING SO LATE.
WARREN?
ARE YOU...
BOBBY!
GO! GO! GO!
MAGNETO'S HERE!
KR-OSH
HE HAS THE PROFESSOR.
THERE'S NOTHING YOU CAN DO--
JUST GO.
...

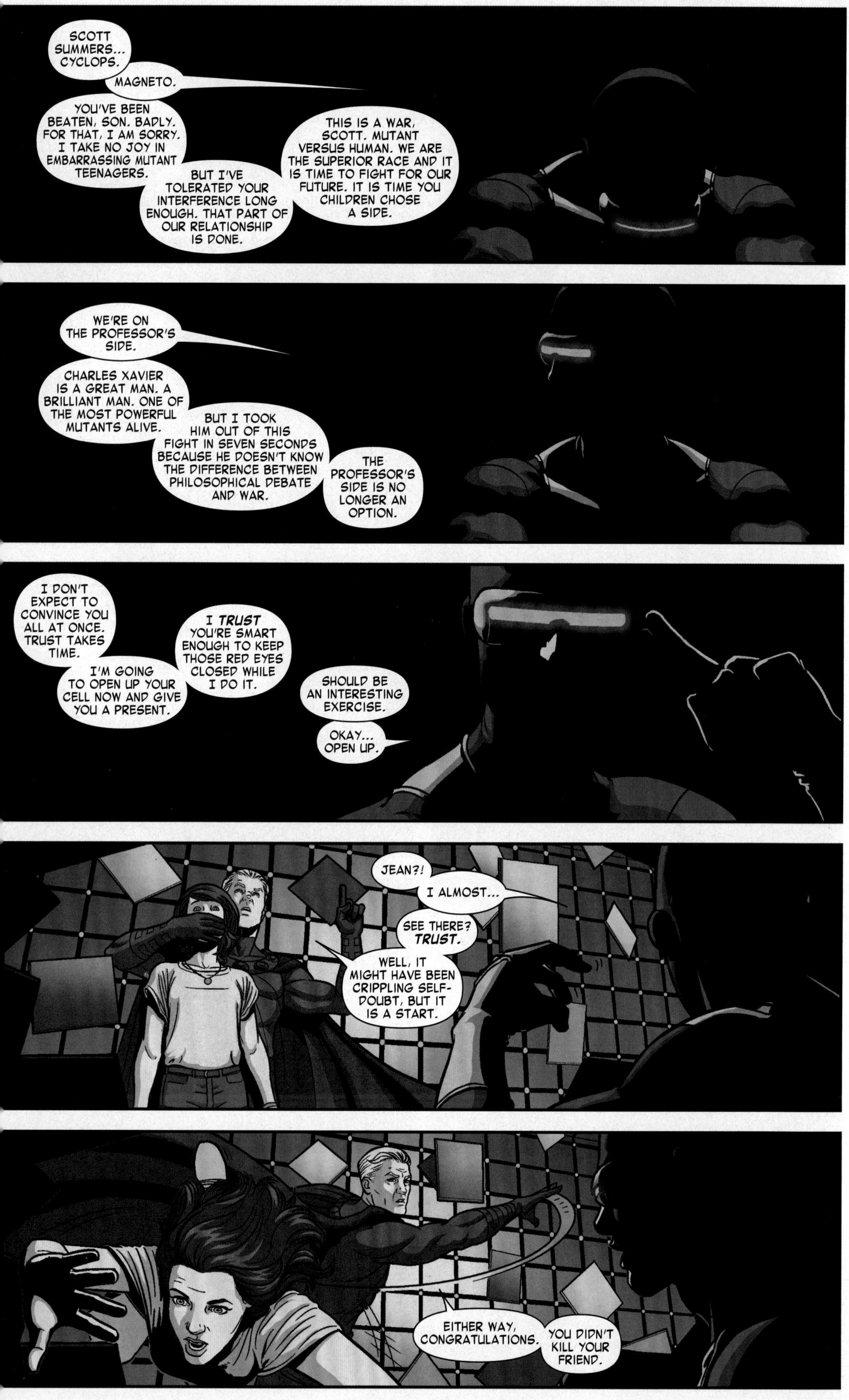
SCOTT SUMMERS... CYCLOPS.
MAGNETO.
YOU'VE BEEN BEATEN, SON. BADLY. FOR THAT, I AM SORRY. I TAKE NO JOY IN EMBARRASSING MUTANT TEENAGERS.
BUT I'VE TOLERATED YOUR INTERFERENCE LONG ENOUGH. THAT PART OF OUR RELATIONSHIP IS DONE.
THIS IS A WAR, SCOTT. MUTANT VERSUS HUMAN. WE ARE THE SUPERIOR RACE AND IT IS TIME TO FIGHT FOR OUR FUTURE. IT IS TIME YOU CHILDREN CHOSE A SIDE.
WE'RE ON THE PROFESSOR'S SIDE.
CHARLES XAVIER IS A GREAT MAN. A BRILLIANT MAN. ONE OF THE MOST POWERFUL MUTANTS ALIVE.
BUT I TOOK HIM OUT OF THIS FIGHT IN SEVEN SECONDS BECAUSE HE DOESN'T KNOW THE DIFFERENCE BETWEEN PHILOSOPHICAL DEBATE AND WAR.
THE PROFESSOR'S SIDE IS NO LONGER AN OPTION.
I DON'T EXPECT TO CONVINCE YOU ALL AT ONCE. TRUST TAKES TIME.
I'M GOING TO OPEN UP YOUR CELL NOW AND GIVE YOU A PRESENT.
I *TRUST* YOU'RE SMART ENOUGH TO KEEP THOSE RED EYES CLOSED WHILE I DO IT.
SHOULD BE AN INTERESTING EXERCISE.
OKAY... OPEN UP.
JEAN?!
I ALMOST...
SEE THERE? *TRUST.*
WELL, IT MIGHT HAVE BEEN CRIPPLING SELF-DOUBT, BUT IT IS A START.
EITHER WAY, CONGRATULATIONS.
YOU DIDN'T KILL YOUR FRIEND.

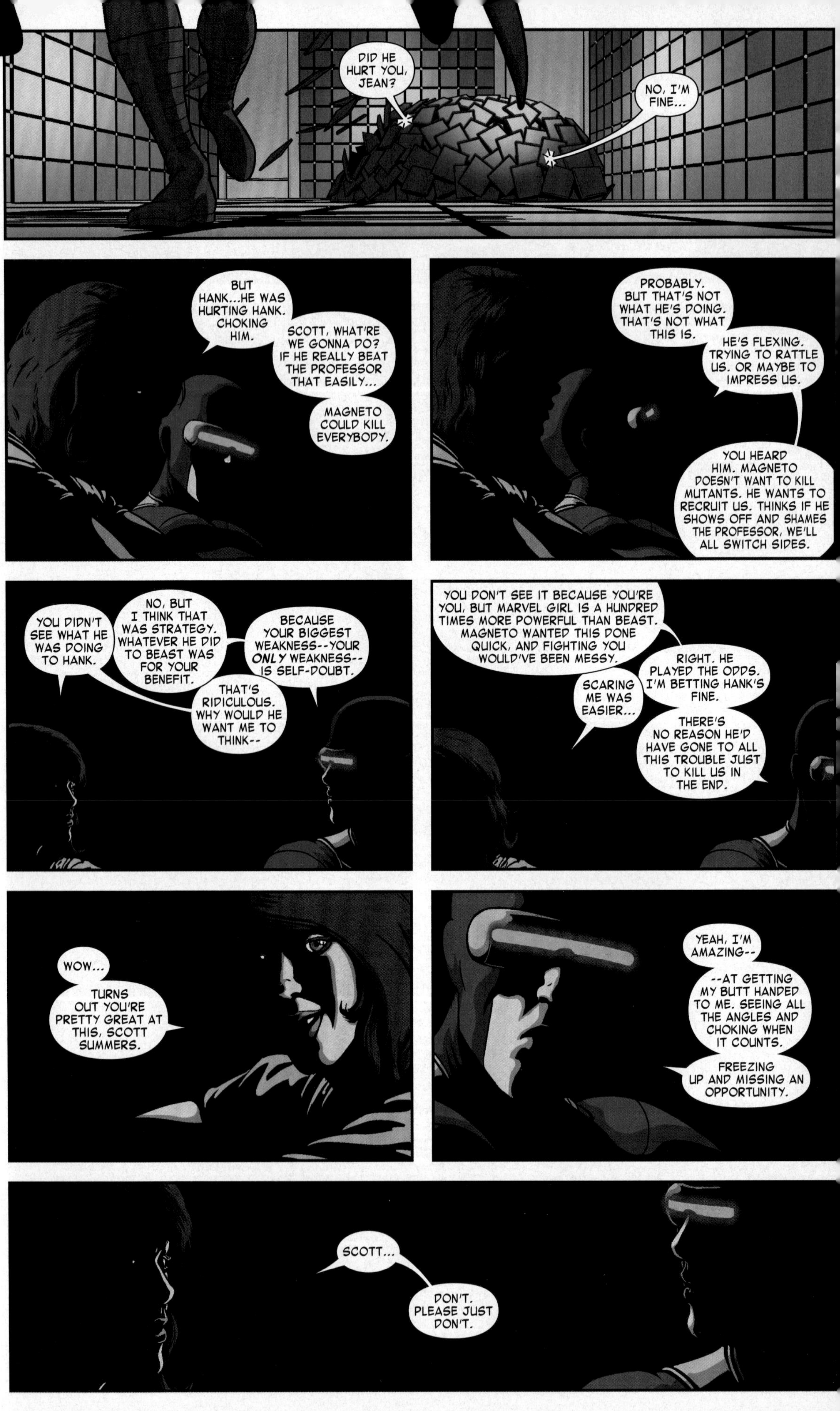
DID HE HURT YOU, JEAN?
NO, I'M FINE...
BUT HANK...HE WAS HURTING HANK. CHOKING HIM.
SCOTT, WHAT'RE WE GONNA DO? IF HE REALLY BEAT THE PROFESSOR THAT EASILY...
MAGNETO COULD KILL EVERYBODY.
PROBABLY. BUT THAT'S NOT WHAT HE'S DOING. THAT'S NOT WHAT THIS IS.
HE'S FLEXING. TRYING TO RATTLE US. OR MAYBE TO IMPRESS US.
YOU HEARD HIM. MAGNETO DOESN'T WANT TO KILL MUTANTS. HE WANTS TO RECRUIT US. THINKS IF HE SHOWS OFF AND SHAMES THE PROFESSOR, WE'LL ALL SWITCH SIDES.
YOU DIDN'T SEE WHAT HE WAS DOING TO HANK.
NO, BUT I THINK THAT WAS STRATEGY. WHATEVER HE DID TO BEAST WAS FOR YOUR BENEFIT.
BECAUSE YOUR BIGGEST WEAKNESS--YOUR *ONLY* WEAKNESS--IS SELF-DOUBT.
THAT'S RIDICULOUS. WHY WOULD HE WANT ME TO THINK--
YOU DON'T SEE IT BECAUSE YOU'RE YOU, BUT MARVEL GIRL IS A HUNDRED TIMES MORE POWERFUL THAN BEAST. MAGNETO WANTED THIS DONE QUICK, AND FIGHTING YOU WOULD'VE BEEN MESSY.
SCARING ME WAS EASIER...
RIGHT. HE PLAYED THE ODDS. I'M BETTING HANK'S FINE.
THERE'S NO REASON HE'D HAVE GONE TO ALL THIS TROUBLE JUST TO KILL US IN THE END.
WOW...
TURNS OUT YOU'RE PRETTY GREAT AT THIS, SCOTT SUMMERS.
YEAH, I'M AMAZING--
--AT GETTING MY BUTT HANDED TO ME. SEEING ALL THE ANGLES AND CHOKING WHEN IT COUNTS.
FREEZING UP AND MISSING AN OPPORTUNITY.
SCOTT...
DON'T. PLEASE JUST DON'T.

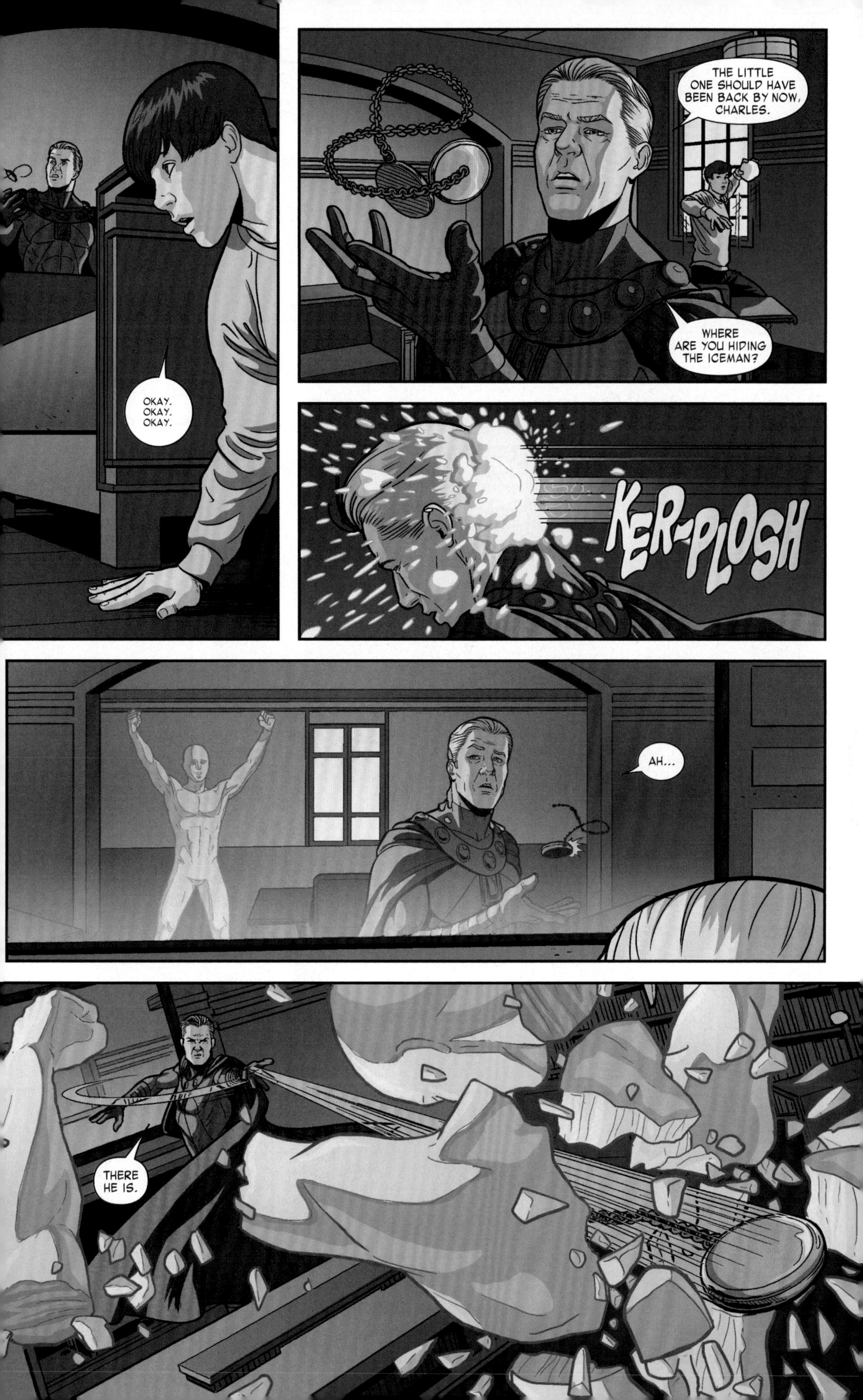
OKAY. OKAY. OKAY.
THE LITTLE ONE SHOULD HAVE BEEN BACK BY NOW, CHARLES.
WHERE ARE YOU HIDING THE ICEMAN?
KER-PLOSH
AH...
THERE HE IS.

NO. I'M BACK HERE.

HONESTLY THOUGHT THERE WAS ZERO CHANCE YOU'D BUY THAT WAS ME.

I MEAN, C'MON...

ICEMAN ALWAYS WEARS BOOTS.

BIG YELLOW ONES.

EVERYBODY KNOWS THAT.

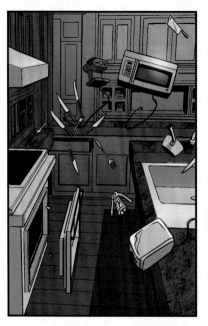

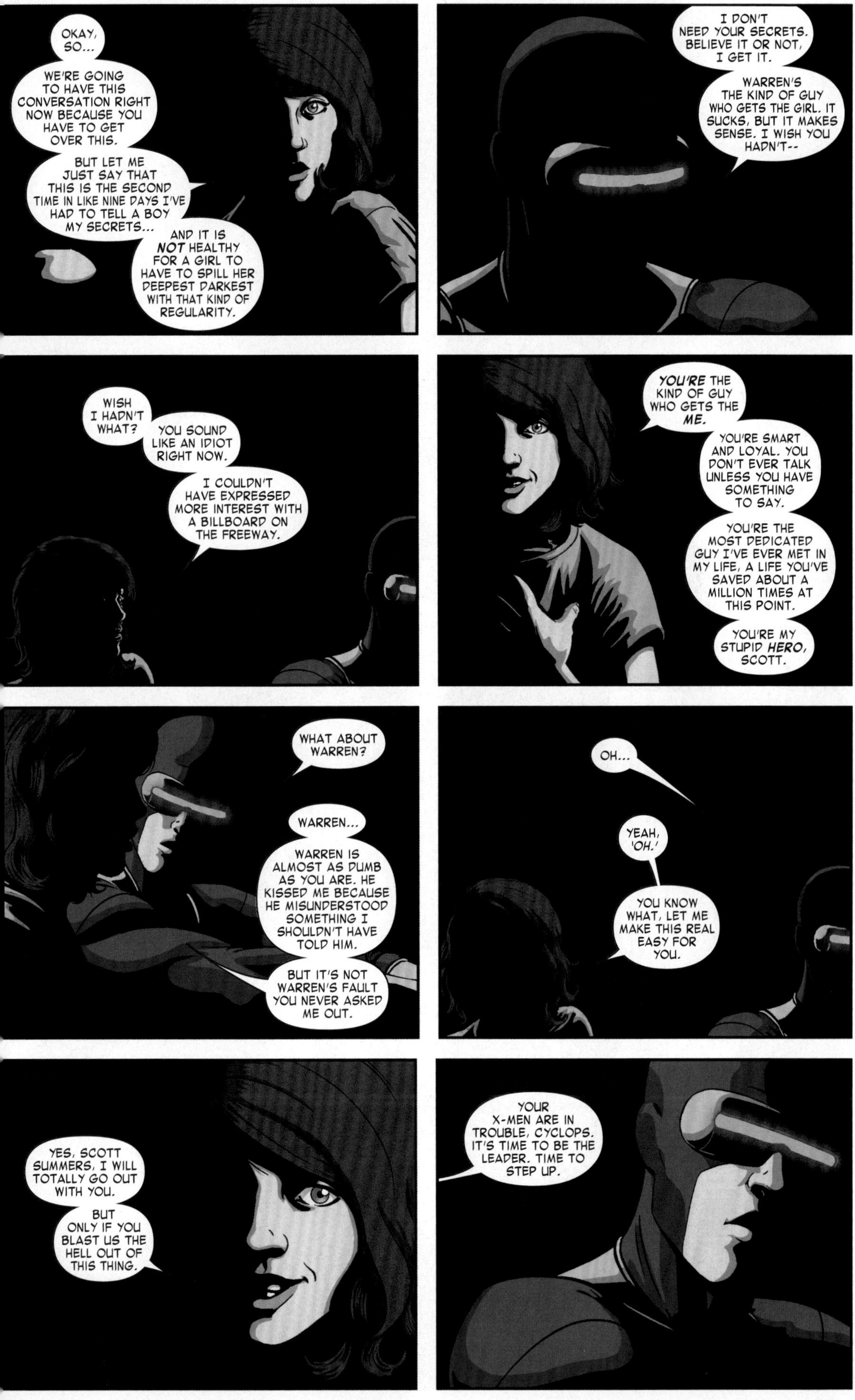
OKAY, SO...
WE'RE GOING TO HAVE THIS CONVERSATION RIGHT NOW BECAUSE YOU HAVE TO GET OVER THIS.
BUT LET ME JUST SAY THAT THIS IS THE SECOND TIME IN LIKE NINE DAYS I'VE HAD TO TELL A BOY MY SECRETS...
AND IT IS *NOT* HEALTHY FOR A GIRL TO HAVE TO SPILL HER DEEPEST DARKEST WITH THAT KIND OF REGULARITY.
I DON'T NEED YOUR SECRETS. BELIEVE IT OR NOT, I GET IT.
WARREN'S THE KIND OF GUY WHO GETS THE GIRL. IT SUCKS, BUT IT MAKES SENSE. I WISH YOU HADN'T--
WISH I HADN'T WHAT?
YOU SOUND LIKE AN IDIOT RIGHT NOW.
I COULDN'T HAVE EXPRESSED MORE INTEREST WITH A BILLBOARD ON THE FREEWAY.
YOU'RE THE KIND OF GUY WHO GETS THE *ME.*
YOU'RE SMART AND LOYAL. YOU DON'T EVER TALK UNLESS YOU HAVE SOMETHING TO SAY.
YOU'RE THE MOST DEDICATED GUY I'VE EVER MET IN MY LIFE, A LIFE YOU'VE SAVED ABOUT A MILLION TIMES AT THIS POINT.
YOU'RE MY STUPID *HERO,* SCOTT.
WHAT ABOUT WARREN?
WARREN...
WARREN IS ALMOST AS DUMB AS YOU ARE. HE KISSED ME BECAUSE HE MISUNDERSTOOD SOMETHING I SHOULDN'T HAVE TOLD HIM.
BUT IT'S NOT WARREN'S FAULT YOU NEVER ASKED ME OUT.
OH...
YEAH, 'OH.'
YOU KNOW WHAT, LET ME MAKE THIS REAL EASY FOR YOU.
YES, SCOTT SUMMERS, I WILL TOTALLY GO OUT WITH YOU.
BUT ONLY IF YOU BLAST US THE HELL OUT OF THIS THING.
YOUR X-MEN ARE IN TROUBLE, CYCLOPS. IT'S TIME TO BE THE LEADER. TIME TO STEP UP.

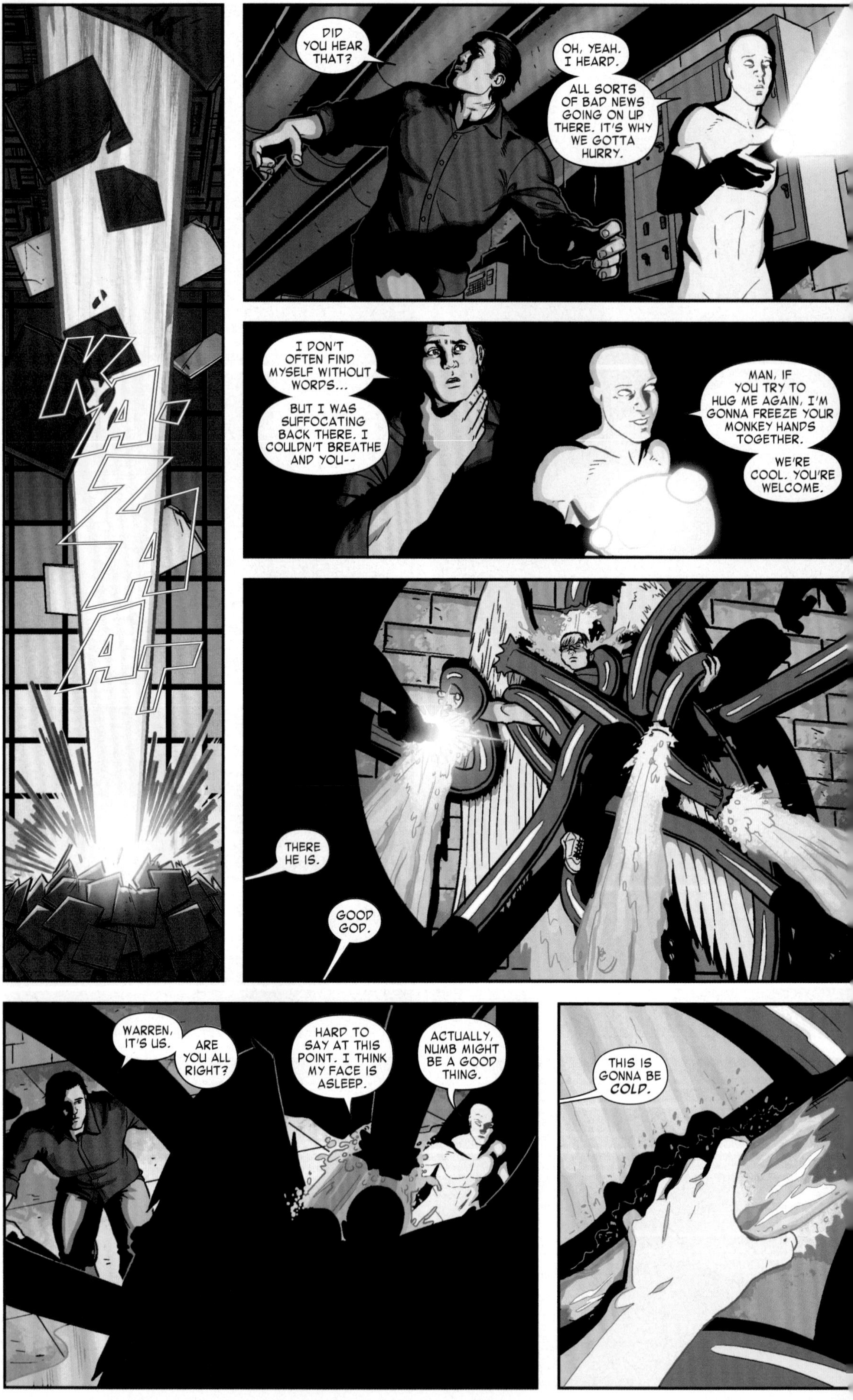
KA-ZA-AT
DID YOU HEAR THAT?
OH, YEAH. I HEARD.
ALL SORTS OF BAD NEWS GOING ON UP THERE. IT'S WHY WE GOTTA HURRY.
I DON'T OFTEN FIND MYSELF WITHOUT WORDS...
BUT I WAS SUFFOCATING BACK THERE. I COULDN'T BREATHE AND YOU--
MAN, IF YOU TRY TO HUG ME AGAIN, I'M GONNA FREEZE YOUR MONKEY HANDS TOGETHER.
WE'RE COOL. YOU'RE WELCOME.
THERE HE IS.
GOOD GOD.
WARREN, IT'S US.
ARE YOU ALL RIGHT?
HARD TO SAY AT THIS POINT. I THINK MY FACE IS ASLEEP.
ACTUALLY, NUMB MIGHT BE A GOOD THING.
THIS IS GONNA BE COLD.

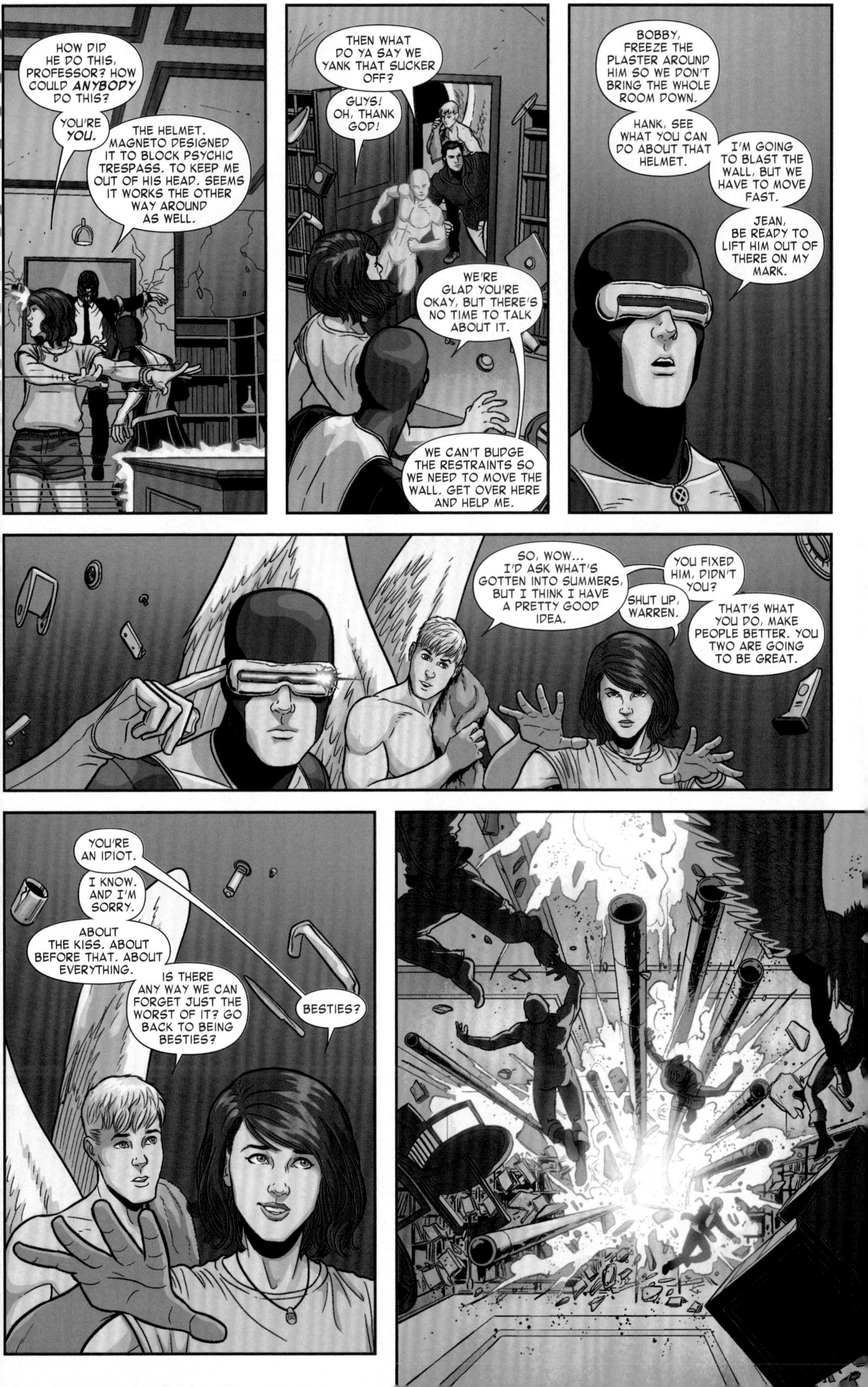
HOW DID HE DO THIS, PROFESSOR? HOW COULD ANYBODY DO THIS?
YOU'RE YOU.
THE HELMET. MAGNETO DESIGNED IT TO BLOCK PSYCHIC TRESPASS. TO KEEP ME OUT OF HIS HEAD. SEEMS IT WORKS THE OTHER WAY AROUND AS WELL.
THEN WHAT DO YA SAY WE YANK THAT SUCKER OFF?
GUYS! OH, THANK GOD!
WE'RE GLAD YOU'RE OKAY, BUT THERE'S NO TIME TO TALK ABOUT IT.
WE CAN'T BUDGE THE RESTRAINTS SO WE NEED TO MOVE THE WALL. GET OVER HERE AND HELP ME.
BOBBY, FREEZE THE PLASTER AROUND HIM SO WE DON'T BRING THE WHOLE ROOM DOWN.
HANK, SEE WHAT YOU CAN DO ABOUT THAT HELMET.
I'M GOING TO BLAST THE WALL, BUT WE HAVE TO MOVE FAST.
JEAN, BE READY TO LIFT HIM OUT OF THERE ON MY MARK.
SO, WOW... I'D ASK WHAT'S GOTTEN INTO SUMMERS, BUT I THINK I HAVE A PRETTY GOOD IDEA.
SHUT UP, WARREN.
YOU FIXED HIM, DIDN'T YOU?
THAT'S WHAT YOU DO, MAKE PEOPLE BETTER. YOU TWO ARE GOING TO BE GREAT.
YOU'RE AN IDIOT.
I KNOW. AND I'M SORRY.
ABOUT THE KISS. ABOUT BEFORE THAT. ABOUT EVERYTHING.
IS THERE ANY WAY WE CAN FORGET JUST THE WORST OF IT? GO BACK TO BEING BESTIES?
BESTIES?

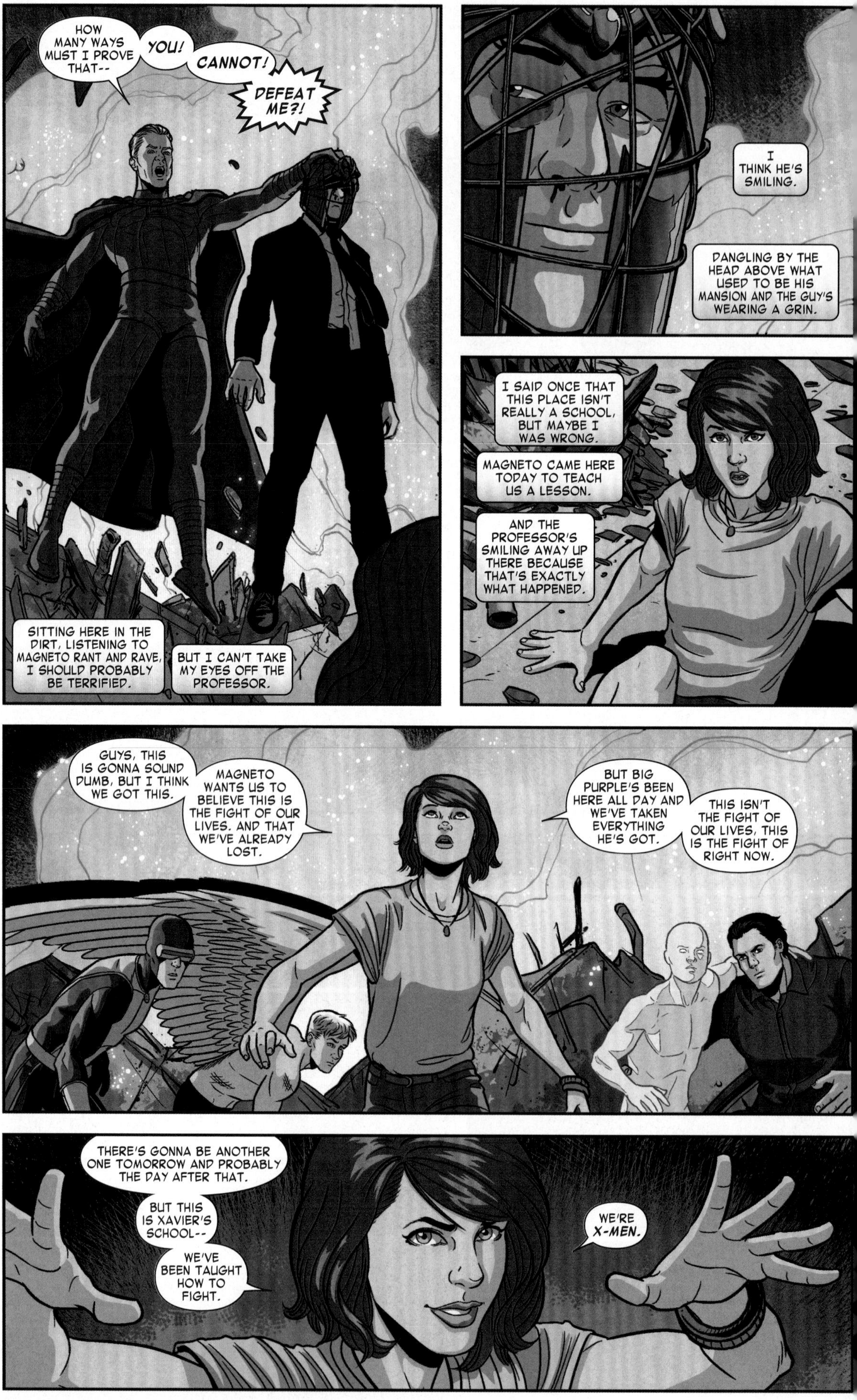
HOW MANY WAYS MUST I PROVE THAT--
YOU!
CANNOT!
DEFEAT ME?!
SITTING HERE IN THE DIRT, LISTENING TO MAGNETO RANT AND RAVE, I SHOULD PROBABLY BE TERRIFIED.
BUT I CAN'T TAKE MY EYES OFF THE PROFESSOR.
I THINK HE'S SMILING.
DANGLING BY THE HEAD ABOVE WHAT USED TO BE HIS MANSION AND THE GUY'S WEARING A GRIN.
I SAID ONCE THAT THIS PLACE ISN'T REALLY A SCHOOL, BUT MAYBE I WAS WRONG.
MAGNETO CAME HERE TODAY TO TEACH US A LESSON.
AND THE PROFESSOR'S SMILING AWAY UP THERE BECAUSE THAT'S EXACTLY WHAT HAPPENED.
GUYS, THIS IS GONNA SOUND DUMB, BUT I THINK WE GOT THIS.
MAGNETO WANTS US TO BELIEVE THIS IS THE FIGHT OF OUR LIVES, AND THAT WE'VE ALREADY LOST.
BUT BIG PURPLE'S BEEN HERE ALL DAY AND WE'VE TAKEN EVERYTHING HE'S GOT.
THIS ISN'T THE FIGHT OF OUR LIVES, THIS IS THE FIGHT OF RIGHT NOW.
THERE'S GONNA BE ANOTHER ONE TOMORROW AND PROBABLY THE DAY AFTER THAT.
BUT THIS IS XAVIER'S SCHOOL--
WE'VE BEEN TAUGHT HOW TO FIGHT.
WE'RE X-MEN.

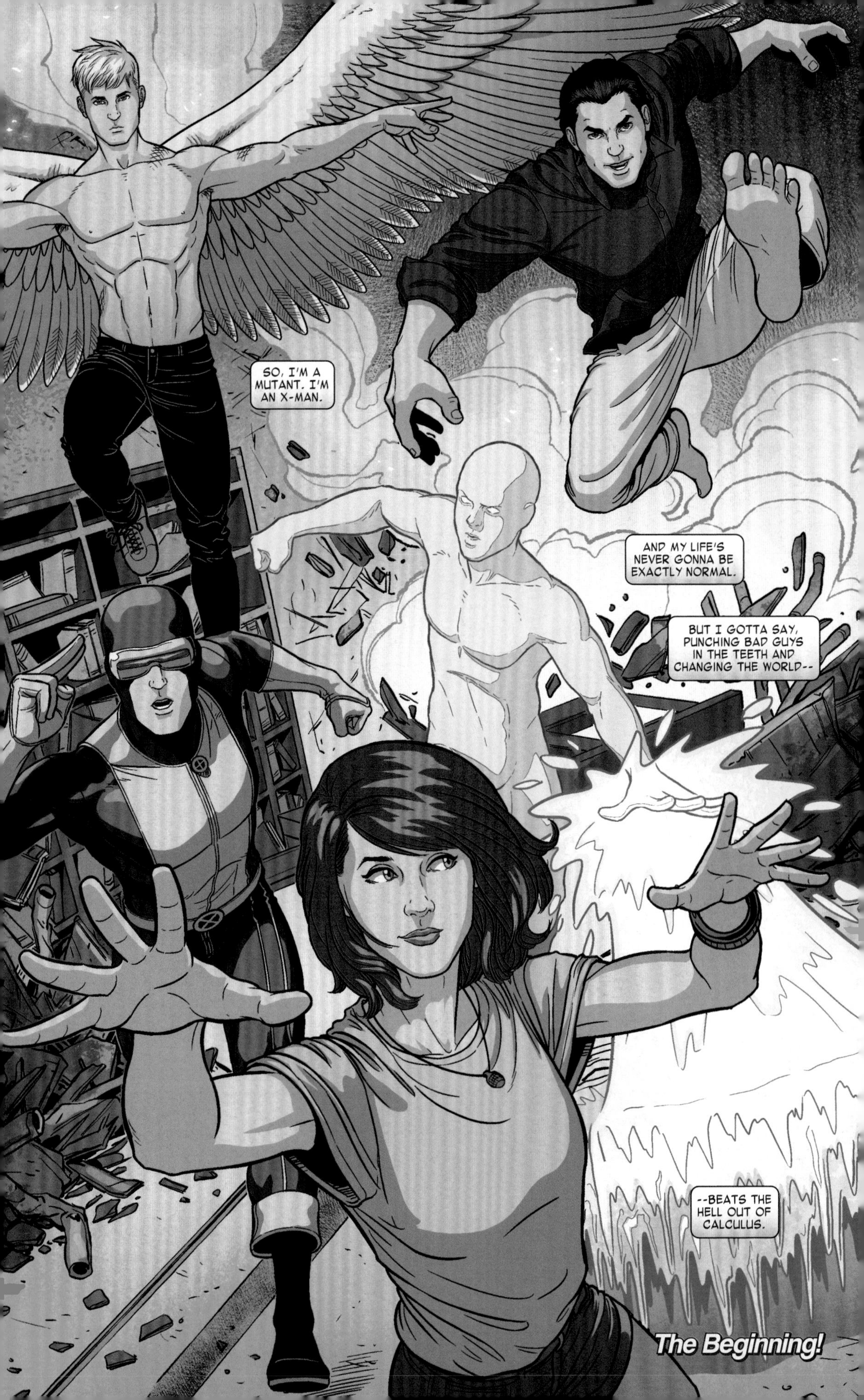
SO, I'M A MUTANT. I'M AN X-MAN.
AND MY LIFE'S NEVER GONNA BE EXACTLY NORMAL.
BUT I GOTTA SAY, PUNCHING BAD GUYS IN THE TEETH AND CHANGING THE WORLD--
--BEATS THE HELL OUT OF CALCULUS.
The Beginning!

UNCANNY X-MEN (2011) #1 THE SHELL-SHOCKED X-MEN HAVE BEEN SUNDERED IN TWO. WHAT IS TO BECOME OF THE MUTANTS WHO SIDE WITH CYCLOPS AFTER THE BIG SPLIT? AND WHAT DOES IT HAVE TO DO WITH THE RESURRECTED MISTER SINISTER?

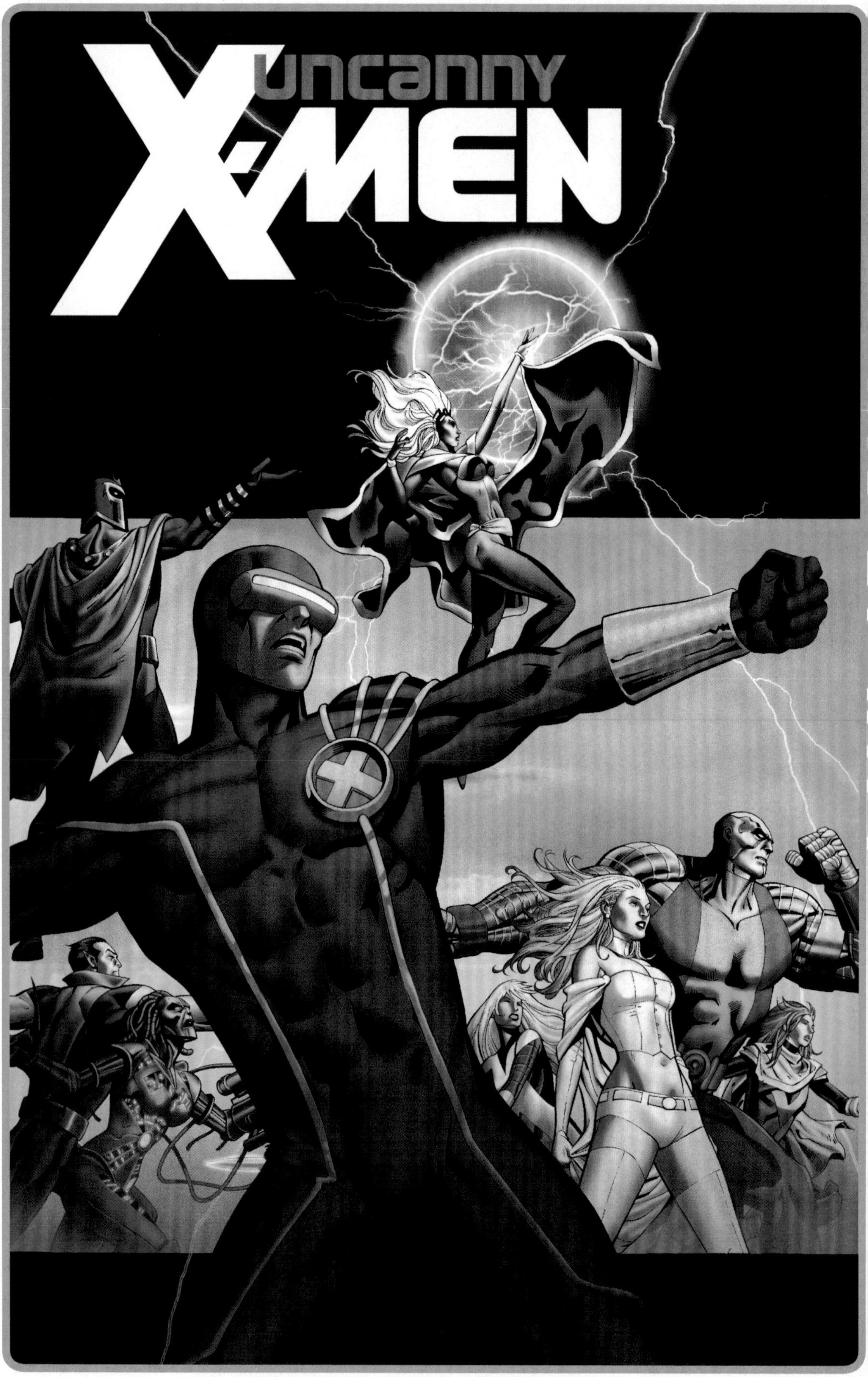
UNCANNY
X-MEN

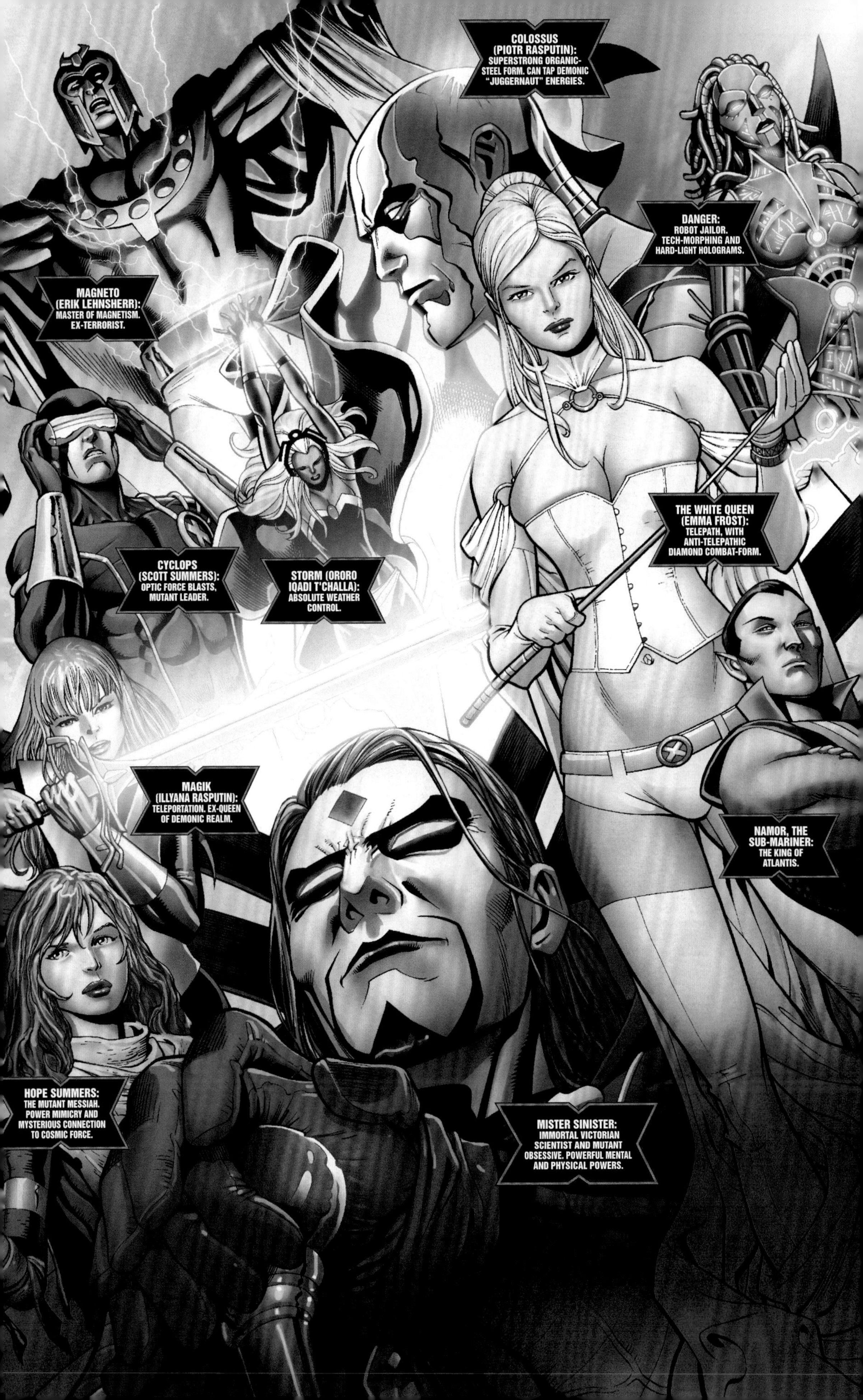

COLOSSUS (PIOTR RASPUTIN): SUPERSTRONG ORGANIC-STEEL FORM. CAN TAP DEMONIC "JUGGERNAUT" ENERGIES.
DANGER: ROBOT JAILOR. TECH-MORPHING AND HARD-LIGHT HOLOGRAMS.
MAGNETO (ERIK LEHNSHERR): MASTER OF MAGNETISM. EX-TERRORIST.
THE WHITE QUEEN (EMMA FROST): TELEPATH, WITH ANTI-TELEPATHIC DIAMOND COMBAT-FORM.
CYCLOPS (SCOTT SUMMERS): OPTIC FORCE BLASTS, MUTANT LEADER.
STORM (ORORO IQADI T'CHALLA): ABSOLUTE WEATHER CONTROL.
MAGIK (ILLYANA RASPUTIN): TELEPORTATION. EX-QUEEN OF DEMONIC REALM.
NAMOR, THE SUB-MARINER: THE KING OF ATLANTIS.
HOPE SUMMERS: THE MUTANT MESSIAH. POWER MIMICRY AND MYSTERIOUS CONNECTION TO COSMIC FORCE.
MISTER SINISTER: IMMORTAL VICTORIAN SCIENTIST AND MUTANT OBSESSIVE. POWERFUL MENTAL AND PHYSICAL POWERS.

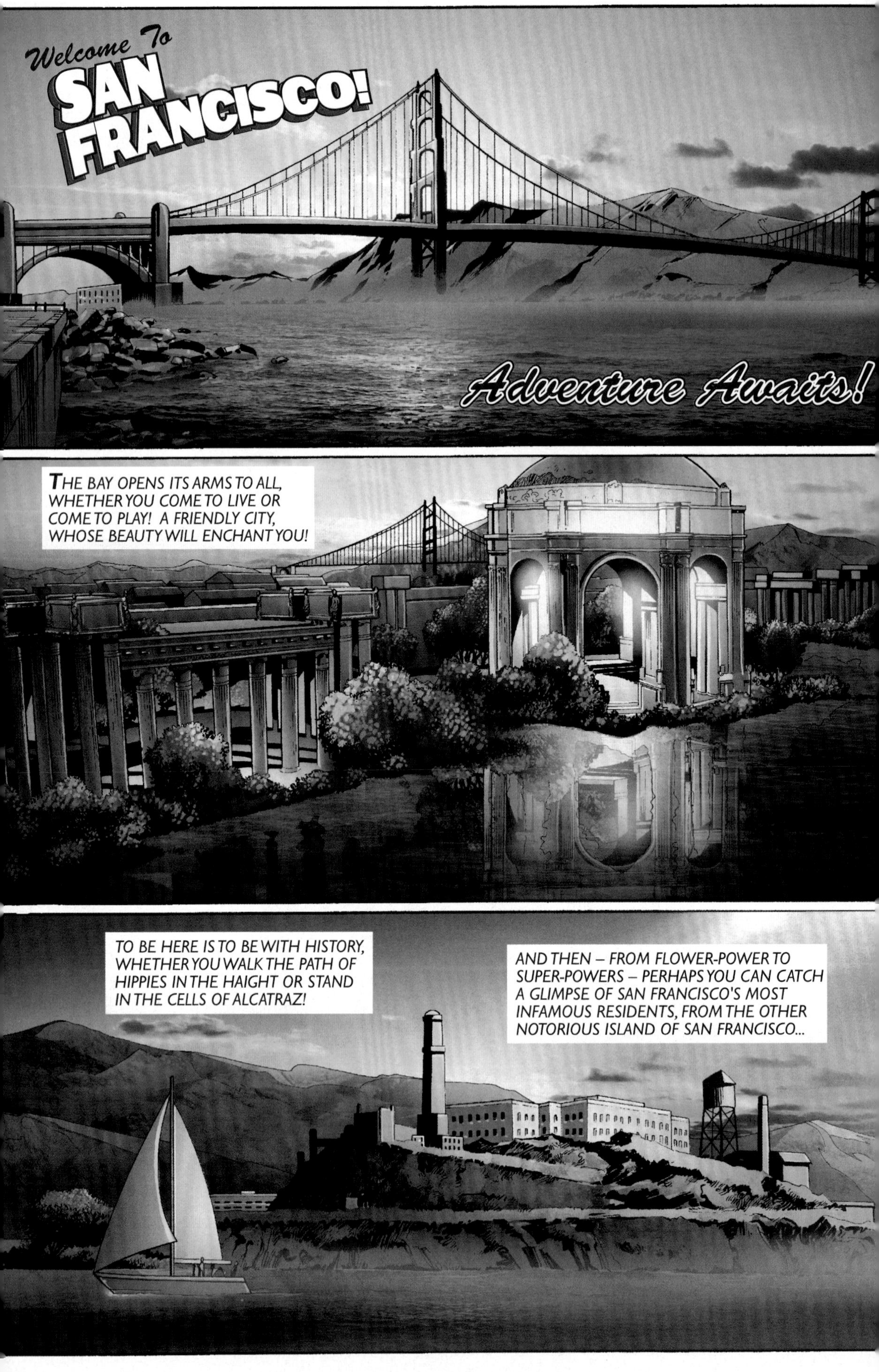
Welcome To
SAN FRANCISCO!
Adventure Awaits!
THE BAY OPENS ITS ARMS TO ALL, WHETHER YOU COME TO LIVE OR COME TO PLAY! A FRIENDLY CITY, WHOSE BEAUTY WILL ENCHANT YOU!
TO BE HERE IS TO BE WITH HISTORY, WHETHER YOU WALK THE PATH OF HIPPIES IN THE HAIGHT OR STAND IN THE CELLS OF ALCATRAZ!
AND THEN – FROM FLOWER-POWER TO SUPER-POWERS – PERHAPS YOU CAN CATCH A GLIMPSE OF SAN FRANCISCO'S MOST INFAMOUS RESIDENTS, FROM THE OTHER NOTORIOUS ISLAND OF SAN FRANCISCO...

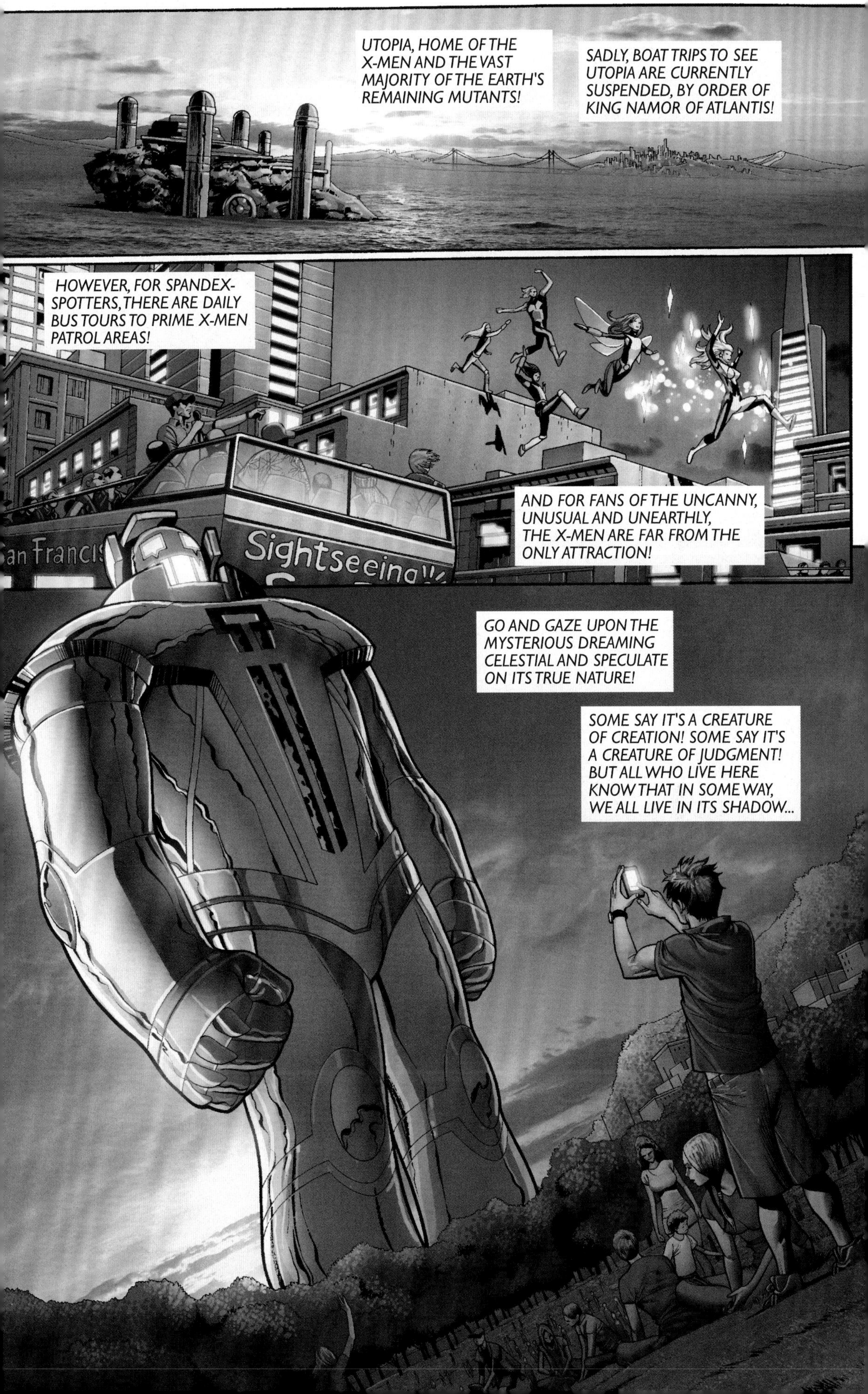
UTOPIA, HOME OF THE X-MEN AND THE VAST MAJORITY OF THE EARTH'S REMAINING MUTANTS!
SADLY, BOAT TRIPS TO SEE UTOPIA ARE CURRENTLY SUSPENDED, BY ORDER OF KING NAMOR OF ATLANTIS!
HOWEVER, FOR SPANDEX-SPOTTERS, THERE ARE DAILY BUS TOURS TO PRIME X-MEN PATROL AREAS!
Sightseeing
AND FOR FANS OF THE UNCANNY, UNUSUAL AND UNEARTHLY, THE X-MEN ARE FAR FROM THE ONLY ATTRACTION!
GO AND GAZE UPON THE MYSTERIOUS DREAMING CELESTIAL AND SPECULATE ON ITS TRUE NATURE!
SOME SAY IT'S A CREATURE OF CREATION! SOME SAY IT'S A CREATURE OF JUDGMENT! BUT ALL WHO LIVE HERE KNOW THAT IN SOME WAY, WE ALL LIVE IN ITS SHADOW...

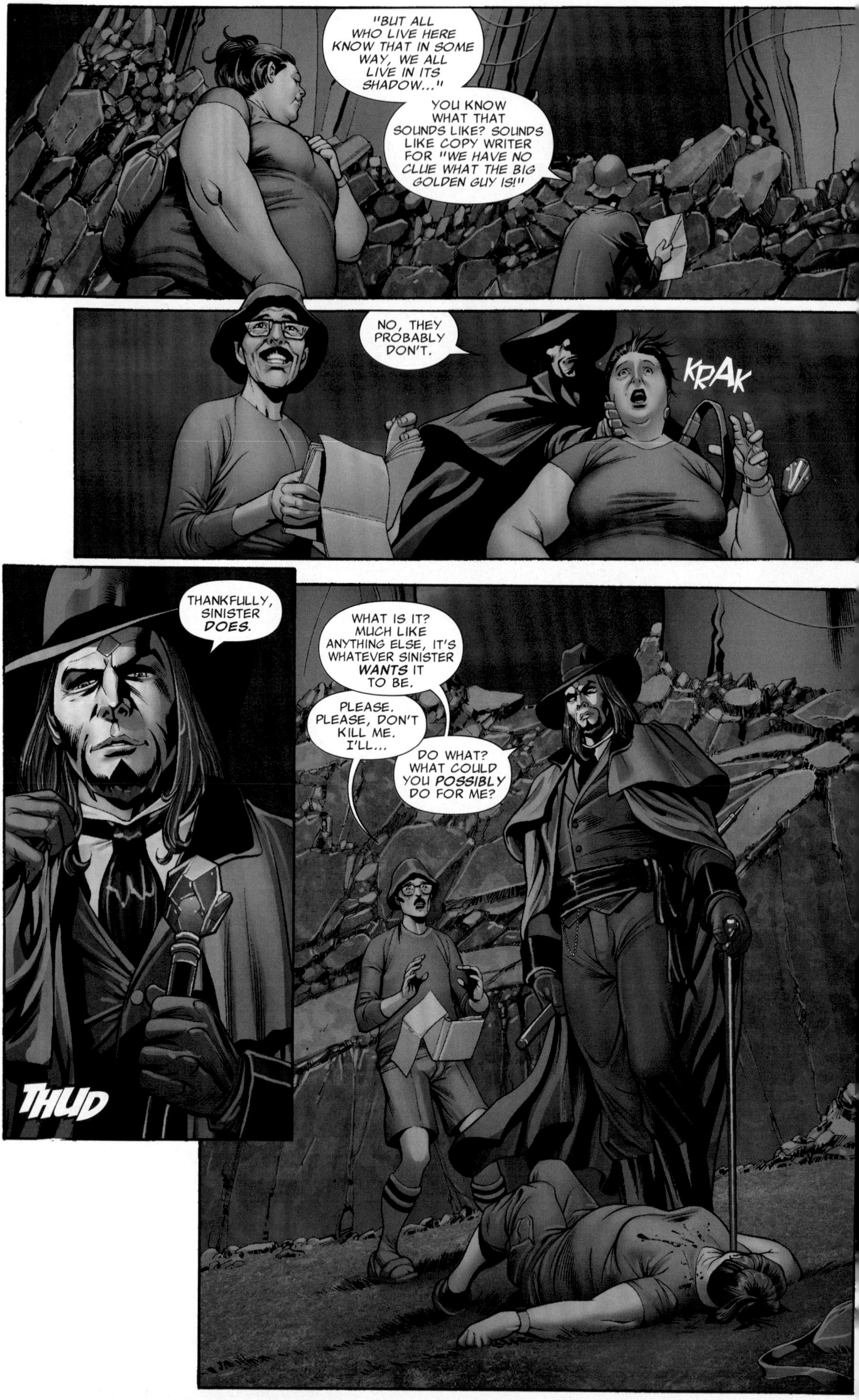
"BUT ALL WHO LIVE HERE KNOW THAT IN SOME WAY, WE ALL LIVE IN ITS SHADOW..."
YOU KNOW WHAT THAT SOUNDS LIKE? SOUNDS LIKE COPY WRITER FOR "WE HAVE NO CLUE WHAT THE BIG GOLDEN GUY IS!"
NO, THEY PROBABLY DON'T.
KRAK
THANKFULLY, SINISTER *DOES.*
THUD
WHAT IS IT? MUCH LIKE ANYTHING ELSE, IT'S WHATEVER SINISTER *WANTS* IT TO BE.
PLEASE. PLEASE, DON'T KILL ME. I'LL...
DO WHAT? WHAT COULD YOU *POSSIBLY* DO FOR ME?

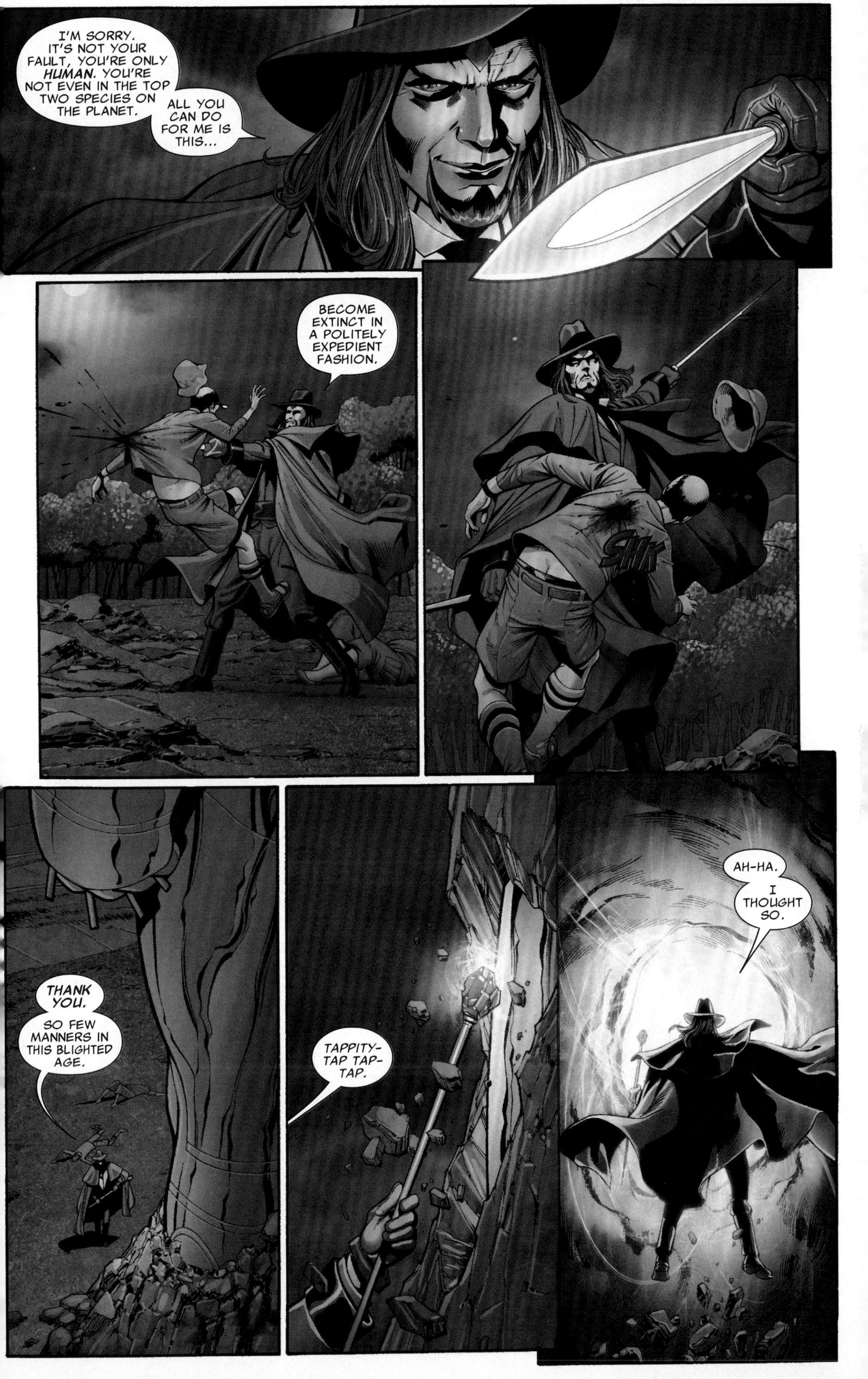
I'M SORRY. IT'S NOT YOUR FAULT, YOU'RE ONLY *HUMAN.* YOU'RE NOT EVEN IN THE TOP TWO SPECIES ON THE PLANET.
ALL YOU CAN DO FOR ME IS THIS...
BECOME EXTINCT IN A POLITELY EXPEDIENT FASHION.
SHK
THANK YOU.
SO FEW MANNERS IN THIS BLIGHTED AGE.
TAPPITY-TAP TAP-TAP.
AH-HA.
I THOUGHT SO.

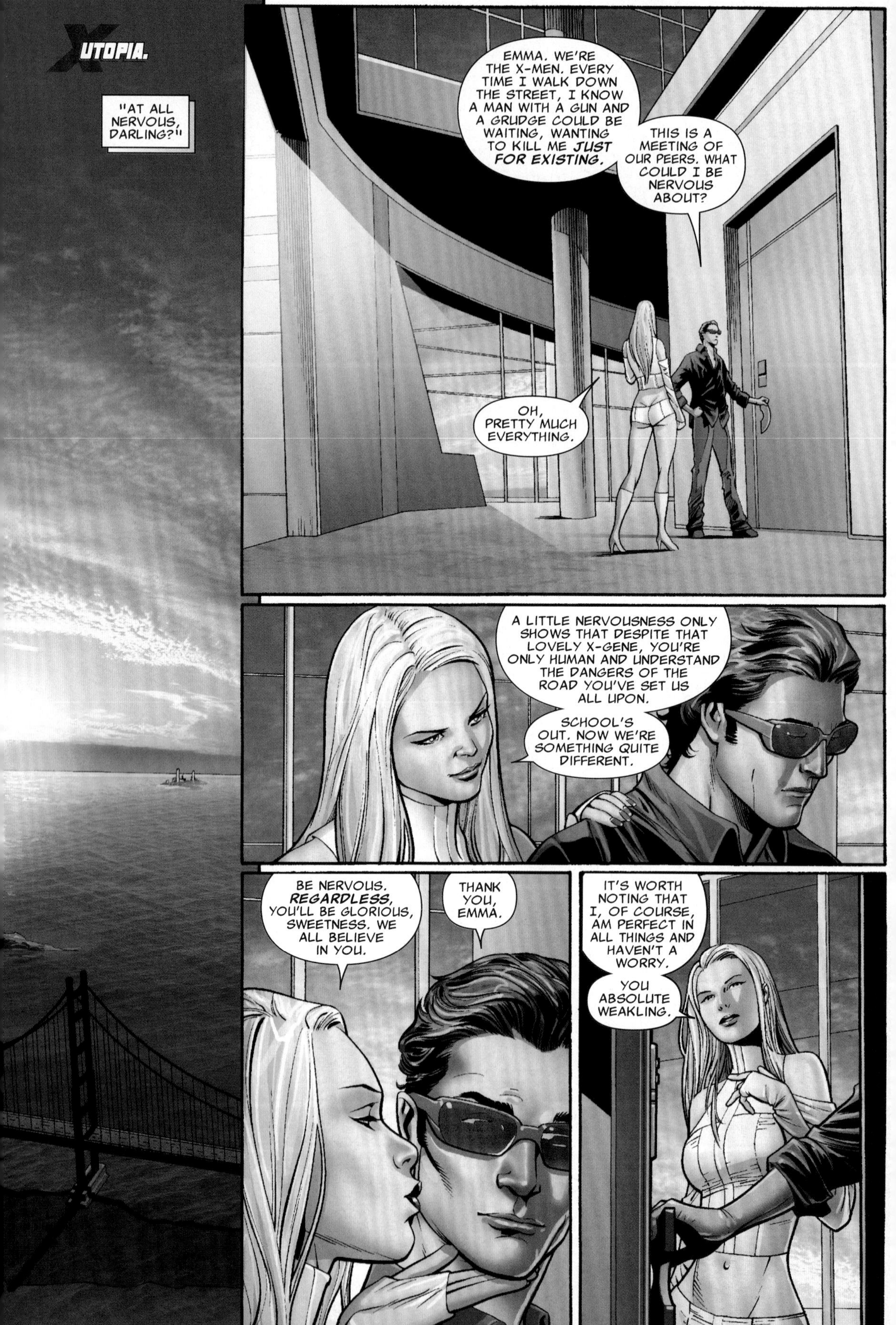
UTOPIA.
"AT ALL NERVOUS, DARLING?"
EMMA. WE'RE THE X-MEN. EVERY TIME I WALK DOWN THE STREET, I KNOW A MAN WITH A GUN AND A GRUDGE COULD BE WAITING, WANTING TO KILL ME JUST FOR EXISTING.
THIS IS A MEETING OF OUR PEERS. WHAT COULD I BE NERVOUS ABOUT?
OH, PRETTY MUCH EVERYTHING.
A LITTLE NERVOUSNESS ONLY SHOWS THAT DESPITE THAT LOVELY X-GENE, YOU'RE ONLY HUMAN AND UNDERSTAND THE DANGERS OF THE ROAD YOU'VE SET US ALL UPON.
SCHOOL'S OUT. NOW WE'RE SOMETHING QUITE DIFFERENT.
BE NERVOUS. REGARDLESS, YOU'LL BE GLORIOUS, SWEETNESS. WE ALL BELIEVE IN YOU.
THANK YOU, EMMA.
IT'S WORTH NOTING THAT I, OF COURSE, AM PERFECT IN ALL THINGS AND HAVEN'T A WORRY.
YOU ABSOLUTE WEAKLING.

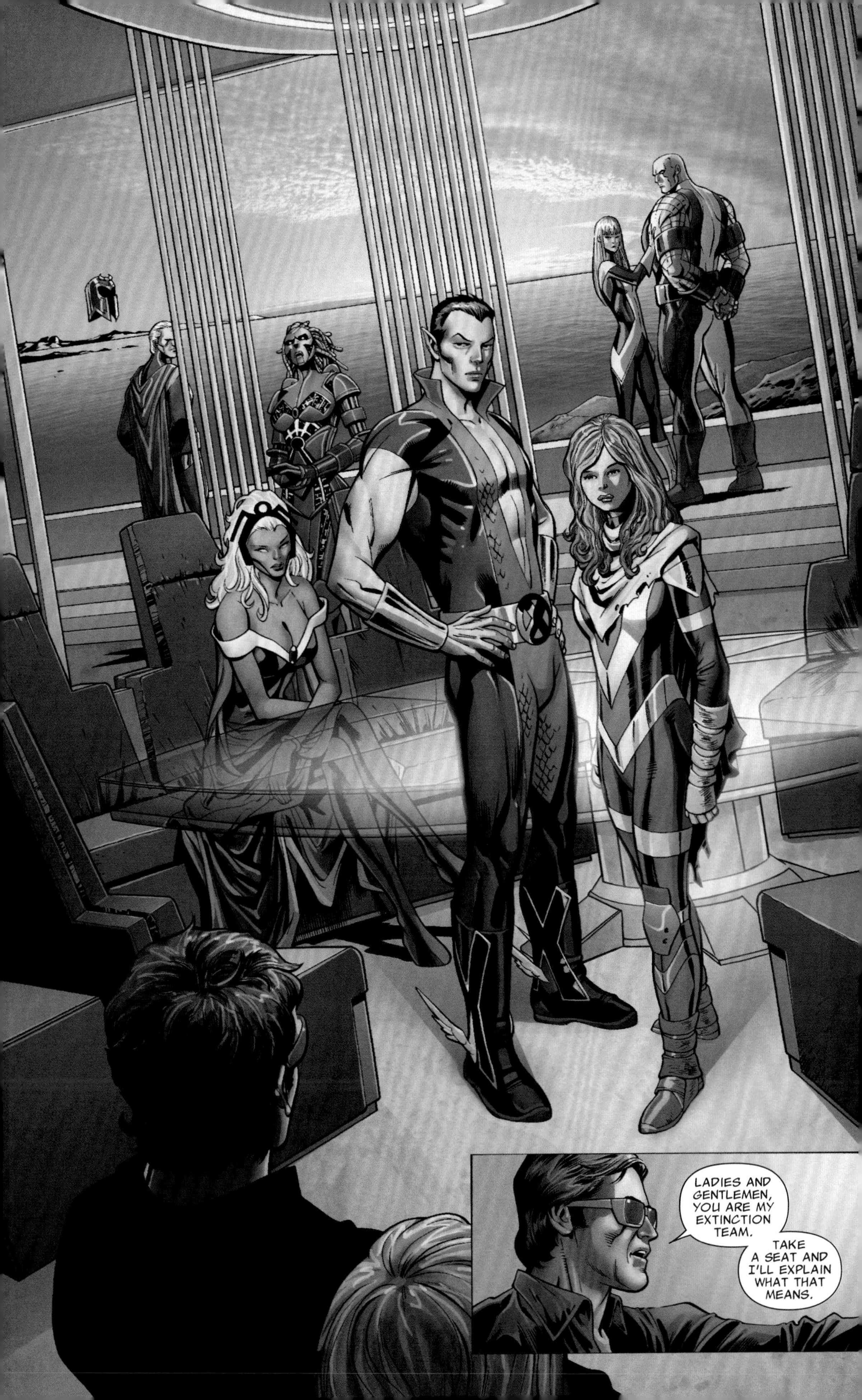

LADIES AND GENTLEMEN, YOU ARE MY EXTINCTION TEAM.
TAKE A SEAT AND I'LL EXPLAIN WHAT THAT MEANS.

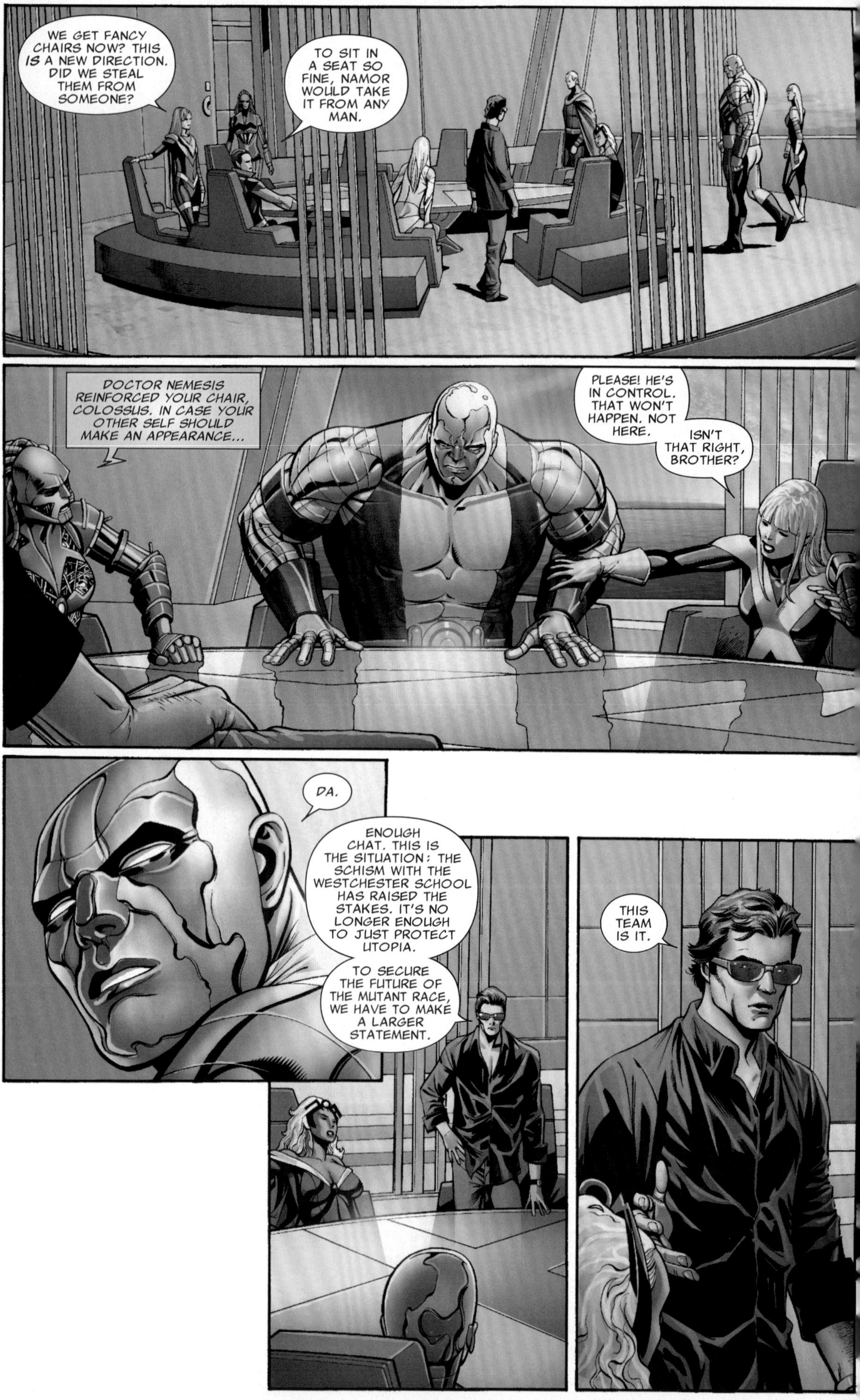
WE GET FANCY CHAIRS NOW? THIS IS A NEW DIRECTION. DID WE STEAL THEM FROM SOMEONE?
TO SIT IN A SEAT SO FINE, NAMOR WOULD TAKE IT FROM ANY MAN.
DOCTOR NEMESIS REINFORCED YOUR CHAIR, COLOSSUS. IN CASE YOUR OTHER SELF SHOULD MAKE AN APPEARANCE...
PLEASE! HE'S IN CONTROL. THAT WON'T HAPPEN. NOT HERE.
ISN'T THAT RIGHT, BROTHER?
DA.
ENOUGH CHAT. THIS IS THE SITUATION: THE SCHISM WITH THE WESTCHESTER SCHOOL HAS RAISED THE STAKES. IT'S NO LONGER ENOUGH TO JUST PROTECT UTOPIA.
TO SECURE THE FUTURE OF THE MUTANT RACE, WE HAVE TO MAKE A LARGER STATEMENT.
THIS TEAM IS IT.

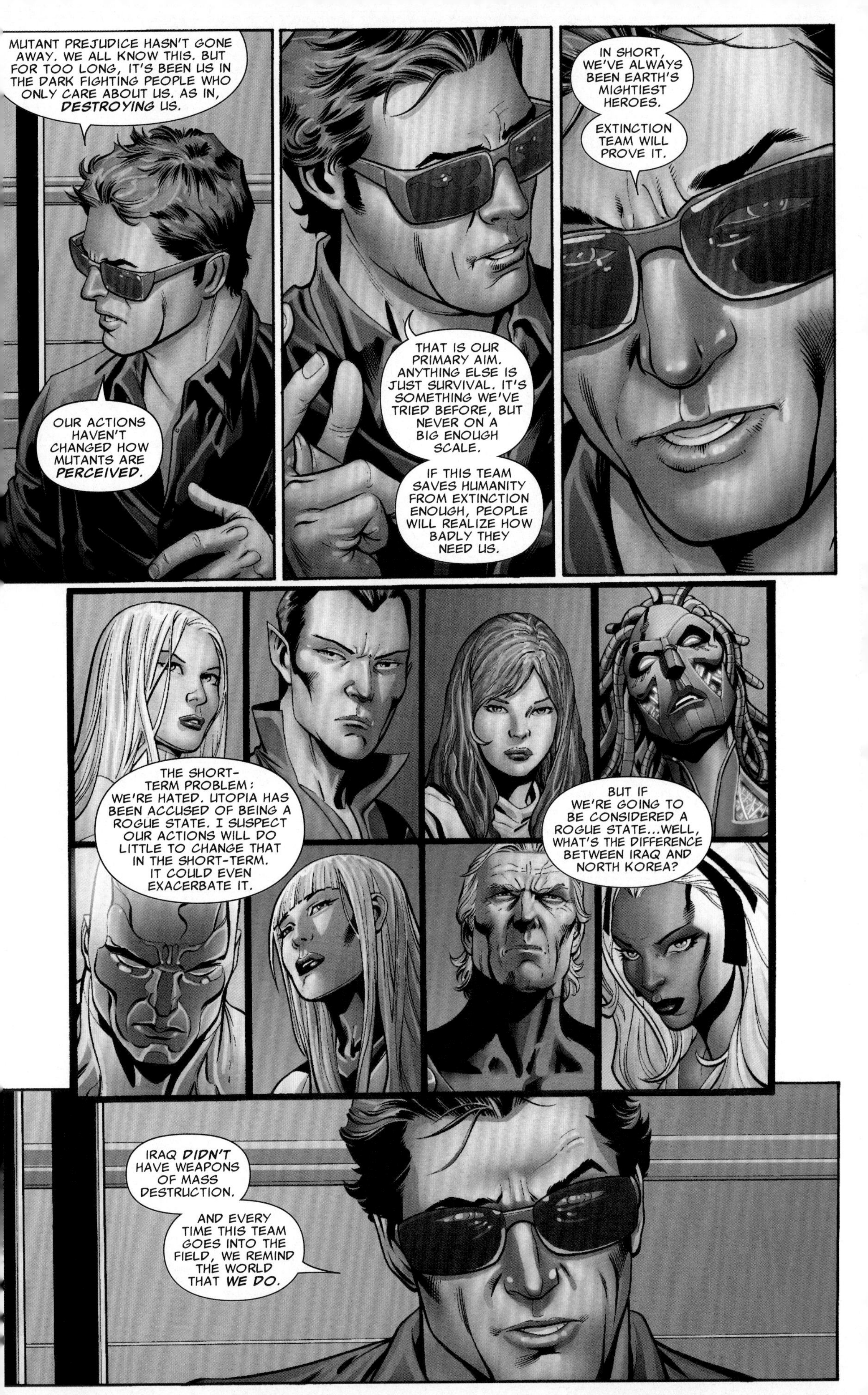
MUTANT PREJUDICE HASN'T GONE AWAY. WE ALL KNOW THIS. BUT FOR TOO LONG, IT'S BEEN US IN THE DARK FIGHTING PEOPLE WHO ONLY CARE ABOUT US. AS IN, DESTROYING US.
OUR ACTIONS HAVEN'T CHANGED HOW MUTANTS ARE PERCEIVED.
THAT IS OUR PRIMARY AIM. ANYTHING ELSE IS JUST SURVIVAL. IT'S SOMETHING WE'VE TRIED BEFORE, BUT NEVER ON A BIG ENOUGH SCALE.
IF THIS TEAM SAVES HUMANITY FROM EXTINCTION ENOUGH, PEOPLE WILL REALIZE HOW BADLY THEY NEED US.
IN SHORT, WE'VE ALWAYS BEEN EARTH'S MIGHTIEST HEROES.
EXTINCTION TEAM WILL PROVE IT.
THE SHORT-TERM PROBLEM: WE'RE HATED. UTOPIA HAS BEEN ACCUSED OF BEING A ROGUE STATE. I SUSPECT OUR ACTIONS WILL DO LITTLE TO CHANGE THAT IN THE SHORT-TERM. IT COULD EVEN EXACERBATE IT.
BUT IF WE'RE GOING TO BE CONSIDERED A ROGUE STATE...WELL, WHAT'S THE DIFFERENCE BETWEEN IRAQ AND NORTH KOREA?
IRAQ DIDN'T HAVE WEAPONS OF MASS DESTRUCTION.
AND EVERY TIME THIS TEAM GOES INTO THE FIELD, WE REMIND THE WORLD THAT WE DO.

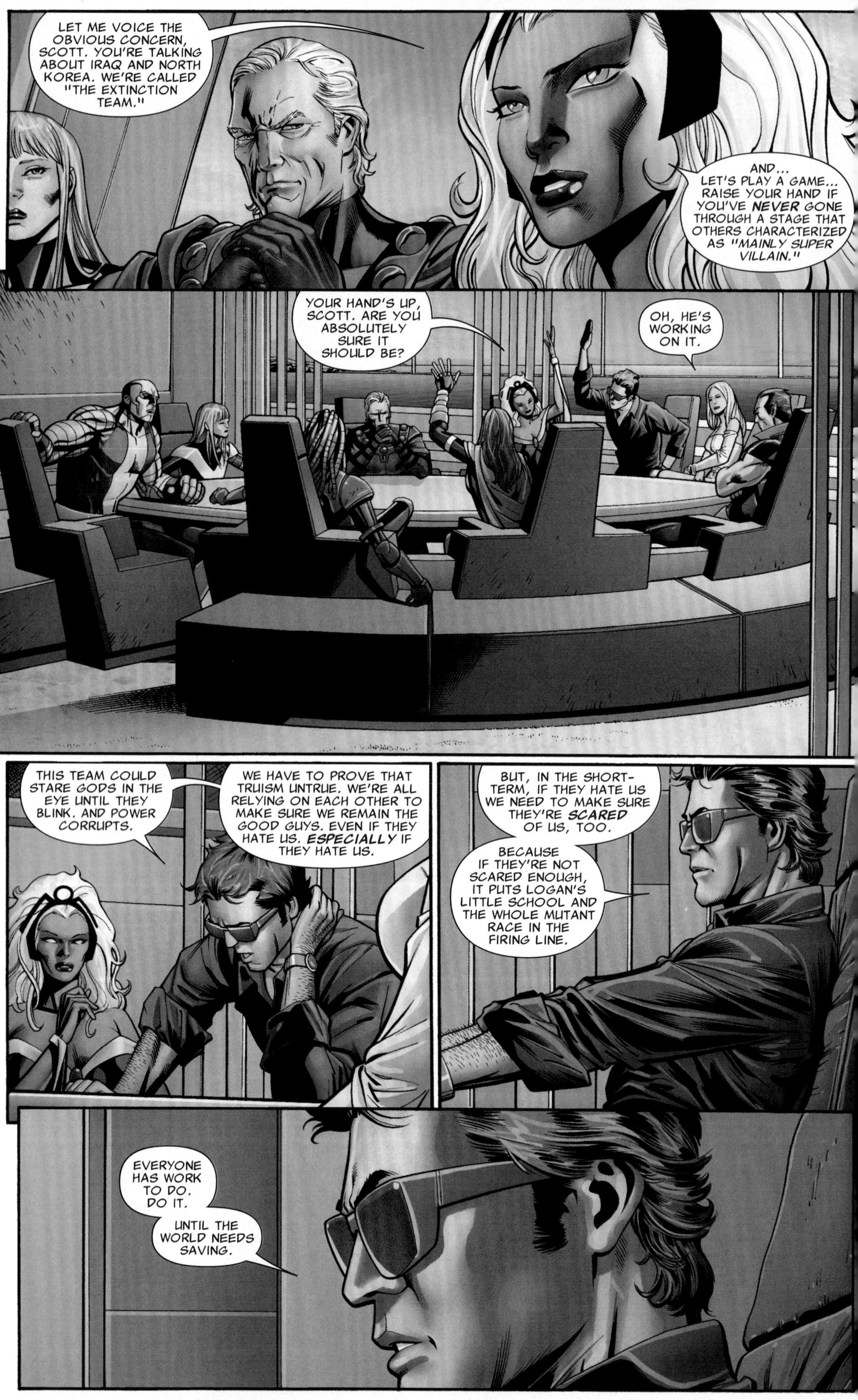
LET ME VOICE THE OBVIOUS CONCERN, SCOTT. YOU'RE TALKING ABOUT IRAQ AND NORTH KOREA. WE'RE CALLED "THE EXTINCTION TEAM."
AND... LET'S PLAY A GAME... RAISE YOUR HAND IF YOU'VE NEVER GONE THROUGH A STAGE THAT OTHERS CHARACTERIZED AS "MAINLY SUPER VILLAIN."
YOUR HAND'S UP, SCOTT. ARE YOU ABSOLUTELY SURE IT SHOULD BE?
OH, HE'S WORKING ON IT.
THIS TEAM COULD STARE GODS IN THE EYE UNTIL THEY BLINK. AND POWER CORRUPTS.
WE HAVE TO PROVE THAT TRUISM UNTRUE. WE'RE ALL RELYING ON EACH OTHER TO MAKE SURE WE REMAIN THE GOOD GUYS. EVEN IF THEY HATE US. ESPECIALLY IF THEY HATE US.
BUT, IN THE SHORT-TERM, IF THEY HATE US WE NEED TO MAKE SURE THEY'RE SCARED OF US, TOO.
BECAUSE IF THEY'RE NOT SCARED ENOUGH, IT PUTS LOGAN'S LITTLE SCHOOL AND THE WHOLE MUTANT RACE IN THE FIRING LINE.
EVERYONE HAS WORK TO DO. DO IT.
UNTIL THE WORLD NEEDS SAVING.

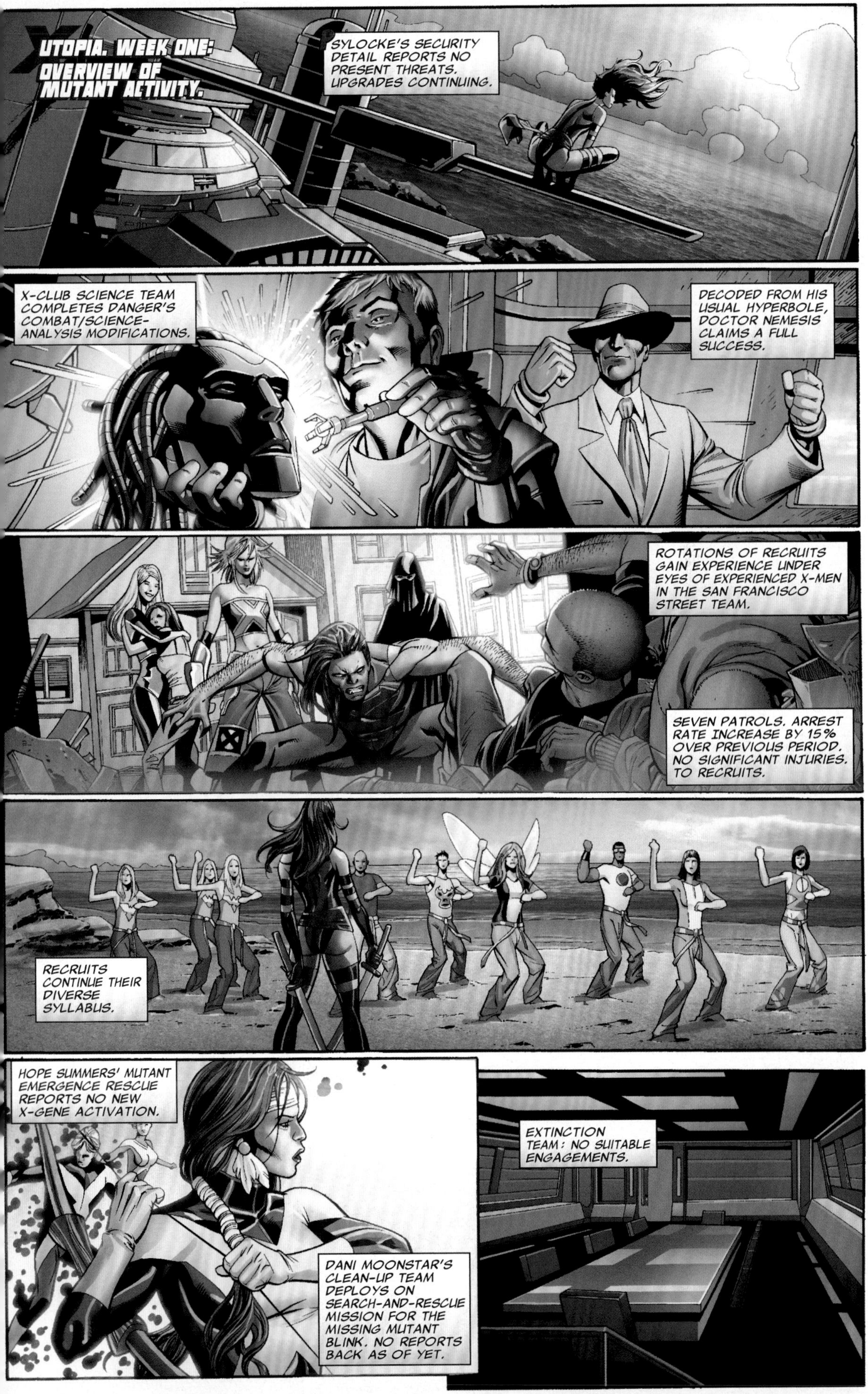
UTOPIA. WEEK ONE:
OVERVIEW OF MUTANT ACTIVITY.
SYLOCKE'S SECURITY DETAIL REPORTS NO PRESENT THREATS. UPGRADES CONTINUING.
X-CLUB SCIENCE TEAM COMPLETES DANGER'S COMBAT/SCIENCE-ANALYSIS MODIFICATIONS.
DECODED FROM HIS USUAL HYPERBOLE, DOCTOR NEMESIS CLAIMS A FULL SUCCESS.
ROTATIONS OF RECRUITS GAIN EXPERIENCE UNDER EYES OF EXPERIENCED X-MEN IN THE SAN FRANCISCO STREET TEAM.
SEVEN PATROLS. ARREST RATE INCREASE BY 15% OVER PREVIOUS PERIOD. NO SIGNIFICANT INJURIES. TO RECRUITS.
RECRUITS CONTINUE THEIR DIVERSE SYLLABUS.
HOPE SUMMERS' MUTANT EMERGENCE RESCUE REPORTS NO NEW X-GENE ACTIVATION.
DANI MOONSTAR'S CLEAN-UP TEAM DEPLOYS ON SEARCH-AND-RESCUE MISSION FOR THE MISSING MUTANT BLINK. NO REPORTS BACK AS OF YET.
EXTINCTION TEAM: NO SUITABLE ENGAGEMENTS.

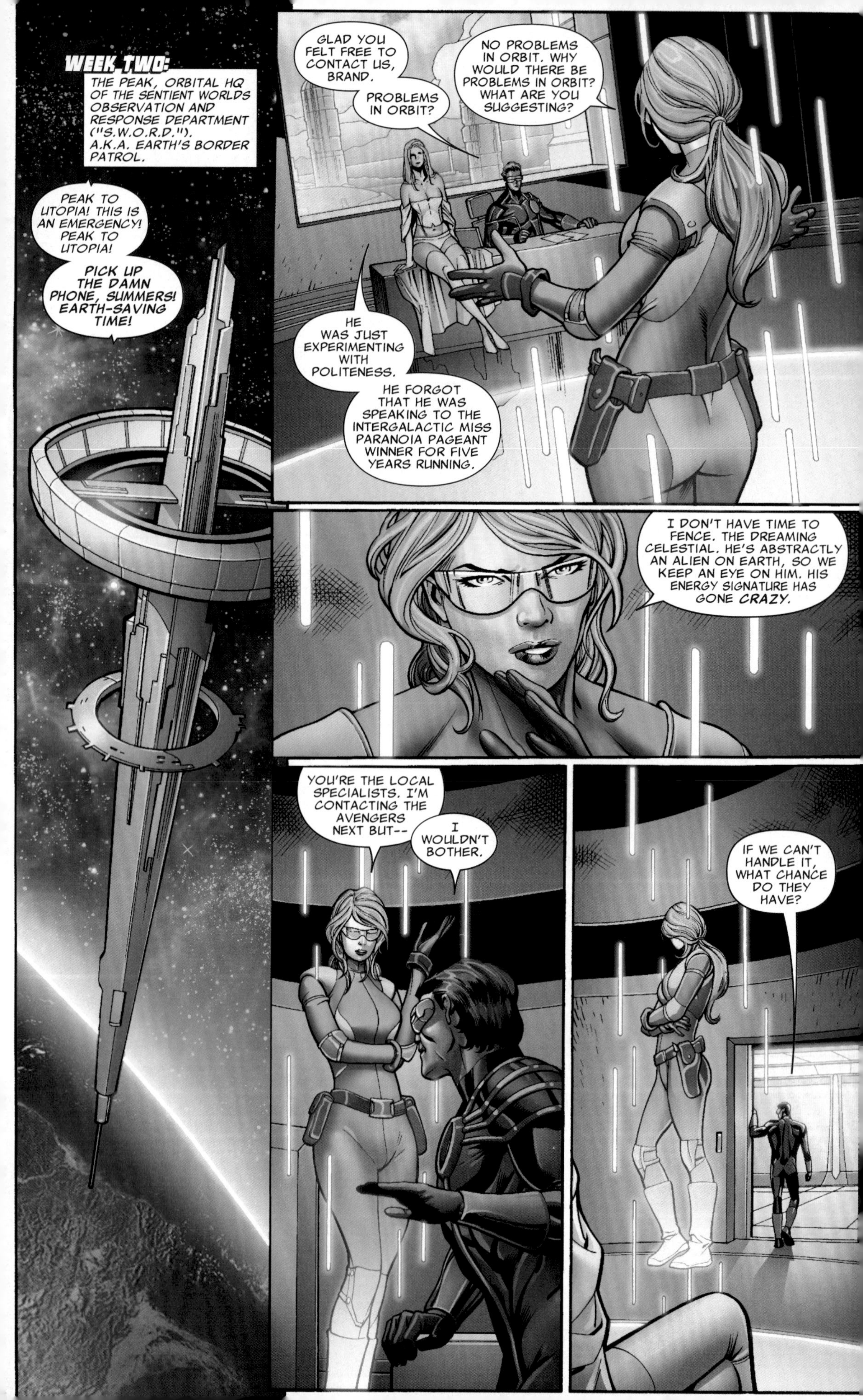
WEEK TWO:
THE PEAK, ORBITAL HQ OF THE SENTIENT WORLDS OBSERVATION AND RESPONSE DEPARTMENT ("S.W.O.R.D."). A.K.A. EARTH'S BORDER PATROL.
PEAK TO UTOPIA! THIS IS AN EMERGENCY! PEAK TO UTOPIA!
PICK UP THE DAMN PHONE, SUMMERS! EARTH-SAVING TIME!
GLAD YOU FELT FREE TO CONTACT US, BRAND.
PROBLEMS IN ORBIT?
NO PROBLEMS IN ORBIT. WHY WOULD THERE BE PROBLEMS IN ORBIT? WHAT ARE YOU SUGGESTING?
HE WAS JUST EXPERIMENTING WITH POLITENESS.
HE FORGOT THAT HE WAS SPEAKING TO THE INTERGALACTIC MISS PARANOIA PAGEANT WINNER FOR FIVE YEARS RUNNING.
I DON'T HAVE TIME TO FENCE. THE DREAMING CELESTIAL. HE'S ABSTRACTLY AN ALIEN ON EARTH, SO WE KEEP AN EYE ON HIM. HIS ENERGY SIGNATURE HAS GONE CRAZY.
YOU'RE THE LOCAL SPECIALISTS. I'M CONTACTING THE AVENGERS NEXT BUT--
I WOULDN'T BOTHER.
IF WE CAN'T HANDLE IT, WHAT CHANCE DO THEY HAVE?

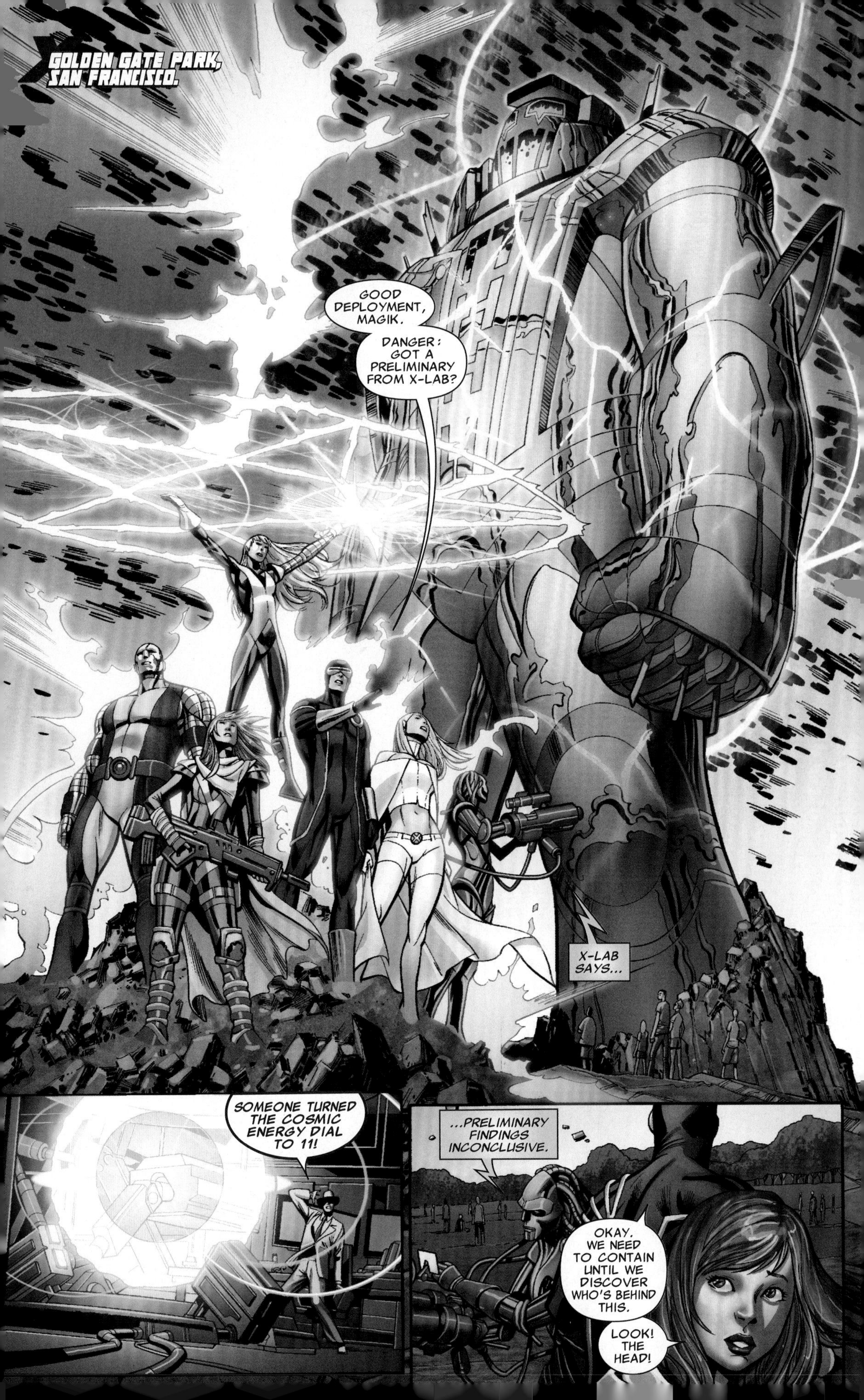
GOLDEN GATE PARK, SAN FRANCISCO.
GOOD DEPLOYMENT, MAGIK.
DANGER: GOT A PRELIMINARY FROM X-LAB?
X-LAB SAYS...
SOMEONE TURNED THE COSMIC ENERGY DIAL TO 11!
...PRELIMINARY FINDINGS INCONCLUSIVE.
OKAY. WE NEED TO CONTAIN UNTIL WE DISCOVER WHO'S BEHIND THIS.
LOOK! THE HEAD!

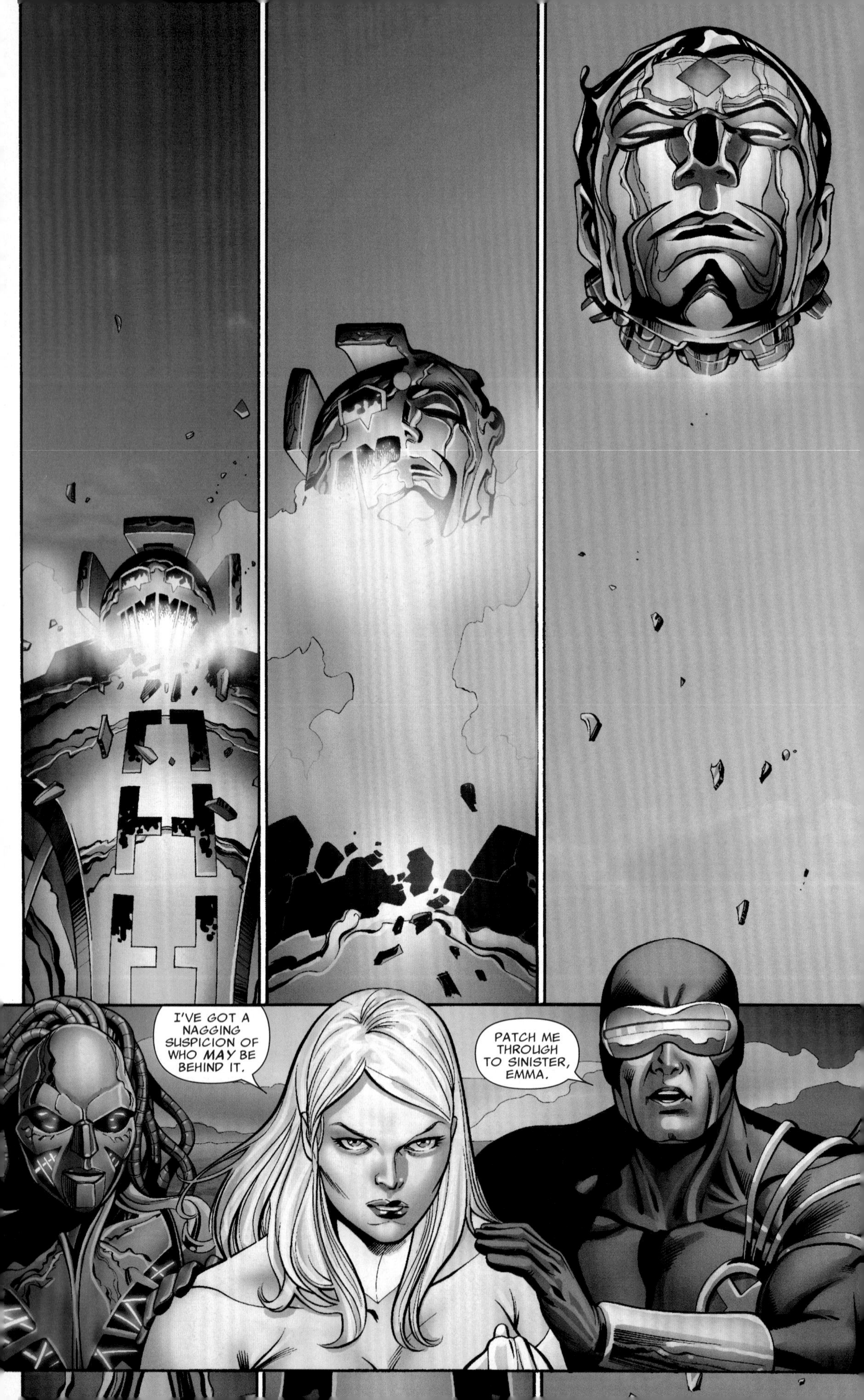
I'VE GOT A NAGGING SUSPICION OF WHO MAY BE BEHIND IT.
PATCH ME THROUGH TO SINISTER, EMMA.

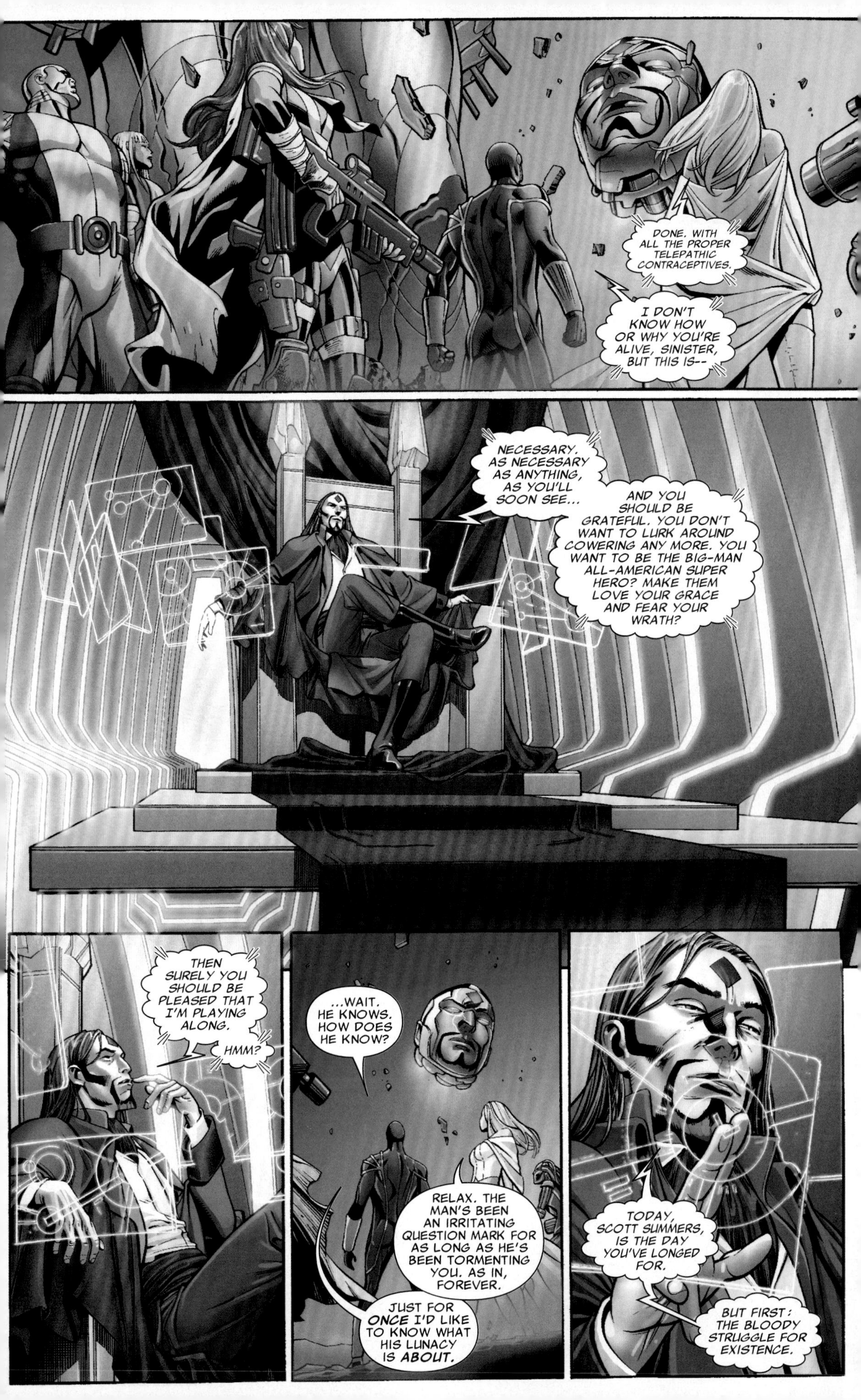
DONE. WITH ALL THE PROPER TELEPATHIC CONTRACEPTIVES.
I DON'T KNOW HOW OR WHY YOU'RE ALIVE, SINISTER, BUT THIS IS--
NECESSARY. AS NECESSARY AS ANYTHING, AS YOU'LL SOON SEE...
AND YOU SHOULD BE GRATEFUL. YOU DON'T WANT TO LURK AROUND COWERING ANY MORE. YOU WANT TO BE THE BIG-MAN ALL-AMERICAN SUPER HERO? MAKE THEM LOVE YOUR GRACE AND FEAR YOUR WRATH?
THEN SURELY YOU SHOULD BE PLEASED THAT I'M PLAYING ALONG.
HMM?
...WAIT. HE KNOWS. HOW DOES HE KNOW?
RELAX. THE MAN'S BEEN AN IRRITATING QUESTION MARK FOR AS LONG AS HE'S BEEN TORMENTING YOU. AS IN, FOREVER.
JUST FOR ONCE I'D LIKE TO KNOW WHAT HIS LUNACY IS ABOUT.
TODAY, SCOTT SUMMERS, IS THE DAY YOU'VE LONGED FOR.
BUT FIRST: THE BLOODY STRUGGLE FOR EXISTENCE.

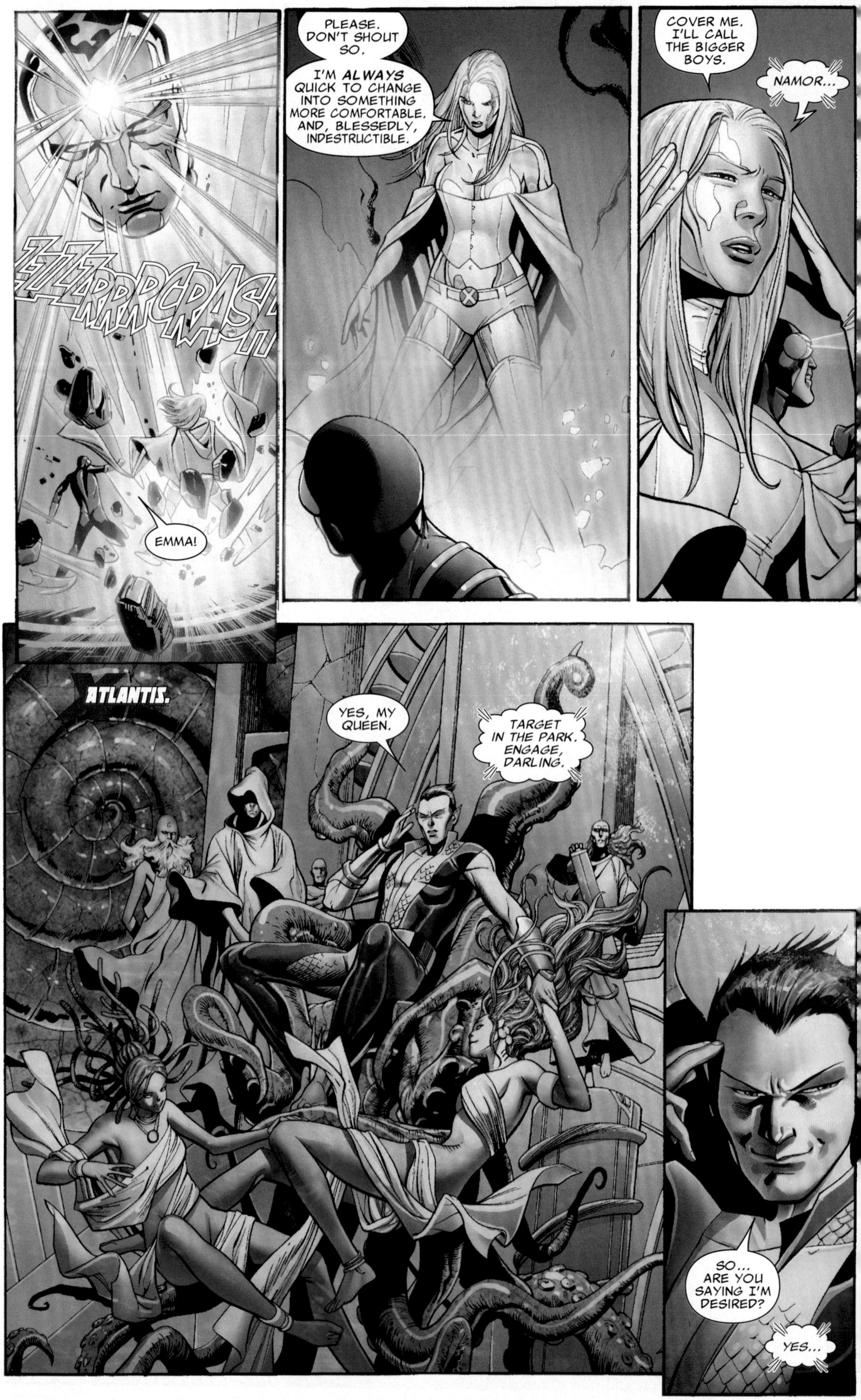
KLARRRCRASH
EMMA!
PLEASE. DON'T SHOUT SO.
I'M ALWAYS QUICK TO CHANGE INTO SOMETHING MORE COMFORTABLE. AND, BLESSEDLY, INDESTRUCTIBLE.
COVER ME. I'LL CALL THE BIGGER BOYS.
NAMOR...
ATLANTIS.
TARGET IN THE PARK. ENGAGE, DARLING.
YES, MY QUEEN.
SO... ARE YOU SAYING I'M DESIRED?
YES...

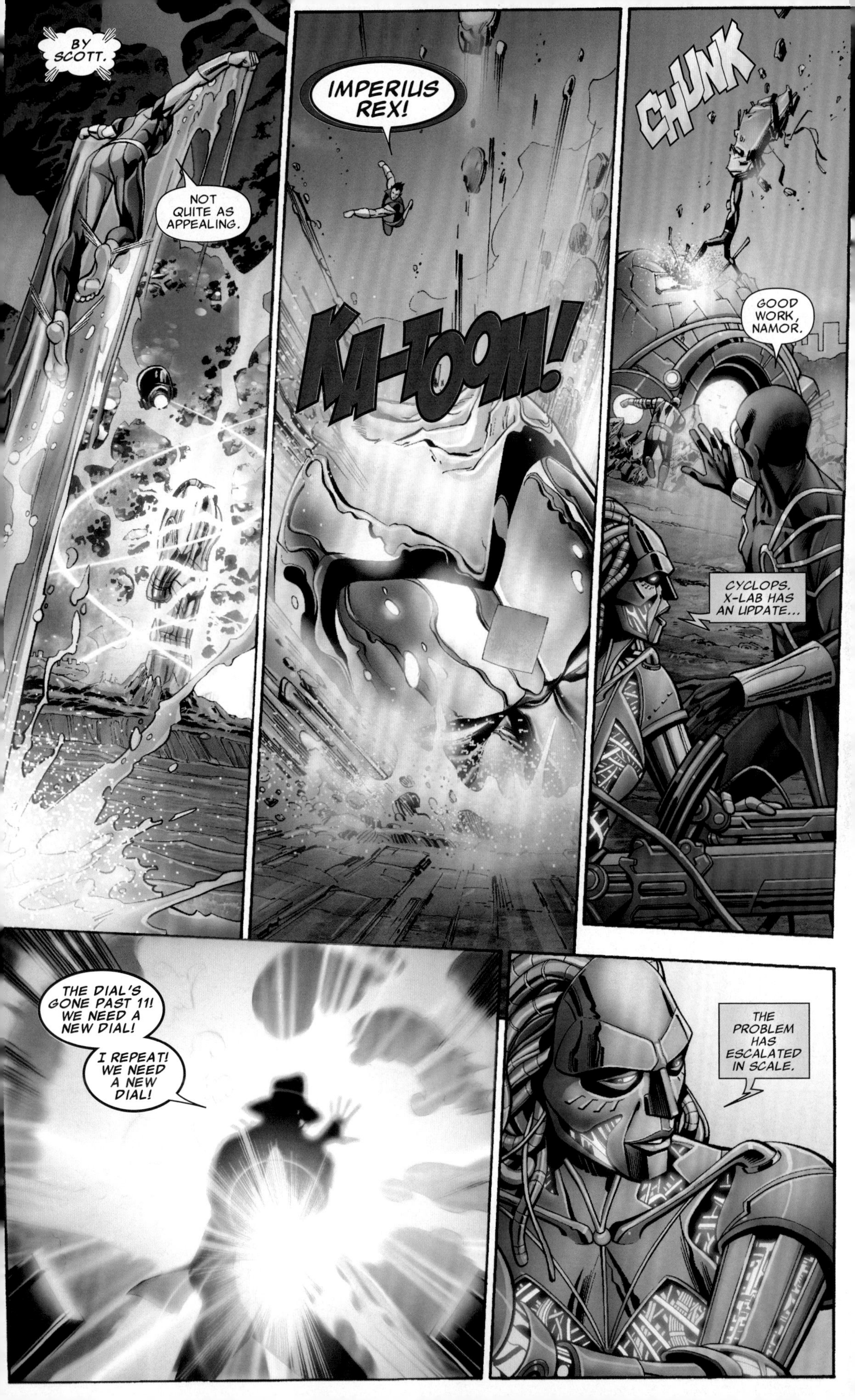
BY SCOTT.
NOT QUITE AS APPEALING.
IMPERIUS REX!
KA-TOOM!
CHUNK
GOOD WORK, NAMOR.
CYCLOPS, X-LAB HAS AN UPDATE...
THE DIAL'S GONE PAST 11! WE NEED A NEW DIAL!
I REPEAT! WE NEED A NEW DIAL!
THE PROBLEM HAS ESCALATED IN SCALE.

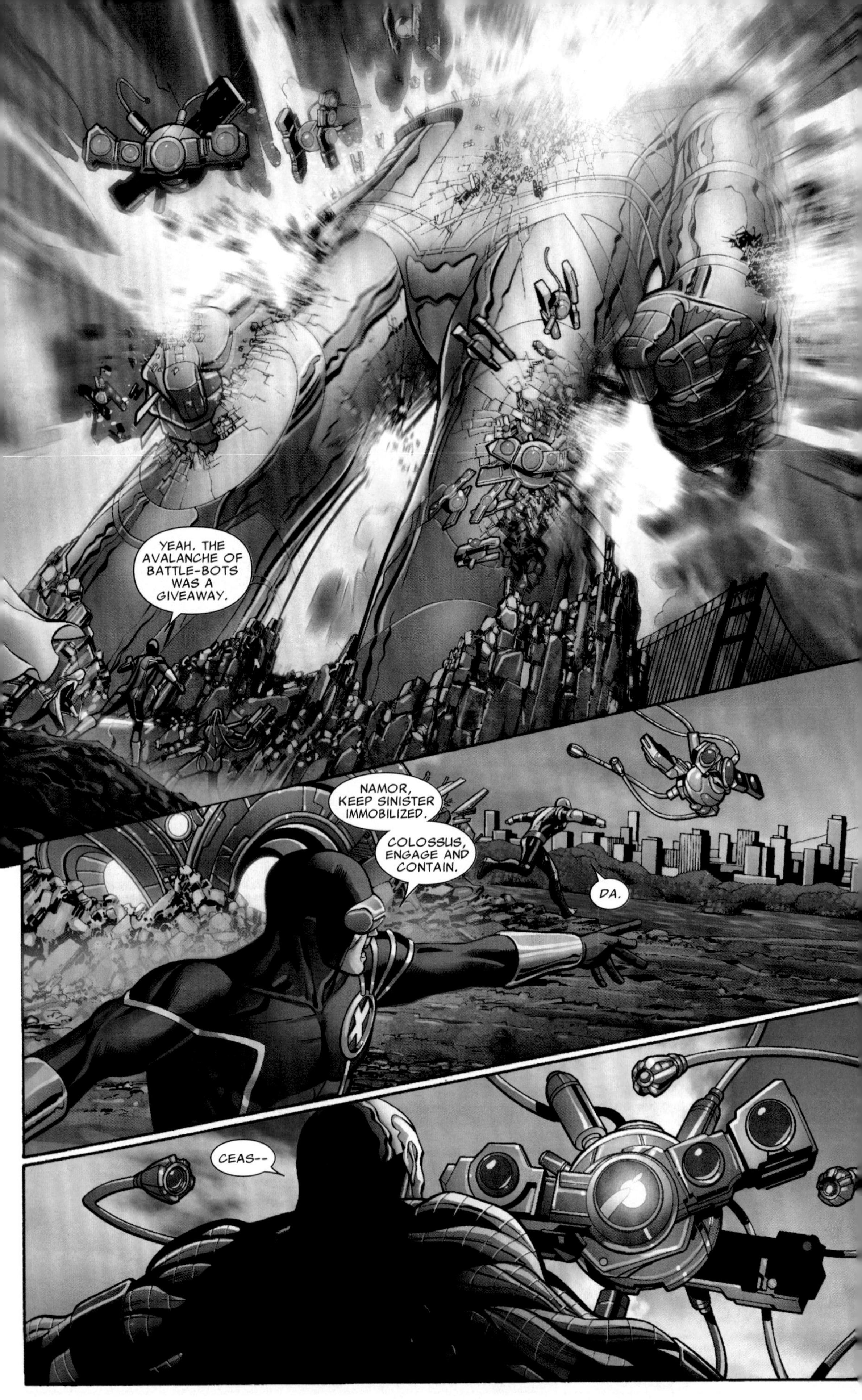
YEAH. THE AVALANCHE OF BATTLE-BOTS WAS A GIVEAWAY.
NAMOR, KEEP SINISTER IMMOBILIZED.
COLOSSUS, ENGAGE AND CONTAIN.
DA.
CEAS--

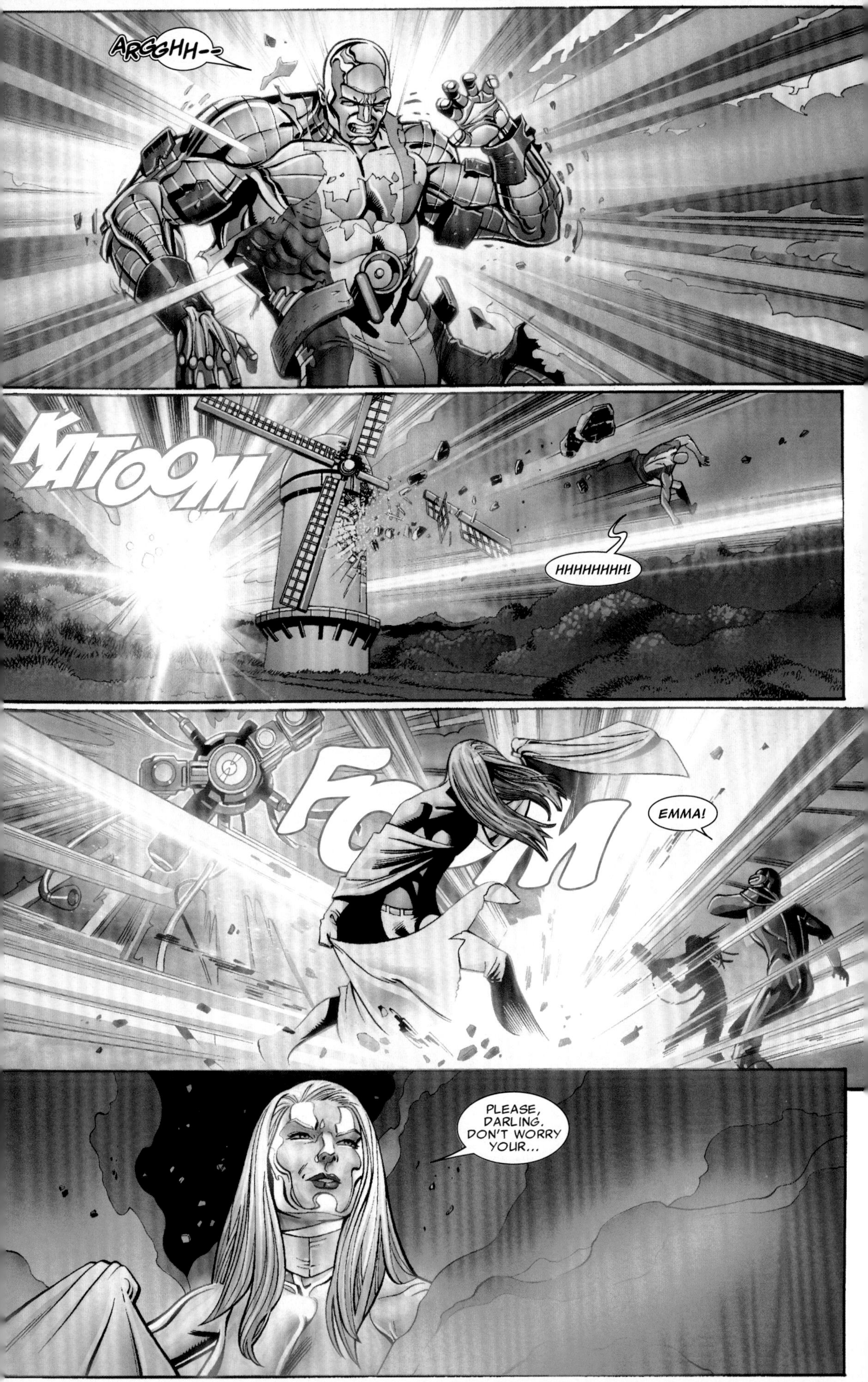
ARGGHH--
KATOOM
HHHHHHHH!
FOOM
EMMA!
PLEASE, DARLING. DON'T WORRY YOUR...

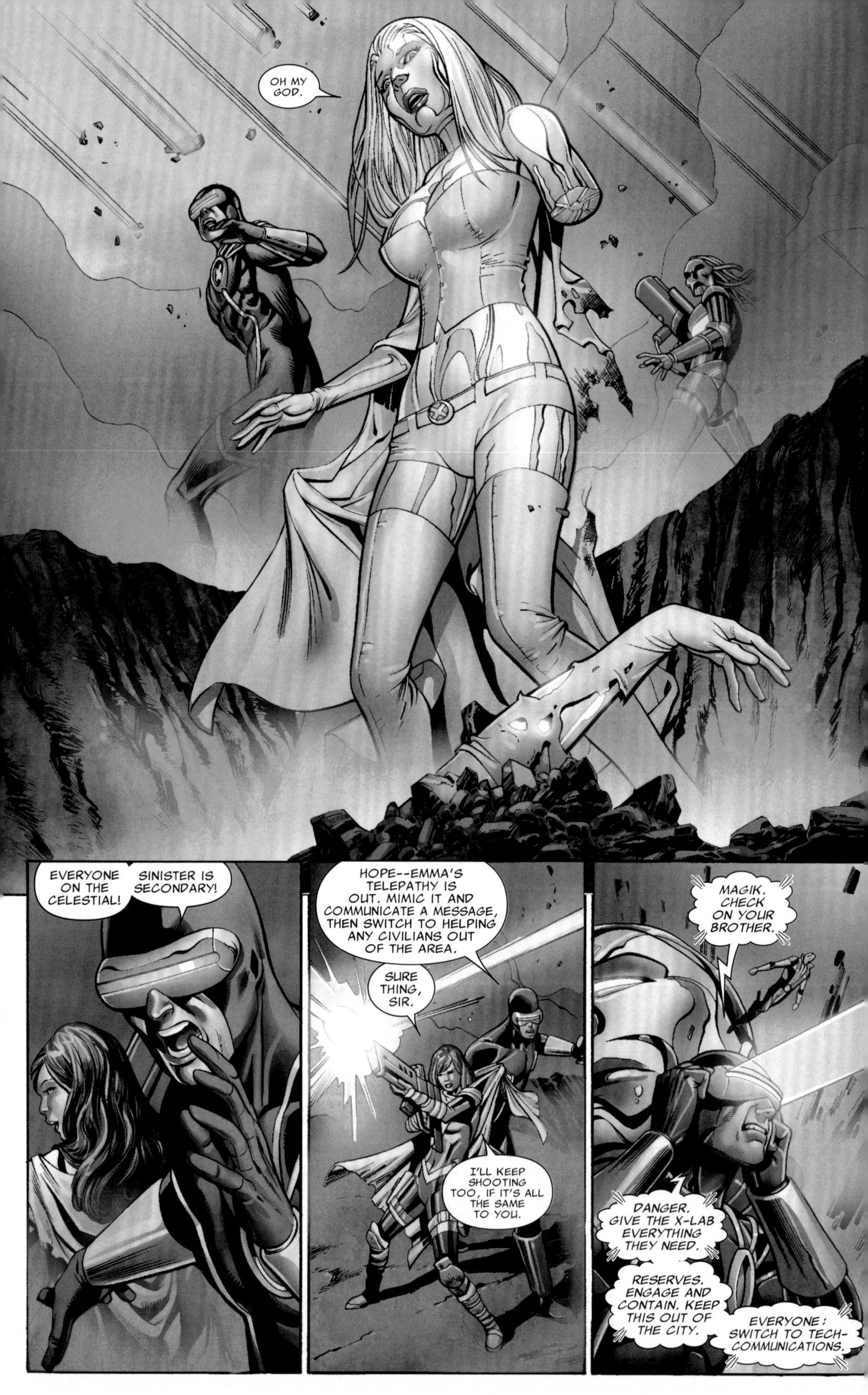
OH MY GOD.
EVERYONE ON THE CELESTIAL!
SINISTER IS SECONDARY!
HOPE--EMMA'S TELEPATHY IS OUT. MIMIC IT AND COMMUNICATE A MESSAGE, THEN SWITCH TO HELPING ANY CIVILIANS OUT OF THE AREA.
SURE THING, SIR.
I'LL KEEP SHOOTING TOO, IF IT'S ALL THE SAME TO YOU.
MAGIK. CHECK ON YOUR BROTHER.
DANGER. GIVE THE X-LAB EVERYTHING THEY NEED.
RESERVES. ENGAGE AND CONTAIN. KEEP THIS OUT OF THE CITY.
EVERYONE: SWITCH TO TECH-COMMUNICATIONS.

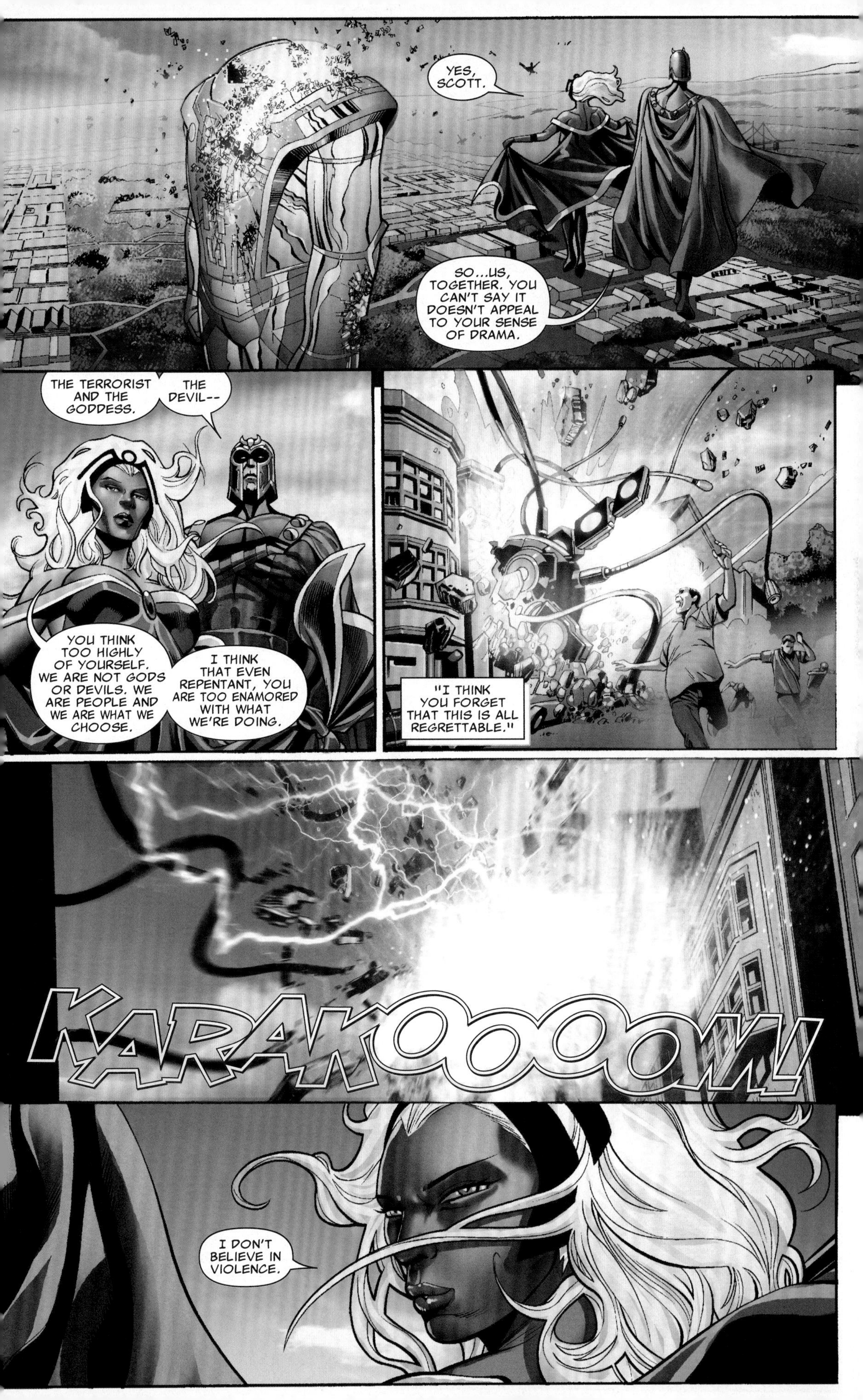
YES, SCOTT.
SO...US, TOGETHER. YOU CAN'T SAY IT DOESN'T APPEAL TO YOUR SENSE OF DRAMA.
THE TERRORIST AND THE GODDESS.
THE DEVIL--
YOU THINK TOO HIGHLY OF YOURSELF. WE ARE NOT GODS OR DEVILS. WE ARE PEOPLE AND WE ARE WHAT WE CHOOSE.
I THINK THAT EVEN REPENTANT, YOU ARE TOO ENAMORED WITH WHAT WE'RE DOING.
"I THINK YOU FORGET THAT THIS IS ALL REGRETTABLE."
KARAKOOOOOM!
I DON'T BELIEVE IN VIOLENCE.

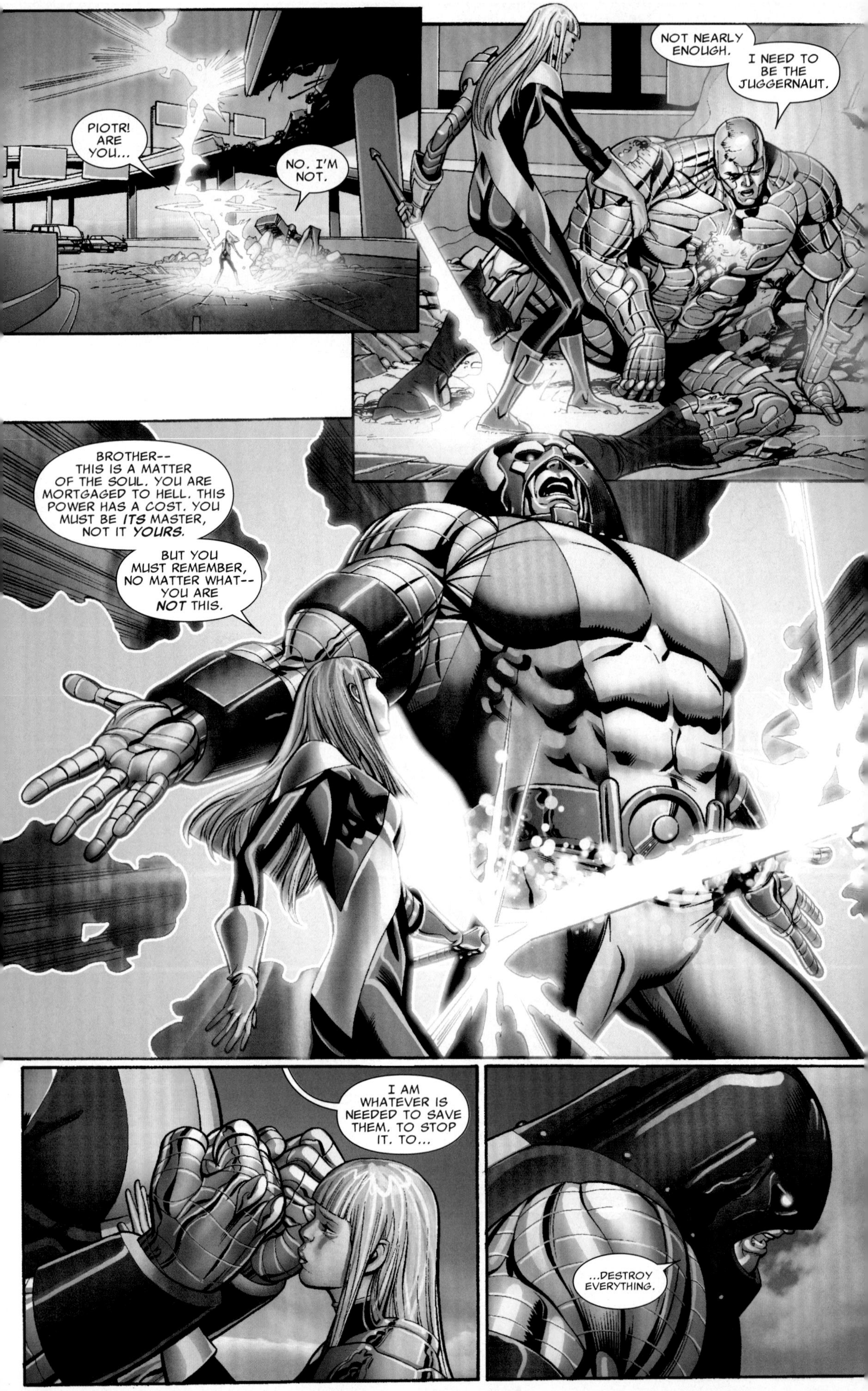
PIOTR! ARE YOU...
NO. I'M NOT.
NOT NEARLY ENOUGH.
I NEED TO BE THE JUGGERNAUT.
BROTHER-- THIS IS A MATTER OF THE SOUL. YOU ARE MORTGAGED TO HELL. THIS POWER HAS A COST. YOU MUST BE ITS MASTER, NOT IT YOURS.
BUT YOU MUST REMEMBER, NO MATTER WHAT-- YOU ARE NOT THIS.
I AM WHATEVER IS NEEDED TO SAVE THEM. TO STOP IT. TO...
...DESTROY EVERYTHING.

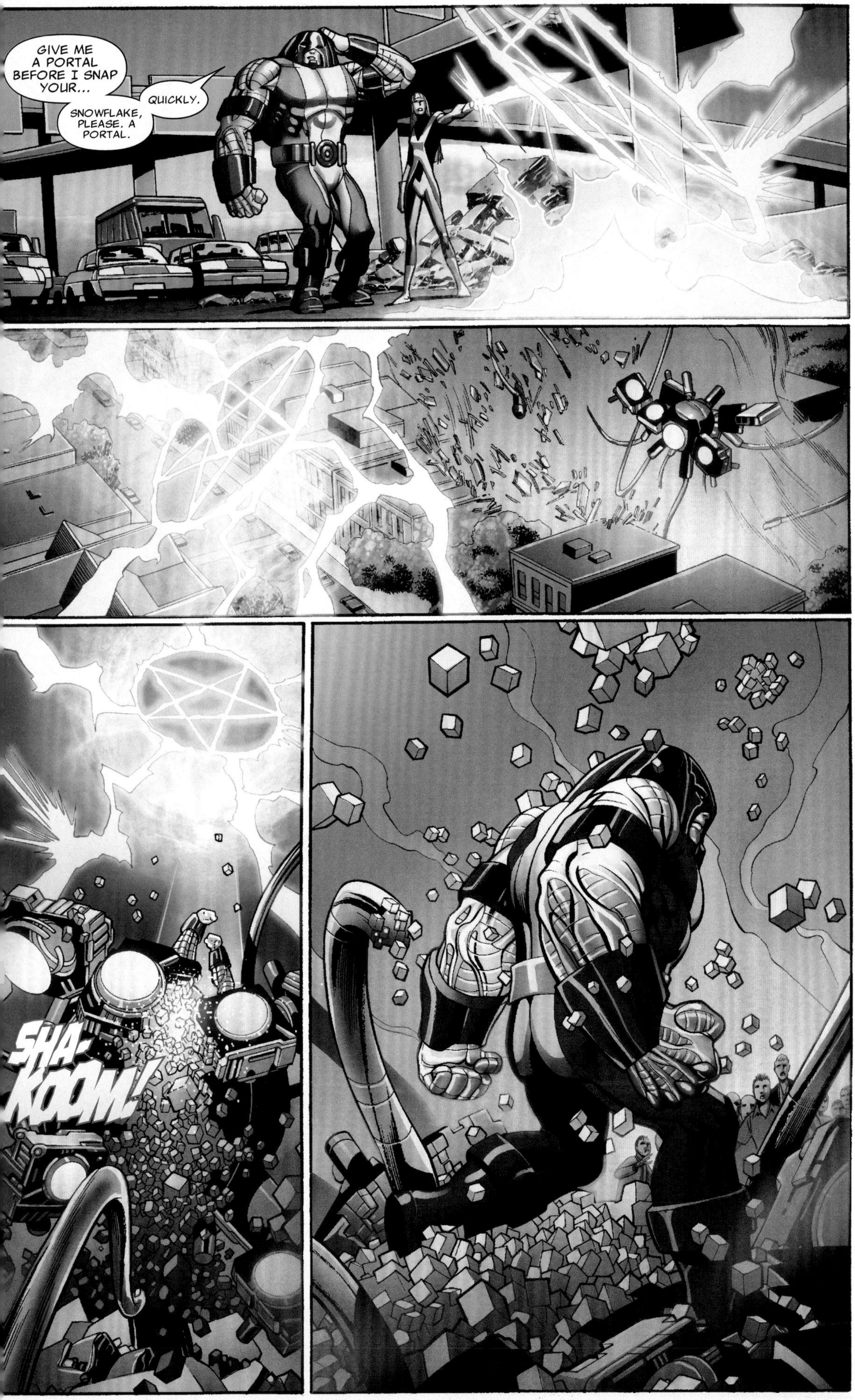
GIVE ME A PORTAL BEFORE I SNAP YOUR...
QUICKLY.
SNOWFLAKE, PLEASE. A PORTAL.
SHA-KOOM!

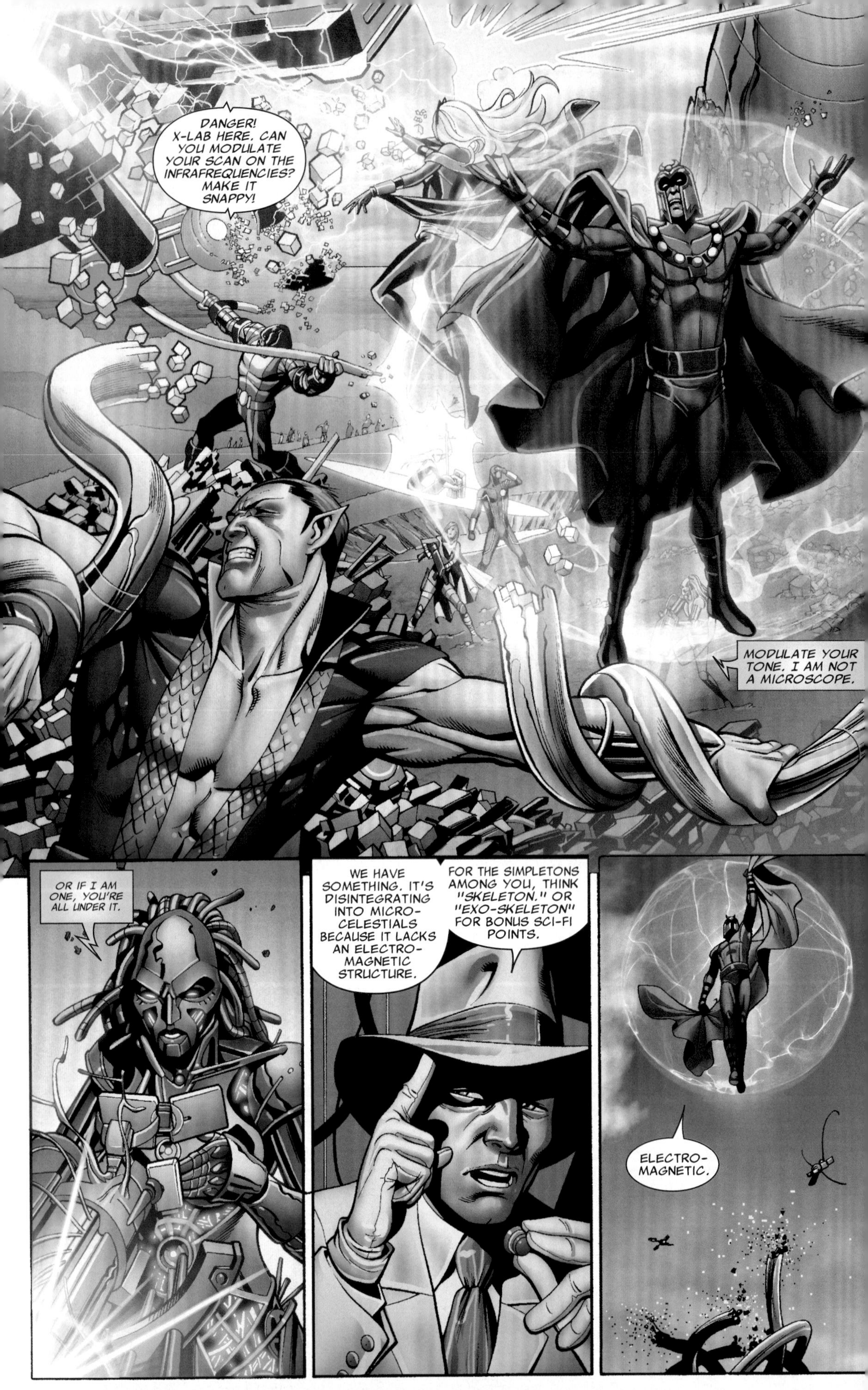
DANGER! X-LAB HERE. CAN YOU MODULATE YOUR SCAN ON THE INFRAFREQUENCIES? MAKE IT SNAPPY!
MODULATE YOUR TONE. I AM NOT A MICROSCOPE.
OR IF I AM ONE, YOU'RE ALL UNDER IT.
WE HAVE SOMETHING. IT'S DISINTEGRATING INTO MICRO-CELESTIALS BECAUSE IT LACKS AN ELECTRO-MAGNETIC STRUCTURE.
FOR THE SIMPLETONS AMONG YOU, THINK "SKELETON." OR "EXO-SKELETON" FOR BONUS SCI-FI POINTS.
ELECTRO-MAGNETIC.

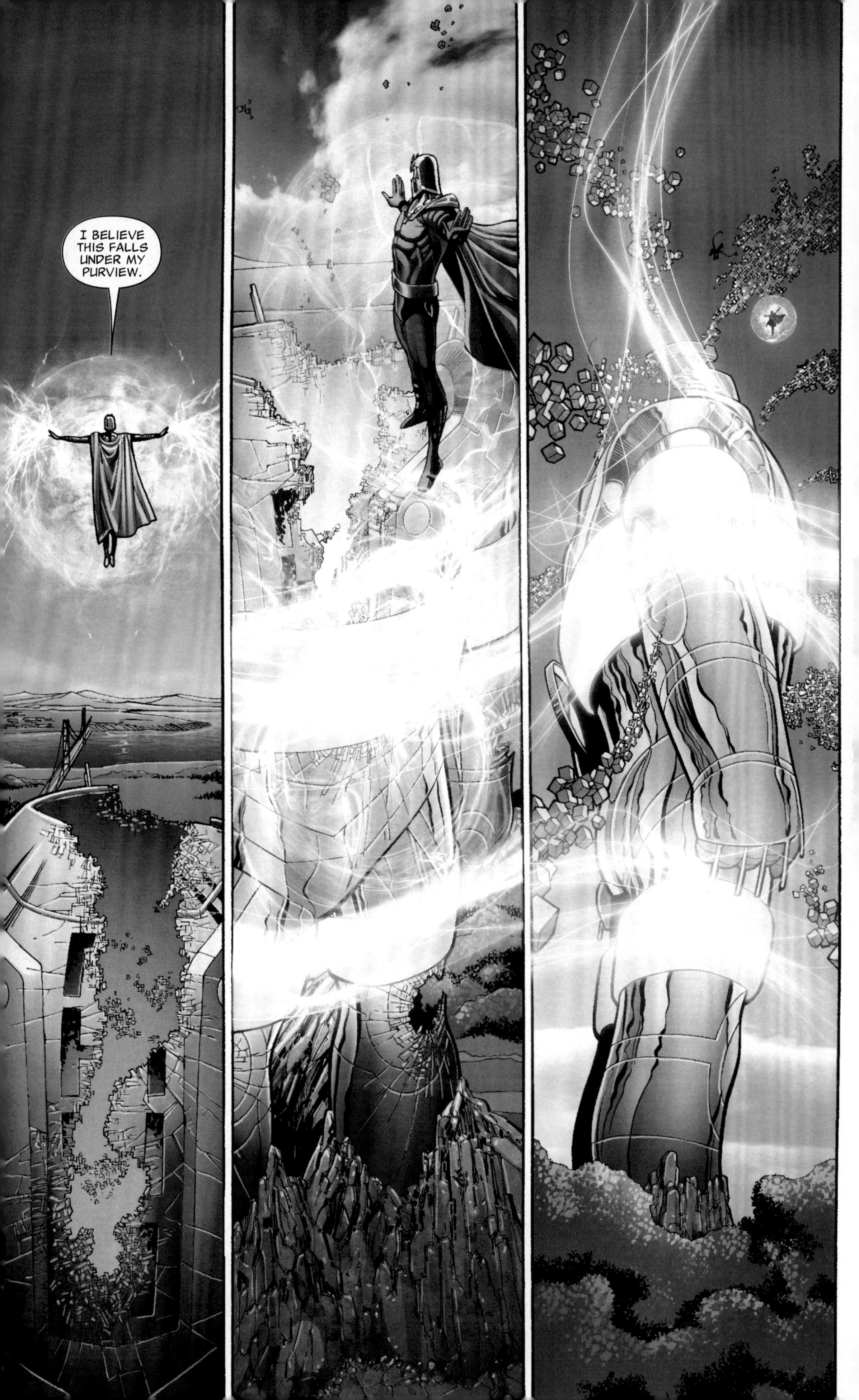
I BELIEVE THIS FALLS UNDER MY PURVIEW.

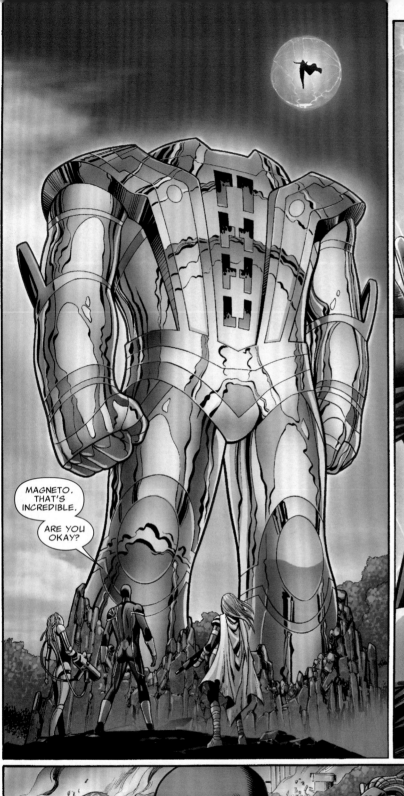

MAGNETO, THAT'S INCREDIBLE.

ARE YOU OKAY?

I'M ACTING AS SURROGATE NERVOUS SYSTEM FOR A COSMIC DEITY.

IF YOU DON'T RESOLVE THIS SITUATION WITH HASTE, EXPECT MY BRAINS TO LEAK FROM MY EYE SOCKETS.

DANGER: TAP SATELLITES AND TRACE. ANY IDEA WHERE SINISTER TOOK THE HEAD? IS THERE ANY CHANCE OF LOCATING HIM?

NO NEED FOR SATELLITES.

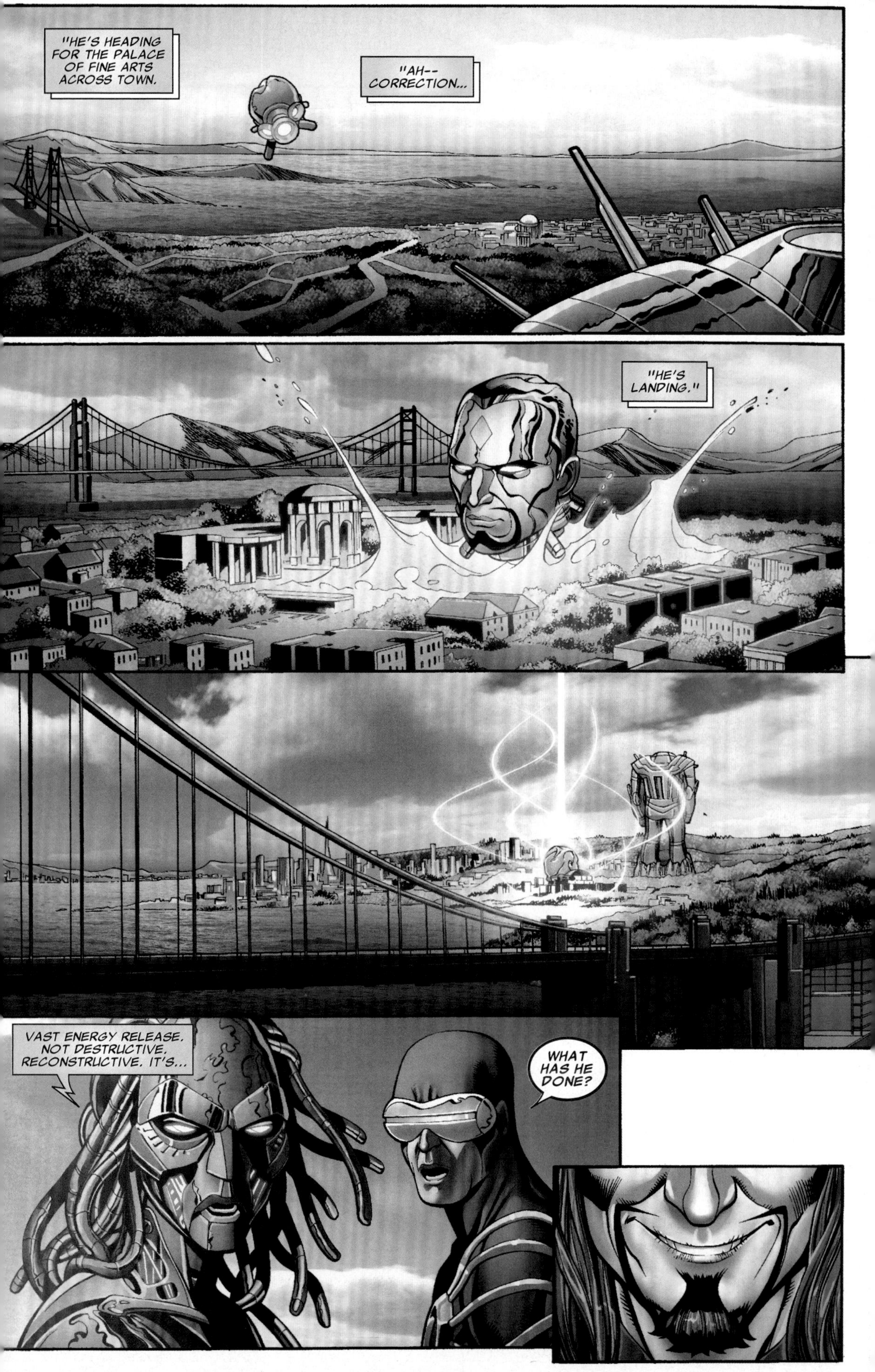
"HE'S HEADING FOR THE PALACE OF FINE ARTS ACROSS TOWN.
"AH-- CORRECTION...
"HE'S LANDING."
VAST ENERGY RELEASE. NOT DESTRUCTIVE. RECONSTRUCTIVE. IT'S...
WHAT HAS HE DONE?

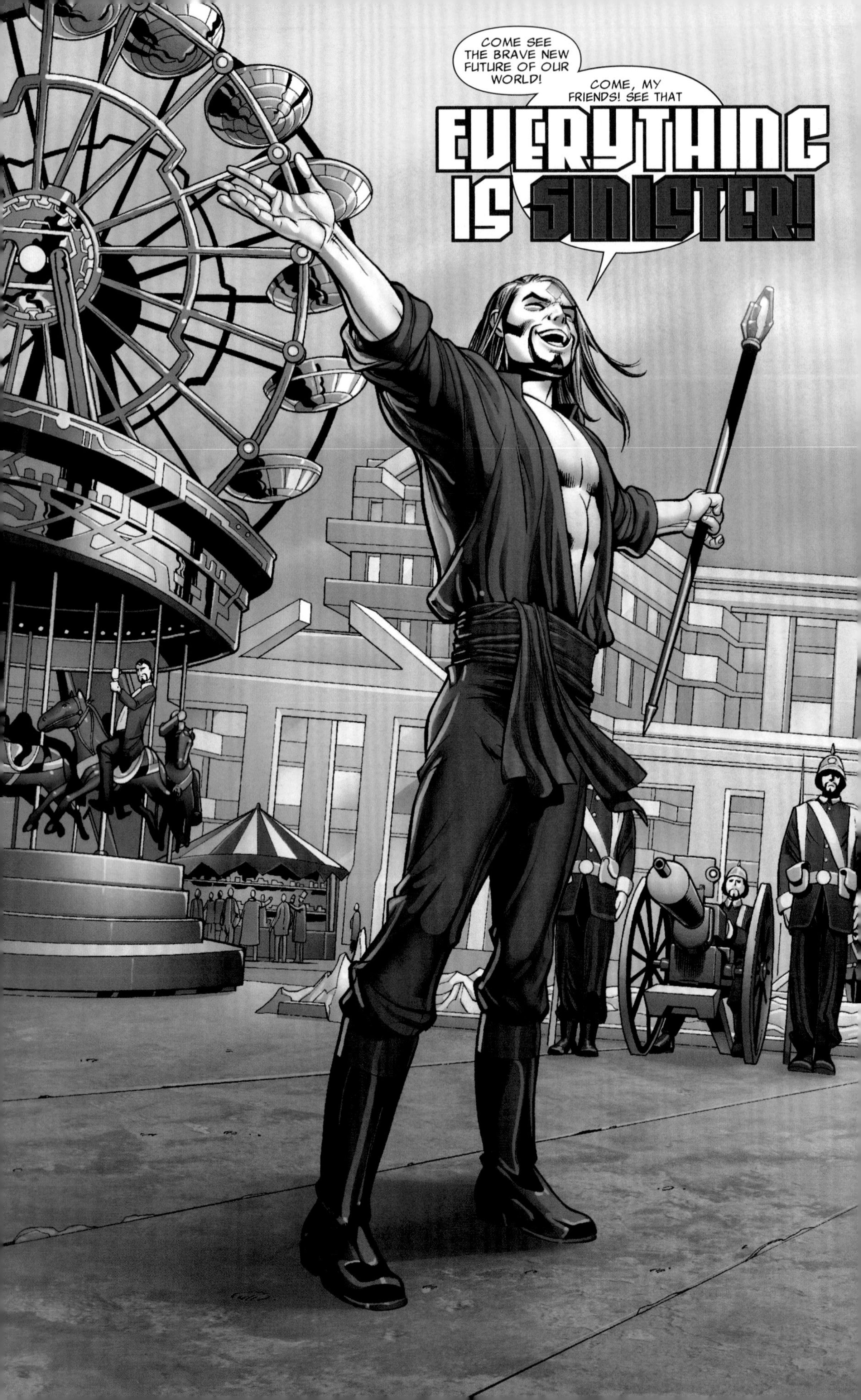
COME SEE THE BRAVE NEW FUTURE OF OUR WORLD!
COME, MY FRIENDS! SEE THAT
EVERYTHING IS SINISTER!

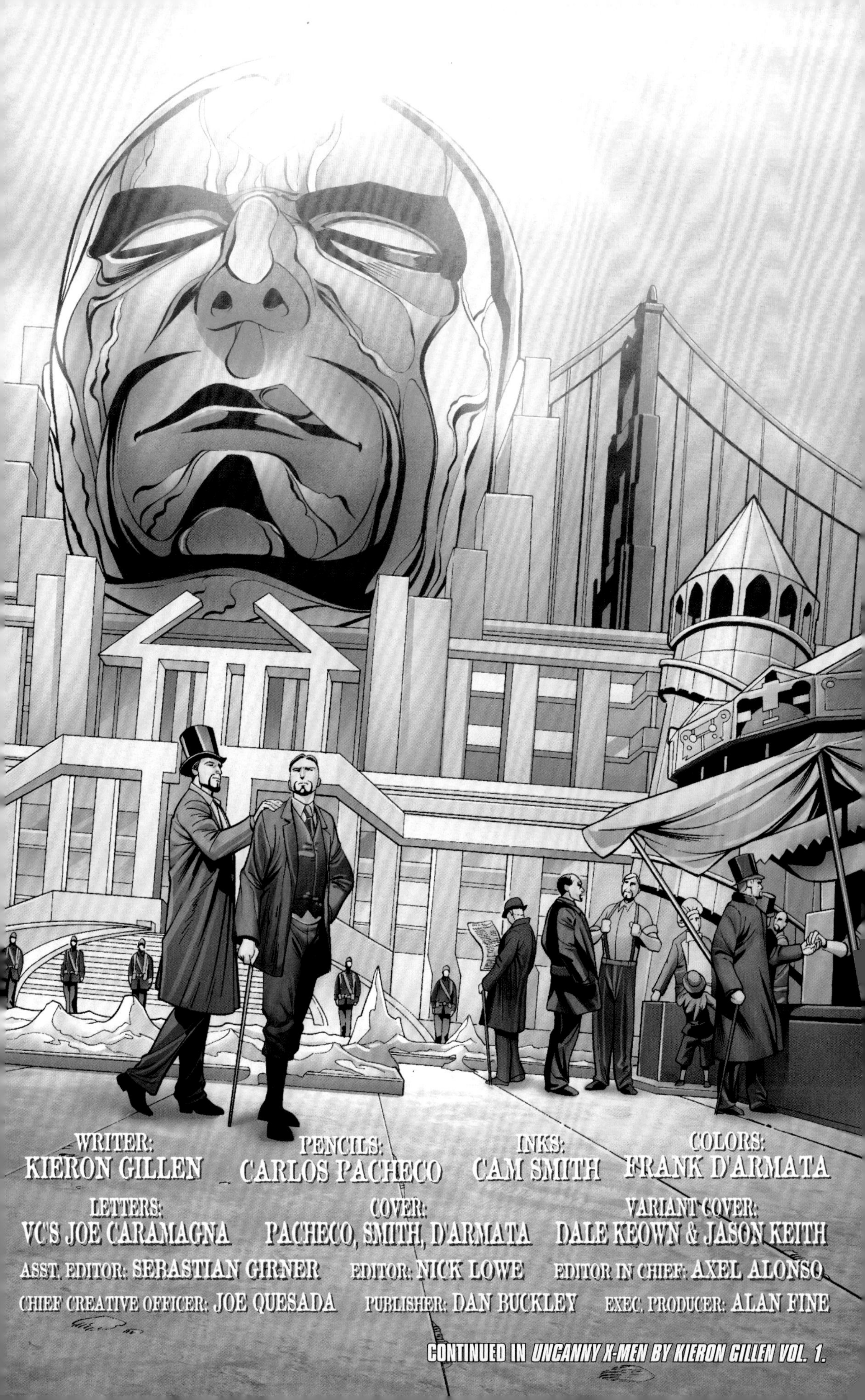
WRITER: KIERON GILLEN
PENCILS: CARLOS PACHECO
INKS: CAM SMITH
COLORS: FRANK D'ARMATA
LETTERS: VC'S JOE CARAMAGNA
COVER: PACHECO, SMITH, D'ARMATA
VARIANT COVER: DALE KEOWN & JASON KEITH
ASST. EDITOR: SEBASTIAN GIRNER
EDITOR: NICK LOWE
EDITOR IN CHIEF: AXEL ALONSO
CHIEF CREATIVE OFFICER: JOE QUESADA
PUBLISHER: DAN BUCKLEY
EXEC. PRODUCER: ALAN FINE

CONTINUED IN *UNCANNY X-MEN BY KIERON GILLEN VOL. 1.*

COSTUME DESIGNS BY JAMIE McKELVIE

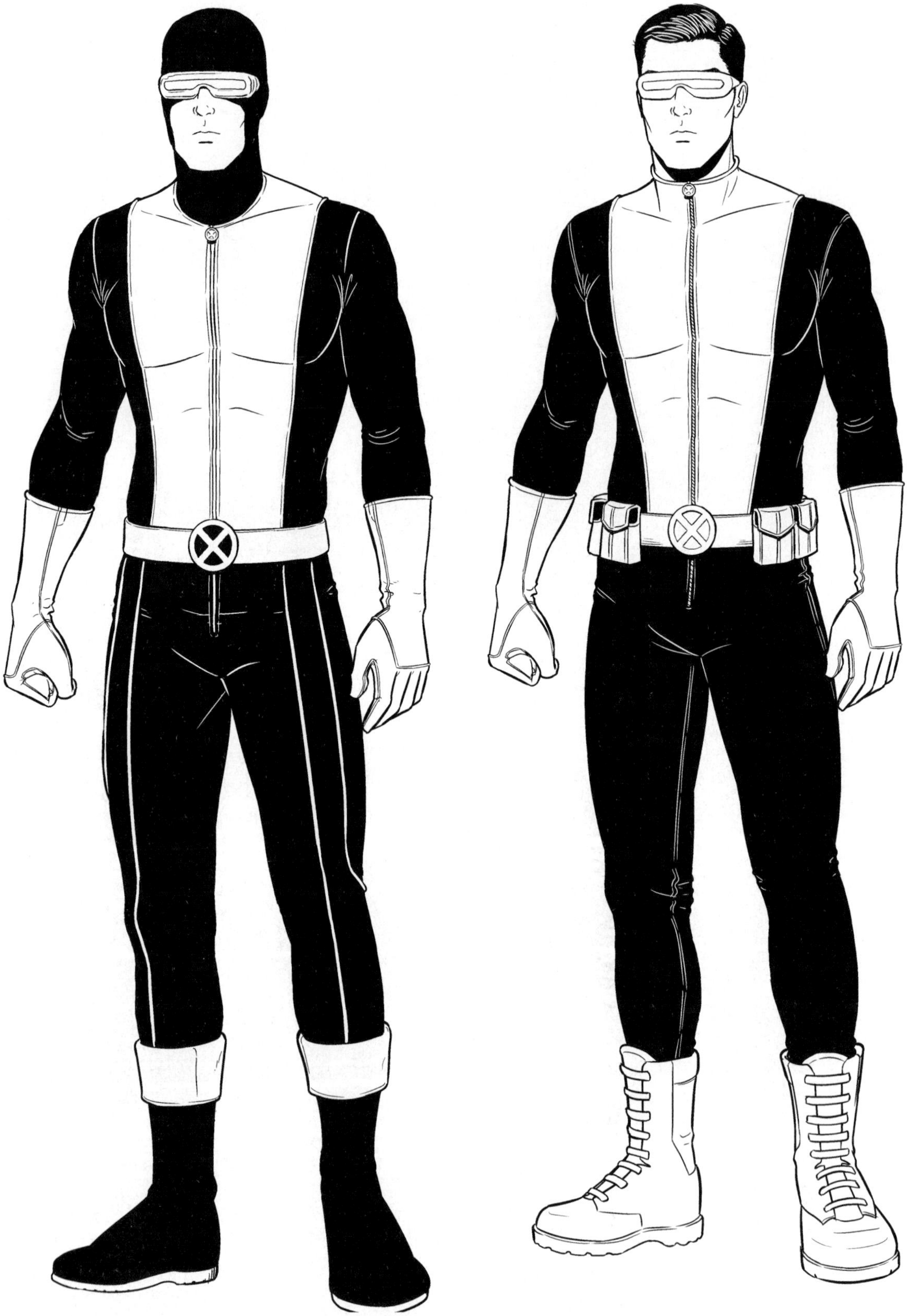

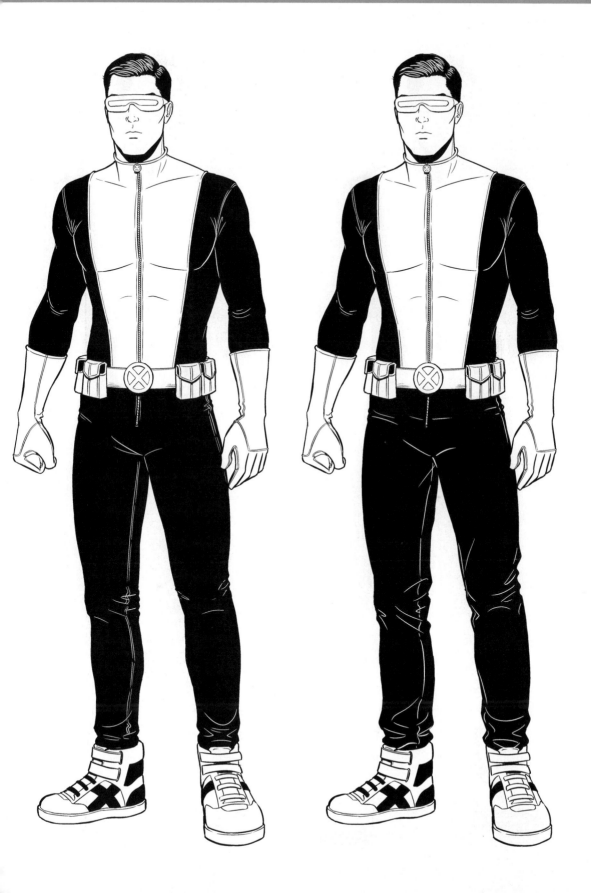

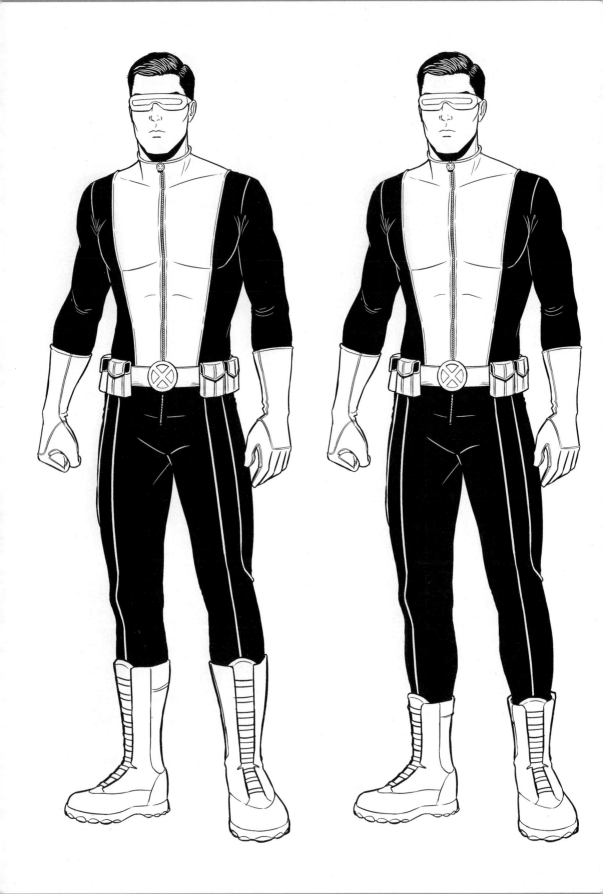